D1797425

EUI – Series C –
Grant (Ed.), Business Interests,
Organizational Development and
Private Interest Government

European University Institute
Institut Universitaire Européen
Europäisches Hochschulinstitut
Istituto Universitario Europeo

Series C

Political and Social Sciences
Sciences Politiques et Sociales
Politik- und Sozialwissenschaften
Scienze Politiche e Sociali

8

Badia Fiesolana — Firenze

Business Interests, Organizational Development and Private Interest Government

An international comparative study
of the food processing industry

Edited by

Wyn Grant

1987

Walter de Gruyter · Berlin · New York

Library of Congress Cataloging-in-Publication Data

Business interests, organizational development, and
  private interest government.

  (Series C--Political and social sciences ; 8)
  Bibliography: p.
  1. Food industry and trade. 2. Food industry and
trade--Societies, etc.   I. Grant, Wyn.   II. Series.
HD9000.5.B87 1987   338.4'7664   87-21403
ISBN 0-89925-380-6 (U. S.)

CIP-Kurztitelaufnahme der Deutschen Bibliothek

*Business interests, organizational development, and
private interest government :* an internat. compara=
tive study of the food processing industry / ed.
by Wyn Grant. – Berlin ; New York : de Gruyter,
1987.
  (European University Institute : Ser. C, Political
  and social sciences ; 8)
  ISBN 3-11-011395-3
NE: Grant, Wyn [Hrsg.]; Istituto Universitario
Europeo ⟨Fiesole⟩: European University Institute / C

Dust Cover Design: Rudolf Hübler, Berlin. – Setting and Printing: Saladruck, Berlin.
Binding: Verlagsbuchbinderei Dieter Mikolai, Berlin.
Printed in Germany.

Preface

This book represents the outcome of a work carried out over a number of years. In that time, very many intellectual debts have been accumulated. Philippe Schmitter and Wolfgang Streeck initiated and organized the international research project on which this book is based with a skill and fortitude that won the admiration of the various national teams. I am, of course, particularly grateful to the contributors to this book who have borne a number of delays in its completion with patience and understanding. I owe a particular debt to William Coleman of McMaster University who gave me considerable assistance at a number of points in the book's gestation.

Editing the book brought me into contact with the work done on the food processing industry by agricultural and other economists. Their work was of considerable assistance to me in developing a better understanding of the industry. I would particularly like to thank Jim Burns, Don Mills and Alan Swinbank of the Department of Agricultural Economics and Management at the University of Reading for their considerable assistance and for inviting me to present an early version of the introduction at a departmental seminar. I would also like to thank Peter Maunder of the University of Loughborough for his assistance.

Although the United States is not one of the countries covered in this book, I have benefitted from contact with a group of scholars at the University of Wisconsin-Madison interested in the political economy of the food processing industry, including Professor Leon Lindberg and Professor Rogers Hollingsworth. I am grateful to them for inviting me to participate in two seminars they organized on the dairy processing and meat processing subsectors in Madison in November 1984. Attending these seminars gave me (and a number of other contributors to this volume) the opportunity to meet with American agricultural economists interested in the food processing industry and also with managers from a number of U.S. firms, cooperatives and associations in dairying and meat processing.

The project also brought me into contact with many association officials in the food processing industry, some of whom gave up their time to attend workshops related to the project. I would particularly likely to thank Cyril Coffin CBE, formerly director general of the Food Manufacturers Federation, and Tim Stocker, deputy director-general of the Food and Drink Federation. I know that they will not agree with many of the points made in this book, but the fact that it has been written is an acknowledgement that their work is important and worthwhile.

The Nuffield Foundation provided funds for an initial workshop which enabled work on the book to be started. The international coordination effort for the whole project was funded by the Volkswagen Foundation. The European University Institute provided funds for a second workshop in Florence to discuss chapter drafts and has, through support for data processing and in many other ways, assisted the completion of the research on which this book in based. Last but not least, I must thank the University of Warwick for providing a congenial intellectual environment for a political scientist interested in the study of political economy and my family for their tolerance and support.

Leamington Spa, February 1986   Wyn Grant

Table of Contents

Chapter 1

Introduction

WYN GRANT

This book utilizes the results of an international comparative research project on the structures and activities of business interest associations in the food processing industry so as to enhance our knowledge and understanding of such associations and their role in the policy making process. The project, which is described more fully below, has been concerned with such questions as why businessmen organize; how they organize; and what they do when they organize. The researchers involved in the project became increasingly interested in the question of whether business interest associations are capable of acting as private interest governments; thas is, whether they are capable of discharging tasks that would otherwise have to be undertaken by the state, thus increasing the load of decision-making responsibilities which modern governments have to bear. (See Streeck and Schmitter, 1985.)

Of course, the question that has to be faced here is not just whether business interest associations have the organizational resources and control over their members that are necessary if they are to function as private interest governments, but whether they are able to discharge tasks allocated to them in a way that is compatible with public policy goals. Are they able to deliver the compliance of their members to arrangements that may involve concessions by the members that conflict with their short-run interests, even if the outcome in the long run is a non-zero-sum game in which all participants in the exchange improve on their initial position? A practical example would be an arrangement between farmers and processors in the dairy industry, licensed by the state, which enabled farmers to obtain an assured outlet and guaranteed prices for their milk; provided assured supplies of milk to processors at a reasonable price; and included provisions for ensuring that the interests of individual consumers were not neglected, and for planning the long-term development of the industry. A number of the countries discussed in this book have arrangements of that kind in the dairy industry.

Thus, this book contributes to the debate about whether there is an 'associative' model of social order which is distinctive from, yet potentially complementary to, the more traditional social orders of state, market and community (see Streeck and Schmitter, 1984). It also reflects a shift in the focus of the debate on neo-corporatism from the macro to the meso or sectoral level (see Cawson, ed. 1985). One advantage of the research strategy adopted in this project is that it facilitates an examination of the conditions at the sectoral level which permit business interest associations to act as effective intermediaries between their members and the state.

Sectoralism and Policy Communities

An implicit theme of this book is that studies of government-industry relations must not only look at 'country styles' in the treatment of industrial policy, but also at how problems, and responses to them, differ from one sector to another. In some cases, similarities of approach in particular sectors (e. g., dairy products) may tend to wash out what are regarded as marked national divergences in policy styles. In studying particular sectors, however, the framework provided by standard industrial classifications provides only a starting point for analysis: political scientists and sociologists are also interested in the distinctive 'policy communities' that develop in particular industrial sectors. As Cawson emphasises:

Most empirical research makes use of various standard industrial classifications to describe the sectoral differentiation of industry ... however, such discussions are only a starting point for the investigation of sectoral interests where actors themselves identify a collective sectoral interest, and organize to defend and promote it. To examine the relationship between structure, organization and political action it may be useful to borrow from Marxist analysis the equivalents of the concepts of 'class-in-itself' and 'class-for-itself'. Like class, sector is a structural concept, and sectoral identity is a necessary but not a sufficient condition for political action. Neither classes nor sectors *as such* act politically; class and sectoral interests are identified, promoted and identified through organization. (Cawson, 1985: 13.)

It is such organizations with which this study is centrally concerned. However, as well as contributing to central theoretical debates on such subjects as neo-corporatism and policy communities, this book also contributes to contemporary public policy debates, in particular about the food and agricultural policies of the EEC, policies which have an impact beyond the boundaries of the Community itself. The value of this aspect of the book's subject matter is enhanced by the fact that it covers three member states (the German Federal Republic, the Netherlands and the United Kingdom), and four non-member states, one in North America (Austria, Canada, Sweden and Switzerland). An area in which there has been increasing public debate in recent years both inside and outside the EEC is the nutritional consequences of a diet with a high component of processed food, and the desirability or otherwise of particular food additives. (For a variety of views on this subject, see Sanderson and Winkler, undated; Stocker, 1985; Wheelcock and Fallows, 1985.) In this book, these issues are raised in particular in Chapter 10 by de Vroom where he points out that consumer interests have become more in the forefront of state regulation of the food processing industry.

Apart from its contribution to these broader social science and public policy debates, the book has a value which arises from the particular topics which it tackles. It examines two neglected subjects — the food processing industry and business interest associations — and it does so on the basis of a rigorous comparative analysis of seven countries. Although the value of comparative studies of interest governance has long been recognized, such studies are still relatively rare in comparison to the number of single country monographs and, when comparisons are made, they are often limited to two countries.

The Organization of Business Interests Project

This book is based on an international research project on the organization of business interests coordinated by Philippe Schmitter from the European University Institute in Florence and by Wolfgang Streeck from the International Institute of Management in West Berlin. The food processing sector was one of four industrial sectors studied; the reasons for its selection are explained more fully below. Each national team collected a standard set of data specified in code books agreed by the participating countries. For each subsector studied in the food processing industry, a considerable body of information was collected in each country on the economic characteristics of the subsector, its pattern of labour relations, and the extent of state involvement in the sector (defined to cover the existence of specialized representative bodies, state regulation and public ownership). This information was collected from published national statistics; from state and para-state agencies with knowledge of the subsector; from business interest associations and trade unions; from market research organizations; from academics specializing in the study of the subsector; and from individual firms. For each association studied, standardized information requiring a code book of some sixty pages was collected from documentary materials and interviews with association officials. In addition, information was collated on the structure of the associational system in each subsector studied.

The Selection of Subsectors for Intensive Study

At an early stage of the research, it became apparent that there was a large number of associations in the food processing sector in many of the countries being studied. Given the resources of time and personnel available for the research, it would not have been practicable to study every association in the industry in every country. It was therefore decided to concentrate on the associations found in three subsectors as defined by the International Standard Industrial Classification: ISIC 3111 (slaughtering, preparing and preserving meat); ISIC 3112 (manufacture of dairy products): and ISIC 3113 (canning and preserving of fruits and vegetables).

As well as studying the associations in each of the three subsectors (whether serving the subsector as a whole, e. g., the dairy industry, or products within it, e. g., particular cheeses), national teams also studied any associations that were not confined in membership to any one of the subsectors, but nevertheless had members in one or more of them. In this way, associations representing the industry as a whole were included in the sample, as well as other associations that crossed subsectoral boundaries such as associations representing producers of frozen foods. Associations extending beyond the food processing industry, but having members in it, were also counted as part of the industry's associational system, e. g., national sector unspecific 'peak' associations such as the CBI in Britain, or branded goods associations such as the *Markenverband* in West Germany. The definition of a 'business interest association' used in the project is discussed in the research design. (Schmitter and Streeck, 1981: 33—36.)

In some countries, the large number of associations even in the subsectors being studied meant that a further sample of organizations to be subjected to intensive study had to be taken. Usually, any association representing the subsector as a whole, or a significant part of it, was selected for detailed study, together with a sample of product associations. It should be noted that basic information still had to be collected on those associations in the subsectors studied which were not selected for intensive analysis so as to build up a picture of the associational system in each subsector.

The choice of subsectors for detailed study did pose some problems which require further discussion. Recent discussions of the food processing industry have placed increasing emphasis on the 'fundamental distinction' (Harris, 1984: 12) between first and second stage processors. In general terms, first stage processors process farm products, whereas second stage processors produce foodstuffs from semi-finished products provided largely by the first stage industry, although they also use farm products. An important difference between the two is that 'The primary processing sector is still closely linked to agriculture, whereas the secondary sector is becoming increasingly similar in structure to other branches of the manufacturing sector.' (OECD, 1983 a: 13.) Product differentiation tends to be more marked in the second stage subsectors. Moreover, first stage processors tend to benefit from the CAP regime because they process the intervenable products, although they also 'face an increased burden of policy pressures and are particularly vulnerable to changes in CAP policies.' (Harris, 1984: 13.) Second stage producers cannot sell into intervention, and are adversely affected by levies and duties placed on essential raw materials not available (or not in sufficient quantities) in the Community e. g., hard wheat (for breadmaking), maize, long-grain rice.

Within the EEC, at any rate, the two types of producer thus face rather different political problems. The first may be inclined to develop and maintain close cooperative arrangements with suppliers of raw materials (in dairy cooperatives, important in a number of the countries studied, suppliers and processors are often united in one organization), while second stage processors may be more interested in exerting political pressure in the conventional ways to modify Community policies. Even outside the Community, first stage processors are likely to have a closer relationship with their raw material suppliers.

It will be noted that all the subsectors chosen for study encompass first stage processors. Why were these particular subsectors selected for detailed study? First, they were chosen because they are of central importance to the industry as a whole and account for a considerable proportion of its output in the countries studied. For example, in the EEC, dairy products and meat products alone account for nearly thirty per cent of all turnover in the food, drink and tobacco industries. Second stage subsectors that were considered for study (e. g., confectionery) are more strongly represented in some countries than in others and therefore the comparative analysis, which was a central objective of the project, would have been rendered more difficult.

Moreover, the decision to focus on first stage industries was not without its serendipity. It is widely accepted that corporatist arrangements are particularly well developed in the agricultural sector. (See, for example, Jackson and van Schendelen, 1985: 10; although for a discussion of new pressures on these arrangements, see Cox, Lowe and Winter, 1985). The closeness of first stage processing industries 'to the farm gate' allows us to examine the extent to which private interest government arrangements found in agriculture 'spill over' into the food processing industry. The evidence presented in this book (see, for example, the chapters by Coleman, Jacek and Pestoff) suggests that such 'spill over' effects are particularly likely to occur in dairy products which, of all the various subsectors in the food processing industry, is perhaps the one most closely linked to agricultural production. For example, milk is not fundamentally transformed in bottling plants, but rather made safe, and packaged suitably for human consumption. Indeed, it is clear that even in countries which are seen as providing hostile environments for neo-corporatist arrangements, such as the United States, private interest governments have flourished in the dairy subsector. (See Young, Lindberg and Hollingsworth, 1985.)

Why Study Business Interest Associations?

Business interest associations have been a relatively neglected subject of study, particularly compared to trade unions. Such studies as have taken place have tended to focus on intersectoral or so-called 'peak associations' within a single country, and to neglect associations operating at sectoral or subsectoral levels. This is unfortunate for, as Deubner has argued, '"sectors" have a highly interesting role in explaining politics.' (Deubner, 1984: 501.) Indeed, it could be argued that the relative importance of 'peak associations' has been declining, and the importance of sectoral associations increasing, in countries such as Britain and West Germany.

The dominant theoretical paradigm has been the American 'pressure group' model which is firmly located within a pluralist tradition of thinking. Defenders of pluralism have claimed that the richness and diversity of that tradition of writing has been underestimated by its detractors. (See, for example, Almond 1983.) However, the fundamental flaw of the traditional pressure group model is that it focusses on the influence exerted by supposedly autonomous organizations on government; it underplays the flow of influence in the other direction, the extent to which governments, often indirectly and unintentionally, shape the structure and content of group activity. (See, for example, Grant and Streeck 1985.) Through this omission, it underestimates the complexity and potential importance of the behaviour of organized interests. The relationship between organized interests and the state must be seen as an essentially reciprocal one in which actors are more interdependent than perhaps they themselves realize.

Neglect is, of itself, not a justification for the study of a subject: some subjects are justifiably neglected, and there are others which have been studied which might have been better left neglected. It could be argued that the relative lack of research simply reflects the unimportance of business interest associations to the workings of western democracies. One response to this position is that it flies in the face of much of what can be empirically observed. Such associations are often well resourced, enjoy high densities of representation, and are engaged in a continual dialogue with government. In country after country, the research teams have observed such major food processing transnationals as Unilever, Nestlé and General Foods not only subscribing to a multiplicity of food processing associations, but also loaning their senior executives for time consuming committee work or to serve as office holders in an association. If business interest associations were unimportant, would profit maximising firms be devoting so much of the time of their senior staff to them?

Why, then, should the owners of capital, possessing as they do the discretionary power to invest, develop a need for collective interest representation? Our study suggests a number of answers to this question: to counter the economic strength of raw material suppliers, as discussed in Chapter 8 by Coleman; to counter the collective strength of the suppliers of labour, as discussed in Chapter 6 by Hilbert and Voelzkow; to counter the strength of the retail trade, as discussed in Chapter 9 by Farago; and to defend the interests of business in areas of state regulation by gaining some control over that regulation, as discussed in Coleman's chapter and Chapter 10 by de Vroom on quality control.

As is made clear in Chapter 3 by Jacek, business interest associations do often function as private interest governments, a tendency that is particularly apparent in the dairy sector — a phenomenon which can be related to the economic structure of the chain of dairy production. Many of the matters with which associations are concerned as private interest governments are, of course, highly technical, but that does not mean that they are unimportant. For example, as well as illustrating the variety of partnership relationships with the state in the area of quality control, de Vroom's chapter is relevant to the increasingly salient public debate about the nutritional value of processed food and the potential effect of its consumption on the health of individuals, and hence on public health in general. More generally, we shall show that the logic of exchange with the state and producer groups enables associations to develop governing properties in areas other than quality control, such as price setting, supply management and occupational training. The precise mix of responsibilities undertaken by associations will vary from country to country, depending on the organizational development of associations (see the chapters by Traxler and Jacek) and the institutional structure of the state (see the chapter by Pestoff).

The Asymmetrey Hypothesis

The neglect of business interest associations by academics is to be particularly regretted given the attention devoted in the academic debate on neo-corporatism to the 'asymmetrey hypothesis'. (See Offe: 1985.) In broad outline, this hypothesis is based on the contention that labour can only exert effective influence through organized collective action, whereas firms can exert direct influence on their own behalf through their operations on the product and labour markets; can, subject to legal constraints, operate in conjunction with other firms to shape the market through cartel action; can exert political influence on their own behalf; or, finally, take political action in conjunction with other firms through associative activity. Thus, it is argued, in the case of labour, 'any constraints imposed on the leadership and the forms in which organizational activities are conducted will have direct consequences for the type of demands that are being made as well as the intensity and unity by which they can be supported.' (Offe, 1981: 150.)

Of course, in return for accepting some restraints on its actions, labour may obtain net gains from the bargaining process which would be greater than those obtained from debilitating conflict with capital. Indeed, it may be the case that the costs of corporatist bargaining are higher in the long run for capital than for labour. The representatives of labour may insist that the agenda of bargaining shifts away from questions of wage and price determination, for example, to issues that impinge more directly on the property rights of capitalists such as investment decisions or forms of workplace organization. Hilbert and Voelzkow note in Chapter 6 how an increasing emphasis on qualitative demands by trade unions in the West German food processing industry led to a response from employers in the form of a new employers' organization for the industry as a whole. The data collected in the broader project on business interests, of which this book represents one part, provides a means of assessing the validity of these alternative hypotheses on the long-run gains and losses from corporatist bargaining. (See the chapter by Hilbert and Voelzkow for a discussion of these issues.)

Discussion of the 'asymmetrey hypothesis' reminds us of the importance of studying business interest associations not just in terms of their reciprocal relationship with the state, but also in terms of their exchanges with the trade unions, which are often simultaneously adversaries and partners. In fact, only a minority of the associations studied in the seven countries function as employers' organizations in the sense that they are directly involved in the process of collective bargaining. Nevertheless, the absence as well as the presence of such functions can shape the overall associational system, as well as the development of particular associations. More generally, one needs to ask whether the collective interest representation of employers is subject to the same dialectical forces which have made workers' organizations, originally set up solely to advance the interests of their constituents in relation to other social groups, subsequently assume governing capacities in relation to their members? These issues are an underlying theme in the chapter by Hilbert and Voelzkow.

There may, however, be asymmetries other than those between capital and labour. In a chapter which makes careful use of admittedly sometimes limited data, Rainbird shows that women have a higher participation rate in the labour force in food processing than in manufacturing in general. Although there are considerable variations in occupational structures between countries, women tend to fill the unskilled, lower paid jobs in the industry. Taking up the theme of the heterogeneity of the industry stressed by other contributors such as van Waarden, Rainbird argues that the combination of heterogeneity with the segmentation of the labour force has been a factor affecting the lack of unity in the organisation of labour in the industry. The implication can be drawn that this, in turn, affects employer organization in the industry. The country with the largest core of skilled labour, the FRG, also has a centrally coordinated union for the industry which has prompted a coordinated response from employers.

Why Study the Food Processing Industry?

The sceptic should by now have been convinced of the value of the study of business interest associations, but might still question the choice of the food processing industry as an arena for such a study. Indeed, an important comparative study of government-industry relationships (Zysman: 1983) makes a case for relative neglect of the industry, breakfast foods being linked with cosmetics in a contrast with the semiconductor sector and the motor industry. Zysman (1983: 43) argues that a distinction must be made between industries 'with extensive linkages to the rest of the economy, which are consequently of substantial national importance, and those which have limited attachments to (or importance for) other sectors.' However, it is somewhat misleading to describe the food processing industry as an 'unlinked industry'. The industry has important links with the agricultural sector, of which it is the main customer, and with the retail sector, of which it is a principal provider of merchandise. Moreover, the food processing industry is linked to a number of other industries, particularly to the suppliers of the machinery which processes food (including significant amounts of specialized microelectronic control equipment) and the suppliers of a variety of packaging materials for food (plastics, glass, card, metal cans etc.).

Zysman has the intellectual courage and honesty to make explicit a latent prejudice which is reflected in a considerable imbalance in the academic analysis of particular industrial sectors (for detailed evidence on this point in the British case, see Young: 1984). On the whole, academics have tended to concentrate their efforts on industries which have experienced dramatic declines in employment and output (such as steel), or on industries based on new technologies which seemingly have the potential to transform the whole pattern of industrial activity (such as microelectronics). The disdain shown for industries such as food processing with more consistent patterns of output fails to reflect their real economic importance and also leads to a potentially misleading emphasis in the study of government-industry relations on crisis ridden or highly promising sectors. Admittedly, there have been valuable studies of the food processing industry by agricultural economists, and industrial economists have paid some attention to the alcoholic drinks sector, but such studies do not offset the relative neglect of the industry by industrial sociologists and by political scientists interested in government-industry relations.

The way in which particular subsectors within the food processing industry were selected for intensive study has already been discussed, but the choice of the food processing industry itself for analysis was also the outcome of a deliberate selection process. The four industries chosen for analysis in the project as a whole (the other three were chemicals, construction and machine tools) were selected with the aid of a sampling matrix. The matrix was made up from two sets of variables: those relating to an industry's economic structure such as concentration and internationalization, and those relating to an industry's interactions with the state, such as its dependence on the state as a customer and the extent to which it is subject to extensive state regulation. The choice of the food processing industry for study thus forms part of a broader intellectual strategy, but there are also particular reasons which make it especially suitable as an arena for the study of business interest associations.

First, it is a very important sector in national economies, even if that importance is often undervalued. Food processing is the largest industry in terms of share of gross output in the EEC (FDIC, 1982: 41) and, of the other countries studied, is the largest manufacturing industry in Canada. Second, it offers a wide mix of subsectors. The outstanding feature of the industry, when compared with other industries, is its heterogeneity, thus allowing useful comparisons to be made *within* the industry. The industry as a whole is, of course, using food as its basic raw material, but that raw material may differ considerably in its origins, the machinery and techniques required for its processing, the packaging of the product, and the product market which it faces. Compare, for example, sausages with yoghurt. The three subsectors we focus on in this study vary considerably in their industrial organization, in relevant state structures, and in the degree of state regulation. (See the chapters by van Waarden and by Pestoff.) In particular, there is more state intervention *and* more self-governance by associations in the dairy subsector. (See the chapters by Jacek and by Coleman.)

The extent of private interest government found in the food processing industry, as established in the chapter by Jacek, is striking and emphasizes well how the traditional treatment of business interest associations as 'pressure groups' is inadequate, and that new theoretical perspectives such as we develop in this book are necessary. It is those new theoretical perspectives that form the focus of the remainder of this introduction; food processing provides a particularly suitable arena in which they can be tested and developed.

Organizational Development and Associative Order

The research project as a whole was informed by the debate on neo-corporatism, and a central concern was the organizational structure of business interest associations as intermediary organizations in potential neo-corporatist arrangements. Even a casual reader of the neo-corporatist literature would quickly become aware that there is a variety of definitions of the term 'neo-corporatism', some of which lead to highly divergent explanations of the concept. (See Grant, ed.: 1985.) There is much to be said for Schmitter's wish 'to conserve the label of corporatism for interest intermediation.' (Schmitter, 1982: 263.) It is thus 'a distinctive mode for organizing ... conflicting functional interests.' (Schmitter, 1982: 263). It seeks to achieve this aim by incorporating formally designated interest associations 'within the process of authoritative decision making and implementation.' (Schmitter, 1981: 295.) The project was concerned with the particular but important question of whether business interest associations are capable of acting as effective intermediaries between their members and the state, and thus developing as private interest governments.

The debate on neo-corporatism has many of the characteristics of a Slough of Despond in which those lacking persistence and wisdom, like Pliable in Bunyan's allegory, end up climbing out in a dishevelled state on the same side as they fell in. The participants in this project have been determined not to stay in the mire, or to climb out on the wrong side, but to 'possess the brave country.' (Bunyan, 1678: 17). In the more prosaic language of social science, this means that neo-corporatism is not to be seen as a final social science paradigm, but one that is capable of being transcended by a new paradigm which goes beyond neo-corporatism by building on the enduring elements of the corporatist debate. Streeck and Schmitter overcome many of the uncertainties and ambiguities surrounding much corporatist terminology by developing an associative model of social order, an exploration of 'arrangements under which an attempt is made to make associative, self-interested collective action contribute to the achievement of public policy objectives.' (Schmitter and Streeck, 1984: 22).

One precondition of such an associative order would be organizationally developed associations, having sufficient autonomy from both their members and the state to enable them to mediate effectively without experiencing destabilization; and possessing sufficient authority over their members to ensure their compliance with agreements arrived at with the state. Such authority may, of course, be derived from the state itself, but this will in turn depend upon the state's recognition of the association as an effective partner. Hence, a virtuous cycle may be set up, in which demonstrated effectiveness in securing the implementation of agreements leads to the delegation of greater authority to an association, thus increasing its importance both to its members and the state.

Organizational Development

Organizational development is the principal dependent variable treated in this book, and it is therefore necessary to explore the concept with some care. As defined by Schmitter and Streeck (1981: 124):

Organizational structures are the more 'developed' the more encompassing they are in scope and purpose (the more 'external effects' and interdependencies they internalize); the more specialized and coordinated they are internally: the more safely their supply of strategic resources is institutionalized; and the greater their autonomous capacity to act and to pursue long-term strategies regardless of short-term environmental constraints and fluctuations.

There are two basic notions involved in this concept: organized complexity and relative autonomy. The first of these notions, organized complexity, is the theme of Chapter 2 by Traxler which looks at the variety of associational systems noted in the different countries studied. The basic question addressed is: what structural arrangements are required, given the basically individualistic and competitive structure of business interest, for owners of capital to be able to associate with each other and form business interest associations?

As Schmitter and Streeck explain (1981: 125), 'an interest association or a system of interest associations is the more *complex* the higher the number and the greater the diversity of the units of which it is composed; and it is the more *organized* the larger the number of institutionalized relations between its components and the greater the extent of the functional coordination achieved through these relations.' Business associations in the food processing industry have to cope with a considerable diversity of underlying interests. For example, if one takes the dairy subsector, one has milk being produced from different animals (cows, goats and sheep); one has processing factories under different forms of ownership (private firms, para-state marketing boards, farmers' cooperatives and consumers' cooperatives); one has to balance the interests of different uses for the raw material (liquid milk versus manufacturing, but also different products); and even within a product category, there may be different identities and market competition (e. g., specialist cheeses). In addition, one has to take account of divergent territorial interests arising from the existence of distinct supply management regimes in different parts of the country, a phenomenon not confined to federal states. (For a fuller discussion of these various heterogeneities in the industry, see the chapter by van Waarden). Interest diversity can be overcome by two routes: through intra-organizational differentiation on the basis of special interests, and through external coordination between independent associations. In both individual associations and associational systems, one may examine the extent to which the arrangements made provide a pattern of functional division of labour and hierarchical coordination, facilitating an effective discharge of tasks, including those of private interest government.

Traxler's chapter shows that there is considerable variety in the coherence of associational systems, not only from country to country, but also from subsector to subsector within particular countries. Examples vary from those in which there is little or no connection between related associations, an overlap of functions and competition for influence, to those in which associations are organized in a clearly structured hierarchy, with an agreed distribution of functions and an absence of competition for members and influence. Whilst pointing to the way in which representation of the Austrian food processing industry is carried out through intra-organizational differentiation and coordination, Traxler notes that in most countries the industry lacks a single focus in the form of one spokesman with an unequivocal superdorinate relationship with subsector and product associations. The industry is consequentially often in a weak position to defend itself against politically strong farmers and economically strong retailers (see also the chapter by Farago on the issue of demand side power).

Private Interest Government

The second aspect of organizational development, the notion of organizational autonomy, forms the focus of Jacek's chapter, although this theme is expanded to take account of the extent to which business interest associations are in practice able to function as private interest governments. As used by Schmitter and Streeck, the concept of organizational autonomy refers both to the input (resources) capacity of an organization, and the output side in terms of an organization's ability to select and pursue strategies of action. Increasing autonomy in both these areas protects an organization from unpredictable turbulence, and hence permits an organization to survive and to orient itself towards long term objectives. (See Schmitter and Streeck, 1981: 128–29.) A stable organization with a long term perspective is more likely to appeal to the state as a prospective partner in governance.

As an organization acquires greater relative autonomy from its membership, not only will its pattern of resource supply change away from a predominant reliance on members, but the outputs of the association will also change. In particular, such organizations will start to supply more monopoly goods, that is, private selective goods supplied through the assistance of other organizations, especially trade unions and the state. 'As far as the state is concerned, such support consists primarily in *monopoly rights* on the provision of certain vital goods or services to (potential) BIA members, or in a share in the *authority* of the state to make legally binding decisions on matters of interest to BIA members.' (Schmitter and Streeck, 1981: 229.) Thus, one can treat the assumption of private interest government functions by a business interest association as both an outcome and an indicator of organizational development.

Jacek shows that associations in the industry are most frequently used to implement general macro-economic and intersectoral policies followed by labour policies, quality standards, measures to stabilize supplier/customer relations and least of all in industry structuring, although the differences among policy areas is not great. The dairy subsector is the most prone to private interest government of the three studied, with fruit and vegetables the least susceptible. When the seven countries studied are placed along a continuum, two countries generally regarded as prone to concertative arrangements (Austria and Sweden) are found to be most likely to develop private interest governments. The position of a North American country, Canada, at the other end of this continuum is not surprising. What is interesting is that West Germany comes closest to Canada, whereas Britain is nearest to the 'neo-corporatist' countries which is a different pattern from what one would expect. In the British case, the reduction of state responsibilities under the Thatcher Government has led to the transfer of some public policy responsibilities, e.g., in training policy, to employers' associations. (See Rainbird and Grant, 1985.)

Jacek also notes that private interest government, especially in what is perhaps its strongest form, that of the provision of authoritative monopoly goods, has developed in the food processing industry at the subsectoral level, particularly in dairying. However, a more integrated system would be necessary if associations were to become important players in questions of industrial structure. Such a dirigiste emphasis may not be welcome to associations themselves, but there may be circumstances in which an industrial policy developed and implemented by associations may be preferable to a state imposed plan. In the meantime there is, as Jacek points out, an underlying tension between the heterogeneity of associational systems in food processing and their assumption of public policy functions.

What is the relationship between structure and function in a virtuous cycle of organizational development? It might seem that associations involved in corporatist structures of representation will be pulled into concertative relationships with the state and that those with pluralist representation structures will be participants in pressure politics. However, as Coleman shows in Chapter 8, in all of the countries except Austria and Sweden the supposedly unstable situation of a pluralist structure of representation and a concertation structure of control occurs. If the associational system is highly developed at the macro level, as in Austria and Sweden, the opportunities for concertation will be channelled upwards to the national peak associations. However, in the absence of such factors promoting the development of associational systems at the macro level, stable concertative arrangements may develop at the meso level. Such subsector structures may be able to manage supply arrangements for particular raw materials, but they do not foster an associational system for the industry as a whole which can deal with broader challenges such as those posed by the nature of the CAP (see the chapter by Pestoff) or the consequences of retailer concentration (see the chapter by Farago).

The Logic of Membership and the Logic of Influence

Why do some associational systems display a greater level of organizational development than others? Chance, particular historical events, even the skills of individual organizational entrepreneurs, may all play their part. Broadly speaking however, two sets of factors seem to be of crucial importance in the longer run: what Schmitter and Streeck (1981) have termed 'the logic of membership' and the 'logic of influence'.

The 'logic of membership' refers to the characteristics of members of an association. Hence, in studying business interest associations, one needs to take account of the characteristics of the interested category which the association or system of associations seeks to represent, and of that subset of the interested category which makes up the membership of the association or system of associations being considered. (In associational systems with compulsory memberships, the two should be identical, but in most of the cases we are considering, membership is voluntary.) In examining the logic of membership one is therefore concerned with such economic phenomena as competition, heterogeneity, profitability and growth in a sector or subsector, as well as with such social phenomena as the social cohesion of the category of interest which is being represented.

The 'logic of influence' is concerned with the various interlocutors with which a business association interacts. Thus, instead of looking inwards to the characteristics of the membership or potential membership, one is looking outwards to a number of external influences on a particular association, or indeed on the associational system of a subsector or whole sector. Most important among these interlocutors is the state; one also has to take account of the EEC, which has some state-like properties. In principle, logic of influence factors might be expected to pull in the opposite direction from logic of membership factors, having an integrating rather than a disintegrating effect. In particular, one might expect governments to prefer to deal with a small number of associations representing comprehensive domains in which interests are aggregated at as high a level as possible.

Reality is a lot more complex than these simple assumptions might lead us to believe. Indeed, as van Waarden points out in this chapter, it is difficult to disentangle the logic of membership and the logic of influence; the two are enmeshed with one another. For example, the dairy subsector is particularly intensely regulated because of the particular characteristics of the sector. Therefore, van Waarden argues, it is difficult to separate the influence of state regulation and sector structure on the associational system.

As van Waarden points out, there is no doubt that the food processing industry is the most heterogeneous of the four industries studied in the International Institute of Management project. One of the most important divisions between firms is that between farmer owned cooperatives and proprietary firms, but there are many others as well. Coleman points out in his chapter that the sub-division of agricultural policy by commodity has had the effect of placing the subsectors of the food processing industry in different policy arenas. There has been a tendency for food processing subsectors (especially, of course, first stage sectors) to become more closely tied with a corresponding group of farmers than with each other. Given all these considerations, it is not surprising that there is (excluding Austria) a fragmented associational system in most countries, as demontrated in the chapter by Traxler.

However, this does not mean that we should treat the logic of membership as a 'given' which inevitably leads to a fragmented associational system. As van Waarden points out, even the most important sector characteristic, heterogeneity, exerts its influence on associative action only because it, in turn, is influenced by state intervention which structures the market. As the OECD has noted (1983 a: 21), 'present agricultural policies make many world markets for agricultural products residual in character'. The market structures which underpin the logic of membership are, therefore, themselves substantially influenced by action by state or para-state bodies; this is particularly the case in the dairy sector. (See OECD: 1983 b.)

Nevertheless, although the influence by state bodies is considerable, it is not consistent and often runs counter to what would be required for organizational development. As Pestoff reminds us in his chapter, the state is not a monolithic institution with a single will, but is rather segmented in character with a composite will of parts which interact with each other through a mixture of conflict and cooperation. Territorial decentralization of the state appears to have a more limited impact on associative activity in food processing than functional decentralization. There are numerous national agencies in each subsector and different agencies exist for different roles and functions. The diversity of state structures dealing with the industry means that they reinforce, rather than counteract, its fundamental heterogeneity. The product-related nature of state structures encourages subsectoral fragmentation of the associations, and 'freezes' the existing pattern of narrow subsectoral associations in the industry.

Membership of the EEC does pose problems for the industry as a whole, or at least for several subsectors at one time, and in the British case, the experience of EEC membership has been a catalyst in leading to a more effective sector wide representational arrangement. However, at the EEC level, the industry faces the problem of the institutional and policy priority given by the Community to agriculture, despite the fact that food processing is a more significant industry. At the EEC level, one again finds a considerable number of product specific associations, with the general sectoral association (CIAA) having experienced a rather slow and uneven pattern of organizational development.

Does Fragmentation Matter?

The general picture that emerges from the study is of a heterogeneous industry facing a diversified state and a multitude of unions. Consequentially, one has a fragmented associational system (with the exception of Austria, where there has been decisive state intervention to shape the framework of associative activity). There are some very effective associations at subsector and product level which are quite capable of functioning as private interest governments or, as Coleman shows, engaging in concertative action with raw materials producers. However, the industry is not always very well represented at the sectoral level, even though there has been progress in that direction in recent years in countries such as Britain and Sweden. Moreover, even when there are sectoral associations, the distribution of authority and responsibility between them and subsector associations often resembles an uneasy partnership, rather than one between a superior body and its subordinates.

If one then asks, 'does fragmentation matter', one has to ask a supplementary question, 'for whom?' After all, one leading firm in the industry told the Dutch project team that the present differentiated pattern of interest representation was very functional. Some interests could be best represented by a small group of concerned firms directly to specialized state and semi-state bodies. (See the chapter by van Waarden.)

No doubt there are many occasions when such specialized representation best serves the interests of firms. However, I would argue that such specialized representation should be viewed as complementary to effective representation at the sectoral level, rather than as a satisfactory alternative. The absence of such sector wide representation is not in the interests of the industry, the state or association officials. Although the full story of the formation of the Food and

Drink Federation in Britain has not yet (and may never be) told, it would seem that both large firms in the industry and civil servants were becoming frustrated by a situation in which there was more than one broadly based association which could be seen as a spokesman for the whole industry. As far as association staff are concerned, overlaps and duplication between associations is likely to make their task more difficult and, in the long run, to discourage the attraction and retention of staff of a high calibre.

The need for effective representation for the industry as a whole is demonstrated by the problems it has faced in coping with the growing economic power of retailers, as discussed in the chapter by Farago. In most of the countries studied, there has been a shift of economic power from food processors to retailers, which the processors have been unable to counteract. This shift adversely affects profits and, ultimately, investment. As Farago points out, the food processing industry is not only faced with the limits to collective reactions set by the market structure and the economic situation of the sector, but also with the limits set by an asymmetry in the organizational development of the industry and of retail trading. The limited capabilities of the relevant associations make it difficult to resolve the problem by agreements between processors and retailers. Farago's chapter is a salutary reminder of the limits of associative activity, particularly when associations are trying to deal with another powerful economic interest rather than the state.

The chapter by de Vroom is also a reminder of the limitations of associative action, as well as of its strenghts. As he points out, the state may, for technical reasons and to ensure compliance, need the participation of business associations in quality regulation. Associations may become involved, in a variety of different ways, in the formulation and implementation of regulations. Indeed, it is clear that in many cases quality regulations are the outcome of a collusion between governments and parts of the industry to protect particular domestic markets against foreign competition. That is not to ignore the importance of public concern about food quality: as de Vroom shows, 'scandals' have played an important historical role in creating pressures for more stringent regulation. In recent years, consumer pressures not related to specific incidents, and the drive for harmonization within the European Community, have assumed a new significance.

Nevertheless, important though associational involvement is in devising and implementing regulations drawn up in response to such pressures, de Vroom points out that quality regulation is a state affair in almost every country; this is the case even in Austria with its marked neo-corporatist traits. He is able to show that across all the industries studied in the project, product quality and safety standards were the most important objects of state intervention, a tendency that is being reinforced by increased consumer pressures. Food additives, in particular, have become a political issue (see Gardner, 1986) and the rather fragmented associational systems to be found in the food processing industry may not be able to cope very well with these general political pressures, any more than they can cope with economic pressures from retailers.

It is one thing to argue that more effective representational arrangements are in the interests of the industry; another to maintain that they serve the general public interest. Nevertheless, one could argue that effective intermediaries are a necessary condition for the efficient conduct of relations between government and industry, relations that are likely to exist even in the most liberal states. Governments need to know that they are talking to bodies which are capable of developing a considered view on behalf of the sectors they purport to represent.

However, it could also be argued that there is a need to develop arrangements which rely neither on state action, nor on the operations of the market mechanism. There are public policy objectives which cannot be achieved through a reliance on the workings of the market, but state action may be rigid, inefficient, and difficult to enforce effectively. There is therefore a case for making use of private interest governments which seek to carry out regulatory activities on behalf of the state through private, albeit state licensed and/or supervised, mechanisms.

The merits or otherwise of such arrangements lie beyond the scope of this discussion. For example, critics of such arrangements might argue that they rely on too narrow a range of interests, and tend to make policy communities even more 'closed' to outside scrutiny and criticism. Their supporters might argue that they are an effective means of achieving public policy objectives without stretching the enforcement capabilities of the state. In practice, much may depend on how well the arrangements are monitored, and whether there is a real threat of direct state action being taken if they do not function properly.

This book does not seek to resolve the controversy about the merits of this form of governance arrangement, but it does provide a considerable body of systematically gathered evidence that is relevant to the discussion. It is clear that there are a considerable number of private interest government arrangements in the food processing industry, often at the subsectoral or product level, and in countries with very different traditions of government-industry interaction. The research reported in this book permits a more systematic and comprehensive examination than has been possible hitherto of the factors which promote and sustain organizational development in business interest associations, and hence the emergence of private business governments.

Chapter 2

Patterns of Associative Action

Franz Traxler

The Management of Diversity

This chapter seeks to investigate the patterns of associative activity among businessmen in the food processing industry. For this purpose, it is, as a first step, necessary to consider the substance of collective business interests and the strategies that can be followed in order to organize them. The scope of interests businessmen have in common extends from particularistic interests (e. g. concerning the very special kind of product or the type of ownership) to class interests which are related to capital as a whole in relation to labour and the state.

Organizing these various interests is complicated by the fact that they are, at least partly, conflicting. On the one hand a multiplicity of divergent group interests exists within the business class such as those of processors and retailers (see the chapter by Farago, this volume); on the other hand it is possible that the particularistic interests of business groups are in competition with encompassing class interests. For example, a declining industry may call for direct subsidies from the state, while business as a whole rejects that kind of industrial policy as a threat to its discretionary power over investment decisions and as a distortion of the conditions of market competition (Traxler and Moser, 1984).

Given this diversity of business interests, the formation of associative action requires the selection from the overall existing interests of those which the respective association intends to represent. This implies a distinction between relevant and irrelevant interests by defining an organizational *domain*. Relevant interests are those, which the association has internalised and, thus, are part of its domain. Irrelevant interests remain outside the scope of the association's activities. Their representation is left to other interest organizations.

The definition of the organizational domain can be done by parameters related to business groups and to tasks (Schmitter and Streeck 1981: 147 ff). Parameters related to business groups identify the potential members of an association. Examples for such parameters are criteria like product, territory and firm size. Parameters related to tasks specify the functions the association claims to fulfil on behalf of their members. The most important mode of task specialization is the distinction between employers' organizations and trade associations. While employers' associations represent the interests of their members in matters of labour relations and the social policy of the state, trade associations articulate their members' interests as producers. The more parameters an association specifies, the more homogenous becomes its group of potential members and the less complex are the interests internalised by it.

As far as the extent of internalised interest complexity is concerned, two alternative forms of associative action can be distinguished. The first alternative means of managing diversity is the formation of encompassing associations organizing as many business groups and performing as many tasks as possible. This form of organizing interests results in an associational system characterized by a low degree of *horizontal* differentiation. Given a particular distribution of interests among business groups, the number of interest associations decreases the more encompassing they are in terms of internalised interests (Schmitter and Streeck 1981: 126). Conversely, a high degree of internalised complexity gives rise to internal differentiation by establishing subunits responding to different member groups and tasks. Internal differentiation of encompassing associations is a central precondition of formulating goals common to all groups within the domain and elaborating strategies appropriate to the problems of goal implementation through coordinating different tasks and unifying divergent interests step by step.

The comprehensiveness of domain affects both the conditions of exerting influence on the environment and of maintaining cohesion among members. The more encompassing the associations' domain, *ceteris paribus,* the greater its possibilities of exerting effective political influence. In the case of industrial relations, employers' associations have to control at least as many segments of the labour market as the corresponding trade unions do. Similarly, the influence of trade associations grows in accordance with the comprehensiveness of their domain. In principle, associations representing a high number of businessmen and a wide range of interests are of greater political relevance than smaller organizations. In addition to this, public authorities will tend to prefer to deal with comprehensive associations, because they can place a lot of the burden of reconciling divergent interests upon the associations' internal decision-making process.[1]

These strategic advantages of a comprehensive associational domain are accompanied by significant problems of internal integration. The more heterogeneous the interests that associations have internalised, the more difficult their internal decision-making process is likely to become. Growing interest diversity creates increasing problems of unifying interests (Staber and Aldrich, 1983: 167). Encompassing associations are forced to unify the interests of all their member groups in order to maintain their ability to articulate unequivocal demands vis-a-vis their interlocutors. As a consequence of this, encompassing associations represent the interests of their members only in a mediated and selective form. During the process of internal compromise it is quite possible that the interests of some member groups are filtered out.

[1] A salient example of transferring problems of interest unification from government bodies to associations is Austria's 'Social Partnership'. In this system of concerted corporatist policy making, the participating 'big four' associations have a privileged position in respect of representing interests via-a-vis the state.

These problems of goal formation within comprehensive associations give rise to domain specialization as the second alternative of associative action. Associations specialized in members and tasks are able to formulate policies more suited to the interests of certain business groups. Therefore, they endanger not only the organizational unity of less specialized associations but also their viability. Why should a firm join an encompassing association, if there are specialized organizations which are capable of articulating its interests in a more authentic way? Furthermore, specialization in domain not only generates *competitive advantages* in relation to other associations but can also serve as a measure to reduce competitive spaces in the relationships between associations (Traxler, 1984). Specialization offers the possibility of defining exclusive domains. In contrast to this, an association, which does not specify its domain, is automatically in competition with *all* other organizations representing business interests. At the level of the associational system, domain specialization leads to a fragmented, highly differentiated pattern of associative action consisting of a multiplicity of small organizations concerned with a narrowly defined scope of interests. From a strategic point of view, fragmented associational systems are subject to a 'particularistic bias' of interest representation, because they highly lack the ability to deal with common interests of groups belonging to different associations. All interests being more general than the narrow domain of the single associations are systematically neglected. The advantages of facilitating internal integration by specialization are connected with difficulties in coordinating interdependent interests.

Thus, the implications of different degress of domain comprehensiveness reflect the competing imperatives of the logic of membership and the logic of influence. While a broadly defined domain is responding to the exertion of influence and colliding with the requirements of internal integration, it is just the opposite in the case of narrow domain.

A way of mediating these competing imperatives is the formation of a pyramid of associations (Schmitter and Streeck 1981: 135 ff). At the bottom of this pyramid are to be found highly specialized *'membership associations'*, organizing firms and/or individual businessmen. At the next-higher level, these associations are integrated into *'peak associations'*. They may also be integrated into peak associations of a 'higher order', which are fewer in number and broader in their domain than the respective associations they are organizing. One may also find *mixed associations* organizing firms/individual businessmen as well as associations.[2]

Such a form of *vertical* associational differentiation permits a stepwise process of unifying interests and coordinating political strategies. Whether one is able to approach the coordination capacity of a single, all groups of business encompassing, membership association, depends on two factors. First, the pyramid of associations must cover the same scope of interests as the single, encompassing

---

[2] Of the associations representing subsector interests in the countries studied, 81 per cent are membership associations, 5 per cent mixed associations and 14 per cent peak associations.

association. This implies that all membership and mixed associations must be affiliated to peak associations representing their interests at a more general, aggregate level. Moreover, all existing mixed associations and peak associations must be integrated into an overall system of interest coordination.[3] That means that all lower order associations are directly or indirectly affiliated to the highest order peak association. Unaffiliated associations indicate a fragmentation of the associational system into several separate subsystems, which are not integrated into the general process of interest aggregation (Schmitter and Streeck 1981: 200). Second, the autonomy of the affiliated associations must not exceed the autonomy of the subunits of the single, all-embracing association.

Under these two circumstances the *inter*-organizational way of unifying interests by vertical differentiation can serve as a functional equivalent of the *intra*-organizational coordination within an all-embracing domain of a single association.

The following sections of this chapter deal with the question of how the process of associational interest aggregation takes place in the countries studied, moving up from the 'bottom' of the level of the three subsectors to the 'top' of the general, intersectoral level of interest representation. The strategy of analysis is as follows. First, the salient features of horizontal differentiation in the associational systems of the three subsectors in each country are investigated. Second, there is a discussion of the vertical differentiation of the associational system and the process of unifying interests. This will be done by reviewing the associational patterns of integrating the subsectors into a more general context of interest representation. Special attention will be focussed on the mode of interest unification at the (sectoral) level of the food processing industry as a whole and on the links between the food processing associations and national business associations representing all sectors of the industry.

Horizontal Differentiation

As mentioned above, horizontal differentiation within associational systems is a function of the number of the single (membership and mixed) associations. In this respect, one might argue that a comparison of the associational systems of different countries has to take into account the different subsector size, especially the different number of potential members. The number of establishments (as an indicator of the national subsector size), the number of membership associations and mixed associations can be seen for the countries studied in Table 2.1. It shows some surprising findings. For instance, in the meat processing subsector the *West German* associational system is complicated by the existence of no less than 474 associations, of which the majority are locally based organizations operating in the *Handwerk* system representing small artisan firms processing meat by non-industrial methods. This pattern does not conform to

---

[3] Since mixed associations are organizing firms/businessmen as well as associations, they must be taken into account for analysing the vertical differentiation at the 'bottom' as well as at the 'top' of the associational pyramid.

the common assumption that West German business interest associations are few in number in each industrial sector. Conversely, *Britain* is characterized by the lowest degree of horizontal differentiation in this subsector, if we take account of subsector size.

Basically, this ratio of subsector size to the number of associations should not be overestimated, because the number of businesses by itself hardly affects the *substance* of collective business interests. Given a certain space of business groups, which is defined in the same way for all countries, a greater number of associations indicates a higher degree of domain specialization, and, as a result of this, a higher degree of inter-organizational differentiation.[4] From this point of view, the number of associations indicates the degree of horizontal differentiation in an associational system more validly than the ratio taking account of the subsector size. Consequently, in the meat processing subsector the *Austrian* associational system, consisting of three sector-unspecific associations is clearly less differentiated than the British system.

Table 2.1 Horizontal Differentiation

Country	Meat Processing			Dairy			Fruits and Vegetables		
	(a)	(b)	(b) (a)	(a)	(b)	(b) (a)	(a)	(b)	(b) (a)
A	3 130*	3	0.10	277	2	0.72	128	3	2.34
CDN	637+	11	1.73	456	9	1.97	232	6	2.59
D	29 000*	474	1.63	817	21	2.57	542	12	2.21
NL	503+	11	2.19	158	14	8.86	101	3	2.97
S	189+	6	3.17	119	2	1.68	43	3	6.98
CH	4 079*	6	0.15	1842	7	0.38	163	6	3.68
GB	29 564*	19	0.08	715	26	3.64	209	14	6.70

(a) Number of establishments (1980); (b) Number of membership associations and mixed associations; * Figure includes butchers; + Figure excludes butchers.

Table 2.1 does not show the full extent of 'Austrian exceptionalism'. In Austria, there are only three associations concerned with the subsectors studied. Their domain is sector unspecific in so far as they are organizing firms notwithstanding the industrial sector to which they belong. Nevertheless, they are not only representing intersectoral but also (sub)sectoral interests stemming from the food processing industry. The *Bundeskammer der gewerblichen Wirtschaft* (Federal Chamber of Business and Commerce) is organizing almost all sections of Austria's capital on the basis of legally guaranteed compulsory membership. The second organization, the *Österreichischer Raiffeisenverband* represents the Raiffeisen cooperatives, which started as a self-help movement of farmers during the last century. The *Konsumverband* engaged in two subsectors embraces the cooperatives of the social democratic labour movement.

---

[4] Similarly, the process of interest unification is the more complicated, the higher the number of associations is irrespective of the subsector size.

Apart from Austria, *Sweden* has the smallest number of associations in the subsectors studied. As in the Austrian case, the type of ownership is an important factor of the formation of associative action. The producer cooperative movement owns nearly fifty per cent of the food processing industry.

Among the smaller countries studied, *the Netherlands* has the largest number of associations in the three subsectors with half the total in the dairy sector. The remaining smaller country studied, *Switzerland,* lies in an intermediate position between Austria and Sweden on the one hand, and the Netherlands on the other.

Of the larger countries studied, *Britain* and *Canada* display some similarities as well as differences. There is more overlap of association domains in Britain and Canada than any of the other countries studied, apart from West Germany. As far as differences are concerned, Britain has over twice as many associations in the three subsectors as Canada; indeed, it has the largest number of associations of any of the countries studied, apart from the special case of West Germany. Second, although both countries have associational systems that are more territorially differentiated than those of any other country, apart from West Germany, that of Canada has more regionally based associations.

Looking at the differences of horizontal differentiation between the three subsectors, it is apparent that there are far fewer associations in the fruits and vegetables subsector than in the other two subsectors. Manufacturers of fruit and vegetable products are either organized in an association covering large parts of the industry as a whole (such as the Food Manufacturers' Federation in Britain) or by an association for fruit and vegetable products. When there is further differentiation, it is either between producers of fruit products and vegetable products (as in Switzerland) or by the process used — i.e. canning versus freezing. One does not generally find in the subsector the differentiation by product one finds in dairying where not only are there associations for particular products such as cheese, but also for particular cheeses. In meat processing, one finds associations for different kinds of meat (bacon, poultry etc.); different stages of the production process (slaughtering, preparation etc.); and different forms of industrial organization (artisan butchers, industrial plants etc.). Some associations are highly specialized, the Association of Swiss Horsebutchers being an extreme case!

One factor contributing to the lower degree of horizontal differentiation in the fruits and vegetables subsector is quality control, which is one of the major agenda items for the food processing industry (see the chapter by de Vroom, this volume); the specialized associations are in particular focus on this issue. Many of the quality control problems in the fruit and vegetable subsector arise on the farm; in particular, it is important to choose exactly the right moment for harvesting the fruit or vegetable, taking account of the time it will take to transport it to the processing plant. Such problems as arise at the plant are related to the *process* rather than the *product*, i.e. they are not specific to fruit and vegetable processing, but might arise in the use of canning or freezing of any product. Hence, associations tend to be organized round the process rather than the product.

Up to this point, the discussion has largely been concerned with the differentiation of associations by product and this is, together with territory, the principal
parameter of specialization (Table 2.2). Associations differentiated by territory
as well as by product are concentrated in West Germany, Canada and Britain
among the countries studied, with some in the Dutch dairy sector and a couple in
Sweden; there are no associations organized on a territorial basis in Austria and,
more surprisingly, Switzerland. Beside these parameters, the type of ownership
is also of relevance as a means of defining potential membership. There were
nearly forty organizations in the countries studied which confined their membership to cooperatives. Conversely, a number of associations confined themselves to private sector firms.

The degree of specialization in tasks is lower than in the dimension of
membership. Many of the associations are combined trade and employers
associations. This can be conceived as one consequence of the efforts of
associations to offer a broad range of outputs to their members.

Most of the associations have defined their domain not only through one, but
several parameters. This high specialization in domain results in a relatively low

Table 2.2 Direction of Specialization
Percentage of associations* whose domain is defined by the following parameters:

| Country | Meat Processing | | | | | |
	T	P	O	EA	TA	EA/TA
A	0.0	0.0	66.7	0.0	0.0	100.0
CDN	63.6	81.8	9.1	0.0	100.0	0.0
D	98.1	1.3	97.3	0.0	0.8	99.2
NL	0.0	72.7	18.2	9.1	36.4	54.5
S	16.7	83.3	33.3	33.3	66.7	0.0
CH	0.0	83.3	0.0	0.0	83.3	16.7
GB	10.5	73.7	5.3	5.3	84.2	10.5
All countries	87.5	11.4	87.5	1.3	10.1	89.1

Table 2.2: Continued

| Country | Dairy | | | | | |
	T	P	O	EA	TA	EA/TA
A	0.0	0.0	50.0	0.0	0.0	100.0
CDN	77.8	88.9	0.0	0.0	100.0	0.0
D	71.4	4.8	76.2	0.0	19.0	81.0
NL	28.6	42.9	100.0	7.1	71.4	21.4
S	50.0	100.0	50.0	50.0	50.0	0.0
CH	0.0	71.4	0.0	0.0	85.7	14.3
GB	23.1	76.9	26.9	0.0	84.6	15.4
All countries	33.3	55.6	46.5	5.1	66.7	28.3

Table 2.2: Continued

Country	Fruits and Vegetables					
	T	P	O	EA	TA	EA/TA
A	0.0	0.0	66.7	0.0	0.0	100.0
CDN	50.0	100.0	0.0	0.0	100.0	0.0
D	41.7	58.3	0.0	0.0	25.0	75.0
NL	0.0	33.3	0.0	33.3	33.3	33.3
S	0.0	66.7	33.3	66.7	33.3	0.0
CH	0.0	66.7	0.0	0.0	83.3	16.7
GB	7.1	85.7	7.1	7.1	92.9	0.0
All countries	17.7	64.7	7.8	9.8	62.8	27.5

T = Territory;
P = Product;
O = Other criteria related to business groups EA/TA = Employers and trade association;
EA = Employers association;
TA = Trade association;
EA/TA = Employers and trade association.
* Calculated only for membership associations and mixed associations.

degree of inter-organizational competitiveness. In all the three sectors in at least 50 per cent of the countries, less than five per cent of possible members have a choice between two or more competing associations.

Vertical Differentiation and Interest Unification

Aggregating Subsector Interests

At this stage, the aggregation of subsector interests by integrating them into a broader interest-political context will be reviewed. Given the multitude of membership associations and mixed associations in most of the countries, the aggregation of interests must primarily take place through *inter*-organizational vertical differentiation. As already discussed above, the degree of inter-organizational coordination decreases with the percentage of membership associations and mixed associations unaffiliated to higher order associations, and the number of mixed associations and peak associations which are not integrated into an association representing their interests at a more general level.

Table 2.3 gives a general view of the degree of vertical differentiation for each subsector and country. In it can be seen the number of membership associations and mixed associations which are potential members of peak associations, the percentage of unaffiliated membership associations and mixed associations, the number of mixed and peak associations and the number of unaffiliated associations of this type. Furthermore, table 2.3 shows a rank order as a composite score of the rank order with respect to the percentage of unaffiliated membership

Table 2.3 Vertical Differentiation

Country				Meat Processing				
	a	b	c	d	e	f	cxf	g
A	3	100	8	0	0	6	48	7
CDN	5	45.5	5	2	2	2	10	4
D	4	0.8	2	29	6	5	10	4
NL	3	27.3	3	8	5	4	12	5
S	2	33.3	4	4	1	1	4	2
CH	3	50	6	1	1	1	6	3
GB	12	63.2	7	5	2	2	14	6

Table 2.3: Continued

Country				Dairy				
	a	b	c	d	e	f	cxf	g
A	2	100	7	0	0	5	35	7
CDN	9	100	7	0	0	5	35	7
D	4	19	4	20	6	4	16	5
NL	4	42.9	6	12	5	3	18	6
S	0	0	1	3	1	1	1	1
CH	1	14.3	3	6	4	2	6	4
GB	9	42.3	5	7	1	1	5	3

Table 2.3: Continued

Country				Fruits and Vegetables				
	a	b	c	d	e	f	cxf	g
A	3	100	5	0	0	5	25	6
CDN	6	100	5	0	0	5	25	6
D	4	33.3	4	10	5	4	16	5
NL	0	0	1	5	3	2	2	1
S	1	33.3	4	4	1	1	4	3
CH	1	16.7	2	7	4	3	6	4
GB	4	28.6	3	5	1	1	3	2

a Number of membership associations and mixed associations that are not affiliated;
b percentage of unaffiliated membership associations and mixed associations;
c rank order of vertical differentiation for b;
d number of mixed and peak associations;
e number of unaffiliated mixed and peak associations;
f rank order of vertical differentiation for e;
g combined rank order of vertical differentiation for cxf.

and mixed associations and to the number of unaffiliated mixed and peak associations.

In comparing the vertical differentiation across countries, *Sweden* is characterized by the highest degree of inter-organizational coordination. The outstanding feature of the Swedish case is that all three subsectors are linked upward to one highest order association encompassing all associations at lower levels. At the other end of the spectrum, there are Canada and Austria which have a remarkably low degree of vertical inter-organizational coordination. Canada has no higher order associations in two of the subsectors, and the two higher order associations in meat processing are hierarchically unaffiliated and specialized in representing territorial interests. Primarily, this lack of coordination is a reflection of the fact that all sector-unspecific business organizations are membership associations which also confine their activities to territorially specialized matters. 'There is no one organization that can speak for business in Canada' (Jacek, 1983 a: 22) but rather five organizations that claim to speak generally for business interests.

A case which is quite different from the Canadian situation is Austria. As mentioned above, all associations concerned with subsector interests are sector-unspecific organizations. Thus, there is a linkage between the subsector interests and the interests of a more general kind. Among these three associations, the Federal Chamber of Business and Commerce is predominant in representing interests of the subsectors as well as of all other sections of Austria's capital. This implies that other employers' associations inside and outside the subsectors guide their wage policy along the lines of the collective agreements concluded by the Chamber and that other trade associations have to address their lobbying to the Chamber rather than to the authorities. As a consequence, a system of vertical inter-organizational coordination is not necessary. The aggregation and unification of interests takes place *within* the Chamber, whose high degree of internalized interest complexity is reflected by an elaborated internal differentiation. There are a multitude of subunits established within the Chamber of which several are related to the different branches of the food processing industry.

Of the other countries studied, *Britain* offsets its large number of associations by a high degree of hierarchical affiliation outside the meat processing sector (where, in any case, there is a strong horizontal coordinating device between the major associations). For instance, in the dairy sector, most organizations are affiliated to the Dairy Trade Federation (Grant 1983 b: 60 ff.), an association of associations which was affiliated to the Food and Drink Federation, a peak association which is affiliated to the CBI. *West Germany* has the highest number of mixed and peak associations of all countries. Although the majority of these associations are integrated into more encompassing organizations, there are more unaffiliated than in other countries, indicating a highly complicated mode of interest aggregation.

The remaining smaller countries, the *Netherlands* and *Switzerland* (except the meat processing industry) show a relatively high number of unaffiliated mixed and peak associations. This results mainly from the existence of several sector-unspecific peak associations which tend to increase the number of unaffiliated organizations of higher order.

Formulating Interests of the Food Processing Industry

Having reviewed the overall patterning of the integration of subsector interests in a more general context of representation, the existence of broadly based food processing associations, which exercise a degree of control over subsector and product specific associations in the countries studied, will be considered in more detail in this section. The term 'formulating interests of the food processing industry' is taken here to refer to organizations reconciling and representing the interests of business in all three subsectors, either through direct membership or through the affiliation of subsector or product associations (or some combination of both). Such associations would usually organize other parts of the food processing industry as well, but associations organizing extensively outside the food processing industry are formally excluded (although marginal cases such as branded goods associations will be discussed). It is also assumed that such associations will have a wide range of concern, so that organizations concerned with highly specific tasks will not be discussed.

The assumption underlying this part of the discussion is that the existence of a sectoral association allows the industry to deal more effectively with problems which are not confined to a particular subsector. However, the mere existence of such an association does not mean that it will necessarily constitute an effective spokesman for the industry. Many such associations may, and do, have considerable difficulty in reconciling the divergent interests of the different subsectors which make up the highly diverse industry we refer to as 'food processing'. In contrast to their claim of unifying interest diversity, they may be unable or unwilling to prevent their affiliates following an independent policy line.

Four broad patterns may be observed in different countries in terms of the organization of food processing sector associations. First, there are those countries where there is no association for the industry as a whole. Second, there are those countries which have sector wide informal arrangements which serve as a weak 'functional equivalent' of a sectoral association. Third, there are those countries where there is more than one broadly based association representing a number of subsectors. Fourth, there are those countries where there are two associations, one dealing with trade association matters, the other with the employers organization function.

Austria does not have an association covering the food processing industry as a whole. Although there is no sectoral association in Austria, not only the food processing industry but also the whole economy is subject to a cohesive system of interest unification within the chamber organization. Moreover, as has been pointed out, there is a grouping within the chamber organizing all firms of the food processing sector. At the sectoral level, the *Fachverband der Nahrungs- und Genußmittelindustrie* is established as a subunit within the chamber. Organizing all industrial firms of the entire food processing sector, it is divided internally into 35 product groups *(Berufsgruppen)*. The product groups of the *Handwerk* (small artisan firms) are organized separately in different subunits.

The Netherlands and *Switzerland* have collaborative arrangements between associations, but no independent sectoral association. The Conference of the Swiss Food Processing Industry is an informal board which attempts to coordinate the activities of its members in relation to government bodies, the mass media and public relations activities generally. However, it has no hierarchical control or sanctioning power over the affiliated associations which, in any case, constitute only a minority of associations in the three subsectors being studied. In the Netherlands, the VAI (Committee for the Food Processing and Agrarian Industry) was set up in the early 1970s as a joint venture of the two national peak associations for business, bringing together their affiliates in the sector unspecific food processing industry. It was originally intended as a forum for internal coordination of the food processing industry, but it has changed into a committee formally representing food processing interests to the government. This change in function is largely due to government and European Community action in the field of quality control and labelling. Rules were becoming less product specific and, as a result, the industry developed a need to aggregate interests at a peak level, while the government wanted a single spokesman for the whole industry.

Britain and *Canada* both have more than one broadly based sectoral association in food processing, although the situation in Canada appears to be more confused. The Grocery Product Manufacturers of Canada has claimed through its president to speak for the industry as a whole but 'This attempt to speak for the industry is resisted, often in quite blunt terms' by organizations such as the National Dairy Council which considers itself to be the only voice of the dairy products industry. (Jacek, 1983: 8.) Britain has an association of associations in the sector (the Food and Drink Federation), although its constitution respects the rights of its members to pursue their own interests at a national level. Its largest member, with whom it shared offices and a director-general, was the Food Manufacturers' Federation which represented a broad range of subsectors in the industry, both through direct membership of firms and affiliated associations. In January 1986 the FDF absorbed the FMF, creating one clearly defined umbrella organization for the food processing industry, the Food and Drink Federation.

West Germany and *Sweden* share the patterns of separate peak associations for trade associations and the employers' organization function. In Sweden, the Swedish Employers' Confederation (SAF) is the principal employers' organization for the food processing industry, organizing private and producer cooperative firms. As far as trade associations are concerned, the representation of the industry has recently been rationalised through the formation of the Association of the Swedish Food Processing Industry (SLIM) through an amalgamation of four trade associations (some consumer cooperatives, but only a few producer cooperatives are members of the new association). The formation of this association enables most of the larger non-producer co-operative firms in the industry to speak with one voice. Before the merger, the main trade association was the food processing section of the Association of Chemical Industries and this relationship caused embarrassment in some quarters because the industry wished to emphasize the pure and natural character of its products. It is interesting that Findus, the largest private firm in the Swedish food processing industry (owned, of course, by the Swiss company Nestlé) pushed actively for a more rational organization of the representative structure of the industry on the trade association side. It should be stressed that the employers organization has no subsector or product associations as members; membership is confined to firms. The new trade association has two product associations as members, the Meat Trade Association and the Brewers' Association.

The German associational system at the sector level consists of four associations. The sectoral peak trade association is the *Bundesverband der Deutschen Ernährungsindustrie* (BVE) which organizes most trade associations in the industry, the exceptions in the subsectors studied being the main meat processing association *(Bundesverband der Deutschen Fleischwarenindustrie)* which left the BVE at the beginning of the 1970s, and three of four associations representing dairies. *The Bund für Lebensmittelrecht und Lebensmittelkunde* is a trade association specialized in representing interests concerning matters of food, drink and health legislation. It is organizing product-specific associations of industrial processors, artisan firms, farmers and retailers as well as firms. The *Markenverband* represents industrial firms (not just in food processing) producing branded articles and tries to defend their interests against the retail sector. It is significant because of the active participation of the largest and most successful food processing firms in its work. The employers association within the food processing industry *(Arbeitgebervereinigung Nahrung und Genuß*, ANG) was only formed in 1977, in response to some new qualitative demands articulated by the food and drink trade union (see Hilbert & Voelzkow, this volume). Not all West German food processing associations which are engaged in representing employers' interests and in negotiating activities are members of the ANG. The ANG does not itself engage in negotiations; rather, it provides a mechanism for coordinating negotiations undertaken by its member associations.

It is evident that at the sectoral level there is considerable divergence in the organization of business interests in the food processing industry in the countries studied. If one looks for broadly based independent associations, which organise all subsectors through direct membership or affiliated associations and which are the unchallenged spokesman for the sector, one is hard pressed to find one. The BVE in Germany does not organize the main meat processing association and shares a part of its tasks with some other task defined associations. The Food and Drink Federation in Britain has to share the task of dealing with broad sectoral questions with some of its more important member associations. The Swedish trade association (SLIM) probably comes nearest to being such a spokesman for the whole sector, although it is a recent development, and it remains to be seen whether its potential is fully realised. In sum, none of the countries studied has a single independent association, combining both employer's organization and trade association functions, and maintaining links with subsector and product organizations through a system of affiliations.

Mediating Sectoral and Intersectoral Interests

The pattern of relationships between food processing industry associations and national intersectoral business associations is varied and complex in the countries studied. Such relationships are important because of the tendency of public and official opinion to undervalue the importance of the food processing industry, and indifference which can be offset to some extent by food processing industry associations drawing attention to the special needs of their sector through national business associations representing all sectors.

In addition, the regulative functions of the European Community affecting the food processing industry require an increased coordination of sectoral and intersectoral associative actions. This may lead to new patterns of organization, as happened with the formation of the Food and Drink Industries Council (the predecessor of the FDF) and the Dairy Trade Federation in Britain, whereas closer cooperation in food processing matters between the intersectoral peak associations in the Netherlands was in part a response to a change in the character of the issues facing the industry as a result of Community membership. (For further discussion of these issues, see the chapter by Pestoff.)

In such a process of reorganizing the representation of food processing interests, national peak associations may play a central role. They may be able to intervene in the system of food processing industry associations in such a way as to promote rationalization of structures or to bring about the operational improvements as in the case of the Netherlands where the two national peak associations have formed a coordinating committee for their food processing members. In Britain, however, the Confederation of British Industry (CBI) seems to have largely lost the interest it displayed in the 1960s in the rationalization of the system of secondary associations. Of course, another possible source of rationalizing pressures can be the largest firms in the industry (as in Sweden) or both the largest firms and national peak associations. This has happened in West Germany where the formation of the ANG was sponsored by the national peak association of employers (*Bundesvereinigung der Deutschen Arbeitgeberverbände*, BDA) as a result of an initiative of some top managers of the largest food processing firms.

The weakest relationship between national business associations and food processing sector associations is to be found where there is a large number of national associations claiming to speak for businesses which have no formal links with food processing industry associations, *Canada* being a classic example (Coleman, 1984: 52 ff). *Britain* is relatively strong at the national peak association level in the sense that it has one principal spokesman for industry (the CBI) which deals with both trade association and industrial relations matters (Grant 1983 a); both the Food and Drink Federation and the Food Manufacturers' Federation were active members of the CBI. *West Germany* has separate national peak associations for trade association and industrial relations questions. The *Swedish* system is complicated by the existence of the cooperatives, and the *Swiss* system by the coexistence of national business and agricultural associations both being relevant to the advancement of food processing interests. The *Netherlands* has three national level intersectoral associations, one for industrial relations matters and two for other questions, one representing Christian employers and the other employers without a religious affiliation.

Austria is a nearly ideal case of integrating particularistic business interests into an all-embracing association; there is the Chamber organizing almost all business groups. For these groups, more than 900 subunits are established responding to different branches, territories and levels of interest aggregation. The Chamber not only embraces nearly the entire economy, but also exerts a strong hierarchical control over its subunits. Each subunit is only allowed to deal autonomously with those matters which exclusively affect itself. Matters which overstep this area of competence must be transferred to the appropriate higher-ranking subunit encompassing all business groups involved. Because of the growing interdependence of business interests, there is an increasing necessity to unify them at the intersectoral, national level through an enormously complex step-wise process of interest aggregation (Traxler, 1984: 303 ff). Thus, the Chamber shows a degree of control capacity in relation to partcularistic interests, which a peak association organizing independent organizations could hardly attain. The Austrian mode of unifying interests by *intra*-organizational differentiation and coordination is more than just a functionally equivalent mechanism for the *inter*-organizational structures, on which the management of diversity mainly rests in the other countries studies.

Conclusion

As Maunder points out, 'There is not one food manufacturing industry but several, and they differ widely in terms of their capital intensity of production, variety of production and the nature of their markets'. (Maunder 1980: 80.) The diversity of product, process and market within the industry is reflected in the system of business interest associations that exists in most countries. It is often fragmented and generally lacks a single focus in the form of one spokesman for the industry as a whole with an unequivocal superordinate relationship with the associations representing particular products and processes. Of course, one must not exaggerate the incoherence of the associational systems in food processing. One theme which has not been pursued intensively in this chapter is the importance of horizontal coordinating arrangements between associations which allow them to work together, either on an 'ad hoc' basis on a particular issue or on a more permanent basis over a whole policy area.

It could be argued that the food processing industry does not need as coherent a system of associations as other industries because many of the issues that arise in its relationships with government are product or technique specific and are best handled by an association (or product section of a larger association) concerning itself with problems at that level. Moreover, it could be argued that in most countries, the relationship the industry's associations enjoy with the relevant government agencies are relatively stable and generally based on mutual respect and a desire for a constructive and well informed dialogue.

However, such a complacent conclusion would overlook two important considerations. First, for three of our countries, the stable relationships referred to have been disrupted by membership of the European Community (and, indeed, the existence of the Community also affects Austria, Sweden and Switzerland and even Canada). It is going to be difficult for the industry to lobby effectively at the Community level if it is not properly organized at the national level. Second, some of the industry's most important relationships are not with government, but with its customers and suppliers. Such relationships are significant in all industries, but they are almost certainly of greater importance in food processing than in any other sector. As a Chairman of the (former) British Food and Drink Industries Council's delegation to the European level organization commented, 'The industry remains caught between the lower millstone of farm prices, and the upper millstone of retailer concentration and consumer price resistance.' One might add that farmers have been very effective at the political defence of their interests, whilst retailers have made increasing use of their economic power.

In referring to the competing imperatives of the logic of membership and the logic of influence, the highly fragmented form of the associational systems indicates the predominance of the logic of membership in the associative activity of business in this sector. Since associative action responding to the logic of influence implies autonomy from the members in order to unify their interests, the fragmented mode of interest representation can be conceived as a lack of associational governability. Conversely, this mode is a result of the power of firms/individual businessmen to design their collective action in accordance with their desire of having their interests represented as authentically as possible.

Considering 'Austrian exceptionalism' draws our attention to the problems of managing interest diversity business associations have to face. The Chamber, whose structure is clearly responding to the logic of influence, can maintain its unity solely by a multitude of guarantees for organizational security (e.g. monopoly of representation, compulsory membership) provided primarily by the state (Traxler, 1984: 390 ff).

From these findings can be drawn the conclusion that business interest associations need *external* support to overcome their members' particularistic orientation and to increase their internal governability. This is a central precondition of the ability not only to adopt a policy line responding to the logic of influence but also to assume public policy functions in corporatist arrangements.

Chapter 3

Business Interest Associations as Private Interest Governments

Henry J. Jacek

Theoretical Focus

This chapter deals with the second of the two aspects of the dependent variable of organizational development, namely the concept of relative autonomy *(Verselbständigung)* which refers to an organization's ability to control its supply of resources and to its capacity to select its goals and the strategies and tactics it believes is necessary to achieve those objectives. As the autonomy of interest associations increases, then these organizations could become private governments[1] or more appropriately 'private interest governments' as defined by Streeck and Schmitter (1984: 21–22). These associations are seen as being given public responsibilities so as to become organizations of 'regulated self-regulation'. In this way special interests ... are made subservient to general interests by appropriately designed institutions. The 'collective self-interest' of these organizations is used to generate and reproduce a stable social/economic/ political order because it is assumed that these associations are capable of being 'transforming agents of individual interests' so as to produce 'responsible associative governance.' So in this chapter 'private interest governments' will be used as 'the concept for arrangements under which an attempt is made to make associative, self-interested collective action contribute to the achievement of public policy objectives'.

The range and character of private interest government functions exist in at least five major policy areas[2] that affect the food processing industry; industry

---

[1] The concept of 'private government' has at least two basic meanings. The second broader understanding will not be used in this chapter. This alternative usage sees hierarchy and authority in private organizations as 'government' and distinct from market relations which are identified as the normal hallmark of the private sector. The objectives and uses of this authority is secondary to its exercise. Thus Gilb (1981: 464) defines a private government as 'the government of a business or industrial corporation, a bank or other financial institution, a trade association, church, or any other limited-purpose organization'.

[2] In developing these five major areas of policy I have built this classification upon my previous analysis (Jacek, 1983 b).

structure, labour, supplier/customer relations, standards, and general macro/intersectoral economic policies. The first purpose of this chapter is to order these five policy areas along a continuum which distinguishes these policy areas in terms of their degree of public character. This exercise hopefully is an elaboration of Streeck and Schmitter's (1984: 37–38) generalization that 'there is growing evidence that there is a certain range of policy areas for which institutions of group self-regulation may produce more socially adjusted and normatively acceptable results than either communal self-help, free trade, or *étatisme.*' An important point to remember is that there is nothing inherent in these five policy areas that make them either public or private. The extent to which each policy area has 'public character' is a question of empirical investigation.

The relationship between organizational development, especially as indicated by the concept of relative autonomy, and private interest government is based on the view that the successful assumption of private interest government functions can lead to the provision of more and more resources by the state. Such provision in turn is likely to lead to greater strategic autonomy from the association's members and to a greater capability to interact with the state, the public government. Thus, as Wyn Grant points out in Chapter One, the functions of private interest government are both an indicator and outcome of organizational development.

The second part of the chapter will examine the extent to which the connections exist between the components of the 'virtuous cycle' described by Wyn Grant in the first chapter. First on the input side questions can be raised about financial resources and public status. Do business interest associations that act as private interest governments have a more diversified financial resource base compared to those associations that lack governing properties? Sources of finance and the relative importance of independent professional staff capacity of associations versus voluntary members assistance are the important indicators here. Also, to what extent is public status[3] attributed to private interest governments vis-a-vis poorly developed associations? The former should be more likely formal participants in para-state bodies. In addition these same organizations are expected to be holders of state-granted licenses to administer particular goods.

Second, do private interest governments provide monopoly goods to a significant extent? Monopoly goods are goods or services to which an association has been granted sole or monopoly rights in their provision (Schmitter and Streeck, 1981: 229–238). What other types of goods are produced by BIAs and what is the balance between these types and monopoly goods? Also, to what extent is there any pattern of provision of goods by different types of subsectors, countries and associational structures? In particular, is the provision of monopoly goods subject to explanation by these other factors?

---

[3] Here I am referring to some de facto imputation of public status by state authorities to an organization that could exist as a private element of civil society. For an analysis in keeping with my meaning see Offe, 1981: 123–158 and Offe, 1985.

Policy Areas and Private Interest Governments

A. The Public Functioning of Associations: An Overview of Policy Areas

The five major policy areas studied in this chapter may be divided into policy subareas. Although three summary charts on each of our food subsectors will be provided, greater elaboration of the form of private interest government for these policy subareas will be provided in sections dealing with each subsector. Analytically, the policy subareas are outlined below.

The shaping of industry structure may be divided into four policy subareas; investment and deinvestment, competition, research and development, and consumer prices and profits. The co-ordination of investment and deinvestment, i. e. rationalization of the industry, if done privately could be accomplished by joint ventures, mergers or possibly by cartels but if there is public involvement BIAs may administer government funds or may promote larger units of production. The second subpolicy area which is possibly an association activity where such behaviour is not illegal is shaping industry structure by regulating competition among firms by forming input prices and the allocation of raw material supplies, appropriate market shares and the development of other competitive or anti-competitive practices such as measures that prevent the entry of new competitors. Of course, these are ways for protecting or preserving the status quo or at least for controlling the pace or direction of change. A third policy subarea that may affect industry structure is research and development. If research and development is solely an activity of the firm then firms can be distinguished from one another on the quality of research and development (R & D) if it is done at all. Firms with high quality R & D can be expected over time to increase sales, assets and profits at the expense of competitors leading to tendencies toward oligopoly. If however a BIA carries out industry research and development then firms, probably small ones, with an individual competitive disadvantage potentially can have access to industry state-of-the-art research and development. The final policy subarea of the general area of policies that affect industry structure is the one involving policies on output or consumer prices. These policies may be the most important because they seem most likely to affect the very profitability of the industry. One might expect capitalism unfettered by either the state or association to be the most profitable.

The second broad category of public functions that business interest associations may perform are policies that regulate the industry's labour market. Possible policy subareas include negotiating binding labour agreements, co-ordinating practices on the hiring and firing of workers, administering state vocational education, and administering worker social insurance programmes. The usual type of labour regulation that first comes to mind is the negotiation of industry-wide, multi-firm labour agreements including binding agreements on minimum wages and conditions, in general the promotion of labour peace. Related to the first policy subareas are policies that involve the hiring and firing of workers. Policies in this subarea may have as goals labour black-listing or attempts to find sources of low-paid guest workers. Third, an association either by itself or in cooperation with state agencies may administer state vocational education and training. The final subarea of policies affecting labour is in the administration of worker social insurance programmes including pension plans.

The third general type of public policies are those that help stabilize the chain of production relations from upstream commodity suppliers to downstream transporters, distributors, domestic retailers and agents for foreign sales. Five policy subtypes will be examined in this section: the *recognized right* (Offe, 1981: 135) to negotiate or participate in decisions on prices, quotas, supplies and allocation of supplies of raw materials with commodity producers and firms covered by their domain and with retailers, wholesalers or buying groups; the promotion of the use of domestic inputs[4]; commercial arbitration; development of industry markets including exports; and the collection of authoritative information from member firms for use by state agencies in the making of public policy. The first subarea could cover the negotiation of binding agreements with all customer or supplier organizations on prices and other conditions. Second, a business interest association may promote on the urging of the state the use of domestic inputs in place of foreign supplies. For example a food processing association particularly one in the first stage sectors covered in this project may promote the use of domestic commodities among its member companies under state pressure even though these may be more expensive than offshore supplies. A third subarea is commercial arbitration while fourth, BIAs may promote the marketing, including exports, of the industry's products. The fifth and final subarea of the 'stabilization of the chain of production relations' general area is the collection of authoritative information from member firms for use of state agencies in the making of public policy.

The fourth broad policy area that may be taken over by business interest associations in the food processing industry is to regulate quality and health standards which in general could be seen as protecting the public interest of consumers. The following subareas will be examined below: food quality; hygienic manufacture and handling of food; standardization of products; labelling; control of the use of labels and hallmarks; the publication of standards and expectations of the industry's products; standardization of business forms and contracts and industry regulation of advertising. The first subarea deals with food quality. A business interest association could be charged with developing, promoting and most importantly enforcing quality standards, grades and standards of conduct. Second, there is the hygienic manufacture and proper handling of food, for example, defining a proper standard of freezing for foodstuffs. This would answer such questions as how frozen is frozen and business interest associations could be involved in training workers to handle properly frozen foods. A third policy subarea is the standardization of products by both qualities

---

[4] The public functioning of BIAs in 'crucially important industrial sectors' outside of the food processing industry is perhaps more well-known. Energy and coal-mining in West Germany is one example. The state's attempt at coal import substitution for the electricity industry was frustrated until 'coal mining and the electrical supply industry associations' took responsibility to make the state policy work (Schmitter and Streeck, 1981: 103).

and quantities available to consumers. Fourth, an industry association can promote the proper listing of ingredients and their relative proportions as a way of overcoming a typical market failure. A fifth and very important set of policies is the control of the use of labels and hallmarks. Sixth, quality and health standards may be promoted by the joint association/state publication of standards and expectations while the seventh policy subarea is the standardization of business forms and contracts followed by the final subarea of industry regulation of advertising.

The fifth and final broad set of public policies are those that are not specific to one particular industrial subsector but involve broad public policy goals either for the food sector as a whole or involve macro-intersectoral domestic economic policy or even international policies. In this policy area BIAs are used as agents to help the state implement its goals. We can identify eight ways by which BIAs can be agents of public policy: encouraging compliance with state laws in general; by routine consultation in drafting state legislation and regulations; helping the state to reach its macro-economic goals; helping to implement state regional policy; helping the state in the attaining of agro- and/or food policies; involvement in pollution control; and participation in formulating their government's position on the development of supranational business policies. The first subtype involves activities that encourage the general compliance with not only the letter but also the spirit of state laws and regulations. This process involves continual education and encouragement of member firms to follow state policies as a matter of course. The association staff may translate public policies from state bureaucratic language into the common language of business. A second specific type of association activity in this broad area of intermediate or macro level state economic policy is the routinized and recognized right to be consulted in drafting state legislation and regulations. This right is important in helping the state implement its public policies by improving compliance because such formal consultation together with agreement or compromises before a government gets committed to laws and regulations is expected to lead to business compliance once the public policy is proclaimed by the state. Third, business interest associations may be mobilized to help the state reach its macro-economic goals such as growth, productivity, the restraint of inflation and the creation of high levels of employment. Fourth is the state's use of associations to implement state regional policy while a fifth general policy subarea is state energy policy goals. Sixth, the state may have a general food policy the implementation of which involves food processing associations. A seventh possible area is to help the state implement state environmental policy. A final public policy subarea would be to help the state in the formulation of its position on supranational food processing policies.

B. Policy Areas and their Degree of Public Character

After a careful examination of the amount and form of private interest government in seven countries three conclusions are clear, namely: (1) associations are most frequently used to implement general macro-economic and intersectoral policies followed by labour policies, quality standards, supplier/ customer relations and least of all in industry structuring although the differences among policy areas is not great, (2) the dairy industry is most prone to private interest government while the fruit and vegetable industry is the least susceptible, and (3) when we order our seven countries along a continuum in terms of the presence of private interest government we find Austria and Sweden most prone to this phenomenon followed by Britain, the Netherlands and Switzerland, West Germany, and Canada as the least likely site.

Austria's dairy and meat processing industries provide us with the most developed system of associational control including the shaping of industry structure by controlling investment and deinvestment. A law, the *Marktordnungsgesetz (MOG)* states the goals of the industries' self-regulation and the method of implementation. Two boards, the *Milchwirtschaftsfonds (MWF)* for the dairy industry and the *Vieh- und Fleischkommission* for the meat processing subsector, are charged with carrying out the law through decision-making bodies containing representatives of business, farmers and employees. All association representatives must agree with the arrived-at decision. Investments are controlled by the industry boards in their decisions to recognize them as proper costs. The evaluation of proper costs is used in controlling dairy and meat products' prices and processors profits. The purpose of this control is to promote industrial concentration, rationalization of production and greater efficiency and productivity in these industries. When a firm intends to make a capital investment which the company wants recognized as a proper cost, the firm must make an application to its industry board. The decision of the board is important since the idea of proper or standard costs are the criteria for the granting of subsidies.

In all sectors of the food industry in Austria we find the negotiation of industry-wide, multi-firm labour agreements including binding agreements on standard wages and conditions of employees. These agreements are negotiated by the *Österreichische Raiffeisenverband (ÖRV)*, a specific interest association of the industrial co-operatives, in a process autonomous from the state but which are declared formally binding by the minister of business, trade and industry. Overall centralized direction of Austrian economic policy is through the *Paritätische Kommission*. Prices for goods such as dairy products are fixed directly by interest associations 'within the framework of their co-operation in the *Paritätische Kommission* for wage and price policies'. (Traxler, 1983 a: 4–5.)[5].

The Swedish system is centralized but in a different way from the Austrian. The food policy of Sweden needs to be understood as the interaction of three price types of food: first, the high-priced producer products protected by state

---

[5] The success of the *Paritätische Kommission* in controlling inflation is demonstrated in the fact that of the eleven countries in the Organization of Business Interests project, Austria had the lowest average increase in consumer food prices, 5.2 to 9.4 for the eleven country average, and the lowest average increase in the consumer price index, 6.1 to 9.8 for the eleven country average in 1981 and 1982 (Organization for Economic Cooperation and Development).

imposed tariffs such as potatoes, eggs and cooking fats; second, the low-priced world market products; and third, medium-priced subsidized products which are also partially protected by trade barriers. This third group of products are subject to seven price regulation associations including four that cover our subsectors, associations for cheese, meat, milk and vegetable oil. These price regulation associations oversee the semi-annual food price negotiations with the goal of 'ensuring that the supply of agricultural produce does not exceed the domestic demand at price levels made possible by import restrictions for the respective products' (Pestoff, 1983: 67). Each of these associations has representatives of the state, the producer co-operatives, the food processors by the trade associations and one from the consumer cooperatives.

The centralization of the Swedish associational system is handled in a somewhat different way in the labour policy area. The Swedish food industry has two employer associations, the Employers' Association for Food Processors (LAF) and the Cooperative Negotiation Association (KFO). 'LAF's product sections function as negotiation groups for different categories of employers during branch-wide collective negotiations ... Members are denied the right to negotiate collective agreements, unless approved by LAF ...' Member firms also have to get LAF's approval if they want to lock out their employees and they have an obligation to provide LAF with an enumeration of the names and ages of workers involved in a strike or lock-out. The 'KFO alone can sign a collective agreement for its members ... In case of a labour conflict members are required to follow KFO's directives ... If members purposely break KFO's statutes they can be expelled' (Pestoff, 1983: 25–27). In addition these employer associations administer large government grants for projects that further state regional localization policy.

The associations of the Swedish food industry are made part of the process of devising and implementing macro-economic policies through the use of *ad hoc* parliamentary Royal Commissions and the process of remitting their reports to the associations for criticisms and revision. This system has similarities with that of the Austrian *Paritätische Kommission*. The Swedish associations are an integral part of these Royal Commissions and the *remiss* process which involves written briefs in response to the Royal Commission reports and the Commissions' study and analysis of the *remiss* briefs (Pestoff, 1983: 57–60, 63–65).

When associations in the remaining countries take on the characteristics of private interest governments it is not on a centralized basis but on a more sectoral or subsectoral basis. But this is not to say that the presence of private interest government is minor in these cases, rather it is the form that is different. Britain is a case in point where there is quite a lot of private interest government by British BIAs in the food processing industry. While this may seem surprising to some, an important element of contemporary politics in Britain is the reduction of the state bureaucracy and the transfering of policy implementation to interest associations (Grant, 1984).

Even before this period the 1947 Agriculture Act directed the Milk Marketing Board for England and Wales to negotiate with the representative organization of the dairy industry, the Dairy Trade Federation (DTF) on the price of milk that goes to processors (Grant, 1983 c). As well there exist special mixed government/industry associations, such as the British Food Manufacturing Industries Research Association and the Campden Food Preservation Research Association, which have been set-up for the purpose of doing industry research and development (Grant, 1983 b: 100).

It is in the area of labour policy, especially worker training, that we can see the clear devolution of state functions to industry controlled bodies. The Food, Drink and Tobacco Industries Training Board (FDTITB), a statutory based government board was abolished in favour of industry organizations. For the food industry as a whole, the Food Manufacturers Federation (FMF) has established the Food Manufacturer's Council for Industrial Training (FMCIT). A somewhat different form is the Dairy Trade Federation's Training Policy Committee which is affiliated to the Dairy Industry Training and Education Committee. In contrast still is a third form, the Meat Industry Training Organization (MITO) which had to be set up as a completely new body because of the associational fragmentation of the meat employers (Rainbird and Grant, 1984: 11–14).

But there are policy areas where sectoral centralization does exist overall. Export policy activity has been an important area of activity in Britain. The lead has been taken by the FMF in cooperation with the Department of Trade. 'The FMF developed an export strategy in 1980 which involved hiring consultants to develop a comprehensive marketing plan for British exports of processed foods to the Netherlands, identifying a range of products for which opportunities exist in the Dutch market. The Minister of Agriculture, Fisheries and Food showed a continuing interest in the development of the strategy, as did the Minister of State for Trade and the Chief Executive of the British Overseas Trade Board. The Department of Trade made available until the end of 1981 the full-time services of an executive on secondment from industry. The Department of Trade together with the Overseas Trade Board funded a seminar at which the consultants' findings were presented. The seminar was opened by the Parliamentary Secretary for Agriculture, Fisheries and Food and the FMF's President also spoke from the platform. The seminar was followed by a campaign to obtain tangible support for the strategy from food manufacturing companies and ensure participation in a programme of events scheduled for 1982. Following the FMF strategy, the Department of Trade initiated and financed a similar study of the French market.' Similarly the FMF 'has cooperated with the Department of Energy's Energy Information Bulletins on the application of energy conservation technology in the food processing industry' (Grant, 1983 b: 99).

There is less private interest government in the Netherlands, primarily as the result of lower than average levels of private interest government in the fruit and vegetable processing industry across all countries. Nonetheless each subsector has a *Produktschap* (Statutory Trade Association) which are more or less the same since they emanate from the same law, the 1950 Act on Statutory Trade Associations. In all three subsectors the *Produktschap* organizes the product column from the raw material producers, i. e. the farmers, to the final retailer. The dairy and meat associations are the most important since these sectors are protected from foreign trade and are highly self-regulated. In contrast the one in fruit and vegetable processing is a little less important as this sector is more open to foreign competition and is hence less regulated. This *Produktschap* develops less activities. In addition in one region, that of the dairy province of Friesland, the voluntary regional dairy business association, the *Bond van Friese Coöperatieve Zuivelfabrieken* regulates the investments of its member firms (van Waarden, 1984: 5, 26–30, 43–44).

In the Netherlands cartels in principal are legal which dates from the 1935 Act on Generally Binding Declaration of Cartels. There are a number of cartels in the Dutch dairy industry including a milk one which is declared generally binding. Other cartels such as in the production of coffee cream (unsweetened condensed milk) where the members get a part of the market dependent on their average market share over the past three years or export cartels in condensed milk and cheese need only be registered with the state. In the Dutch dairy industry there is also collective research and development for which the *Produktschap Zuivel* taxes the industry. The funds collected are handed over to a private foundation, the Netherlands Institute for Dairy Research (NIZO) which 'originated in 1950 out of a state Agricultural Research Station. Here a former state activity was privatized' (van Waarden, 1984: 13–16, 24–25).

The involvement of Dutch food processing associations in labour policy is substantial because of the generally binding agreements that are made. Collective wage agreements are well established. The legal basis is the 1937 Act on the Generally Binding Declaration of Collective Wage Agreements. Any negotiated agreement though originally a private contract which only binds the members of the association negotiating the contract can get a public law character and become binding for an industry including those employers and employees not represented in the negotiation process. It is up to the negotiators to request state confirmation on the basis of the 1937 Act. However, some industry organiz-ations are so strong that such state sanction is not needed as is the case of the dairy industry although the collective wage agreements are registered with the state. Second, self-regulatory agreement on social security is present in the entire food processing industry. These agreements 'are formulated and implemented by privately governed social security sector associations *(Bedrijfsverenigingen)*. Third, there are *Bedrijfscommissie* (sector committees), that are made up of representatives of employers' associations and trade unions, which supervise and settle disputes between Works Councils and employers. These *Bedrijfscommissie* are set up under the authority of the 1950 Act on Works Councils. All 'firms with more than 100 employees' must have 'a works council, made up of elected representatives of employees' (van Waarden, 1984: 16–18, 36–43).

All three Dutch subsectors have quality control boards with a semi-public status, governed by representatives of the BIAs in the subsector. Dairy has also an institution for the control of fresh milk, the *Centraal Orgaan voor Melkhy-giëne*, the raw material for the dairy factories. The control boards in meat and fruit and vegetable processing are not so important as in dairy. Only in the latter is there a privately governed compulsory system of quality control. This quality control system is described more fully by Bert de Vroom in Chapter 10.

The presence of private interest government is about the same in Switzerland with the differences being that private interest government is more important in the labour policy field and in the meat processing industry in the Netherlands compared to Switzerland while BIAs in the latter country are more likely to be involved in helping the state implement intersectoral economic policies and in regulating the fruit and vegetable processing industry. In the latter industry the vertically integrated Swiss Fruit Association and Swiss Vegetables Union organize farmers, processors and dealers and these associations set and promulgate minimum prices in the food chain. As well they propose import restrictions to the Special Commissions for fruits and vegetables on which they both sit and control. A similar process occurs in the dairy industry. The milk producer associations, the Cheese Union, the Association of Swiss Food Manufacturers, and cheese manufacturers are represented on the Special Commission on Milk, a consultative board which regulates prices among other things.

The West German food processing industry has a little less private interest government but a number of interesting forms generally not found elsewhere. Although there were some restructuring plans concerning slaughterhouses in the beginning of the 1970s, which plans were administered with the help of meat processing associations, rationalizing the industry by coordinating investment or deinvestment programs is now only relevant in the dairy processing industry. First, there are *Landesvereinigungen der Milchwirtschaft* on the *Länder* level administering dairy industry restructuring programmes. These *Landesvereinigungen* operate with legal sanction and are financed by compulsory levies. Their members are associations representing dairy interests along the entire food chain from farmers through processors to consumers. Second, there are associations of farmers cooperatives. These cooperatives operate dairies. These associations through their access to their members' financial accounts and their relations with cooperative banks, *Genossenschaftsbanken,* and farmers who are the shareholders of the cooperatives are able to pressure dairy cooperatives to merge. Comparatively, when business interest associations do get involved in the subpolicy area of investment/disinvestment, it is within the dairy industry such action occurs while there are no cases of similar activity in the fruit and vegetable processing industry and virtually none in meat processing.

In these latter two subsectors some collective research and development is carried out. There are some product-specific research projects coordinated by a higher order association representing the food processing industry as a whole. This involves promotion and encouraging collective research activities by groups of firms and administering state research subsidies. These subsidies allow the financing of approximately half of the expected research expenditure.

There are minor instances of private interest government concerning labour policy especially in the subarea of occupational training. In the meat subsector the *Deutscher Fleischerverband (DFV)* has control of members' behaviour in this subarea and its institutional cooperation with the *Handwerk* chamber system which is backed up with legal authority. As well occupational training is provided by the *Bundesinstitut für Berufsbildung* for the dairy industry and by the *Arbeitgebervereinigung Nahrung und Genuß* for the fruit and vegetable processing industry.

The chain of product relations is stabilized by the promotion of domestic inputs into the food processing industry. This is enforced by legislative regulations either by EEC market regulation schemes or by the food ingredients and food processing legislation.[6] As well this public policy is promoted by the *Centrale Marketinggesellschaft der Deutschen Agrarwirtschaft (CMA)* which was established at the end of the sixties by the *Absatzförderungsgesetz*, a sales promotion law. Together with representatives of farmers' and retailers' interest associations and some state executives, product specific business interest associations of the food processing industry, such as with milk and other dairy products, are engaged in developing sales promotion programmes for domestic raw materials as well as for processed products.

Private interest government in the West German food processing industry is most important in the policy area of standards. In Germany the representatives of business interest associations supplement the more important government regulations. They are involved in developing the composition of certain foods by the *Deutsche Lebensmittelbuchkommission*. This commission has representatives of interest associations from all parts of the food chain. The final results of its work is a more or less binding and obligatory *Leitsatz*. Those members of the *Lebensmittelbuchkommission* representing the industry are delegated by the *Bund für Lebensmittelrecht und Lebensmittelkunde (BLL)*. Among other activities the *BLL* develops *Verkehrsauffassungen*, i. e. something like an informal, non-obligatory but nonetheless written common understanding of what, e. g. a sausage could and should contain. The importance of these *Verkehrsauffassungen* lies in the fact that they often become obligatory and binding via *Richterrecht* (case law).

Product standards are not the only standards subject to self-regulation in West Germany. Advertising standards are also subject to private interest government. Some German food processing interest associations in all three subsectors are associated with the *Zentrale gegen unlauteren Wettbewerb* (central association combatting unfair competition). If a firm complains about improper or illegal trade or advertising practices of a competitor it can give the relevant information to its first-order association. If this association is unable to persuade the accused

---

[6] This evaluation of the effect of the food and drink legislation is the view of Josef Hilbert, the OBI's specialist on the West German food processing industry, in a letter to the author on June 14, 1984. His interpretation is not necessarily accepted by the respective associations. His argument is that the high level of domestic inputs seen in some product groups such as meat processing is an outcome of market regulation schemes and food ingredients and food processing legislation. The agro-protectionist character of these regulations is an outcome of the interaction of an agro-protectionist food and drink administration and the more or less institutionalized involvement of associations in the policy formulation and implementation process.

firm to alter its behaviour the association hands over the information to the *Zentrale* which has its own arbitration procedure. If this procedure also fails the *Zentrale* has the right to take the accused firm to court. In the food processing industry most of the complaints by one firm against a competitor deal with advertising activities.

Pluralist Canada is the least likely site for private interest government but even here there are instances of this. This is strongest in the dairy industry with the forum being the Canadian Milk Supply Management Committee which meets under the auspices of the Canadian Dairy Commission (CDC). The committee is composed of representatives of the producer-controlled provincial marketing boards, of provincial departments of agriculture, and of the CDC. This committee decides the amount of industrial milk to be produced in Canada for a given year and recommends to cabinet the amount of production to be assigned to each province. The National Dairy Council of Canada (NDC) and the provincial processors associations such as the Ontario Dairy Council (ODC) are extensively involved in the whole supply-management system. The president of the NDC is a permanent observer with the right to speak at meetings of the Committee. In Ontario the ODC has four representatives on a 14 member committee, whose other representation are from government and the Ontario Milk Marketing Board (OMMB), and whose function is to ensure that dairy processing plants use their milk quota for the stated purpose. The milk prices are set by the OMMB with the advice and apparent consent of the Ontario Dairy Council. The ODC 'also represents its members before the Ontario Farm Products Appeals Tribunal, a body which hears appeals from prospective processors who have been denied entry to the industry by the marketing board. The role of the association here has been to support the position of the Board arguing that the declining milk supply in Ontario leaves no room for new entrants to the industry. Therefore the association, which already represents a fairly oligopolistic industry, is able to use its relations with the marketing board to help restrict entry to the industry' (Coleman and Jacek, 1983 b: 272–273). The Ontario Creamerymen's Association also negotiates prices and terms but with the Ontario Cream Producers Marketing Board. Even in the Canadian fruit and vegetable processing industry there is private interest government in that the Canadian Food Processors Association (CFPA) 'negotiates the amount of remitted duty on eligible imports with the Canadian Horticultural Council' (Coleman, 1984: 69).

It is in the latter industry that we find the only instance of private interest government in the labour policy area. Two fruit and vegetable processing associations, the CFPA and the Ontario Food Processors Association (OFPA) deal with this policy subtype. 'The federal and Ontario governments have developed a program called the Caribbean Workers Programme to bring labour from countries in the Caribbean to work in the fields and processing plants at peak periods in the growing season. The OFPA through its Labour Committee negotiates with the province the wages to be paid to those workers who are employed by processors. The CFPA liaises on matters related to this program and on other more general issues with the Canadian Employment and Insurance

Commission and with the Department of Labour' (Coleman and Jacek, 1982: 22–23).[7]

Private interest government helps to stabilize supplier/customer relations most especially in the dairy and fruit and vegetable processing industries but also in the meat processing subsector. The work of the Canadian Milk Supply Management Committee has already been discussed. As well under the auspices of the Department of Regional Industrial Expansion, Government of Canada and the National Dairy Council of Canada, dairy processing companies have been encouraged to market new dairy products.[8] The role of the Canadian Food Processors Association in deciding the level of fruit and vegetable imports has been mentioned but also important is the negotiation by the Ontario Food Processors Association with the important Ontario commodity marketing boards. Of somewhat less importance are the poultry associations' role in dealing with the Canadian Chicken Marketing Agency and the Canadian Turkey Marketing Agency as they set the national production quotas for their products.

In the policy area of quality standards private interest government in the food processing industry is of minor importance although there are some interesting cases of this. The Canadian Frozen Food Association, an industry-wide association, has developed a code of handling practices for frozen food. This code was developed because of a fear of state-imposed regulations. The small five member Handling and Distribution Development Committee of the association that developed this code had as one of its key members an important Canadian state official, the person in charge of the Processed Products Section, Dairy, Fruit and Vegetable Division, Food Inspection Directorate, Food Production and Inspection Branch of Agriculture Canada. This code is the accepted norm of the food processing firms that manufacture frozen foods in Canada, not only the association's members but non-members as well. In addition a number of BIAs have had metric committees for the purpose of mobilizing their member firms to meet the Canadian government's goal of converting weights and measures from

[7] This programme not only draws workers from the Caribbean islands but also from Mexico. The harvest season which begins in early September and lasts two months rules out students who are returning to school and unemployed Canadian workers receive relatively generous unemployment insurance payments compared to the wage rates paid in fruit and vegetable processing plants.

[8] At a recent 'New Dairy Products Marketing Seminar' a number of non-Canadian dairy specialists were brought in to help suggest ways Canadian dairy processors could expand their domestic market. These were included in a seminar on European Dairy Products Marketing which featured presentations on '*Melkunie Holland* — Example of a Modern Dutch Dairy Cooperative' by Dr. C. Timmer, Chairman, *Melkunie Holland*, 'NIZO; Collective Dairy Research in the Netherlands For More Than 35 Years' by Dr. W. I. J. Aalbersberg, General Director, Netherlands Institute for Dairy Research, and 'Market Development — The Express Dairy Recipe for Success' by Mr. Peter Ohlson, Chief Executive, Express Dairy U. K. Limited. At another session there were papers on 'Trends in the Development of New Dairy Products in the Federal Republic of Germany' by Dr. H. Graf Zu Solms-Baruth, *Graf Zu Solms-Baruth GmbH* and 'Trends in the Swiss Dairy Industry' by Mr. H. R. Felix, Manager, Marketing, *Milchverband Winterthur*.

imperial to metric. Finally in the Canadian red meat industry we have an instance of an association/state joint publication explaining quality and health standards and the use of state hallmarks in the industry.[9]

It is in the policy subarea of general macro-economic policies that food processing associations are important agents of the state. These BIAs perform the important role of gaining corporate compliance with state policy. As an example drawn from the Canadian dairy processing industry shows, a seemingly specific issue concerning milk containers became an occasion to educate a member firm on the importance of following the spirit and intention of state regulations because a deviation would violate an understanding on the economic rules of the game between business and the state. A Canadian dairy set the tolerance of its milk-package filling machines so that its containers of fluid milk were filled at somewhat less than the stated quantity but within the range of error state policy would allow. When this became known to the association staff, pressure was put on the firm to reset their machines to fill quantities as stated on their packages. The association president reported that the milk containers of that particular dairy a short while after resumed having quantities equal to those milk containers of other member firms and in keeping with their labels and government regulations.

Even more dramatic are those instances when BIAs are recruited by the state to help the state reach its macro economic goals such as growth, productivity, restrain inflation and create high levels of employment as in the early 1980s. The Canadian government announced target guidelines in its budget of June 28, 1982 to reduce inflation by holding wage and salary increases in the public sector to six per cent during the 12 months ending July 1983 and five per cent in the next 12 month period. However, the first steps were to implement this two year target in the private sector by ministerial meetings with business sectors. On August 17th, 1982 the ministers of Agriculture and Consumer and Corporate Affairs met with 25 major associations in the food industry. Among those attending the meeting at cabinet's request were the Canadian Poultry and Egg Processors Council, the Canadian Food Processors Association, the Canadian Meat Council, the Grocery Products Manufacturers of Canada (GPMC) and the National Dairy Council. These associations were asked to restrain 'voluntarily' prices as well to within the guideline targets. The response to this ministerial pressure was that a number quickly agreed to go along with the government guidelines. As an example the largest of Canada's food associations, the GPMC with 18 full-time staff and a budget of $900,000 in 1980, was led by the executive committee of the board of directors in urging all member firms to comply with the government's request in their firms' pricing policy. The president of the GPMC, himself a former senior civil servant, wrote a few days before the upcoming ministerial meeting to CEO's and presidents of all member firms. He urged them to follow the federal target guidelines in setting prices by conveying a threat from the federal government, 'I am still of the opinion that, if the business

[9] Agriculture Canada and the Canadian Meat Council, *Federal Inspection Ensures Quality* (Ottawa, Ontario: no date).

community is not clearly seen to be cooperating, the Fall Budget may include compulsory price controls and a host of anti-business measures'.[10]

Overall, it is clear that the dairy processing subsector is most prone to 'private interest government' in all countries. Why is it that the dairy processing industry is most likely to be the site of 'private interest government'? Wyn Grant has given three general reasons that set milk production and processing apart from some other agricultural and food products; the perishability of the product, milk does not need a complex grading system and milk producers are not likely to be marginal producers who are expected to be hostile to 'private interest government' (Grant, 1983 c: 8–9). Other additional reasons include the facts that dairy farming requires fixed assets that are specialized in technology unlike horticulture, that entry and exit involves major shifts in capital structure, that 'The necessity for such [health] inspection to protect the public health does not exist for any other farm product' and that milk production and marketing is inherently unstable (Manchester, 1983: 3–16).

Private Interest Government and Organizational Development

How is it that business interest associations can develop the properties of private interest government? The answer would seem to lie in the concept of the relative autonomy of the business interest organization. As the organization develops from a purely member-dependent voluntary association concerned with urgent, immediate problem-solving to one with a diversified and dependable financial, personnel and status resource base and with an increasing attention to important, long-term planning, then the organization staff develops sufficient autonomy to influence both members and potential members. In this way the special interests of current association members are replaced by more general public interests.

There is another important characteristic, that is the difference between rules affecting only the members of the voluntary association and rules affecting also non-members but firms and individuals belonging to a certain category or domain, e. g. firms in a sector or subsector. Thus, any organization can regulate the behaviour of its members, whether it be a firm, a church, an aquarium club or a business association. But that is not what we would call private interest government. The latter concept refers to private associations creating regulations which have a similar status as state regulations, that is, regulations which are *generally binding* for a certain category in society *(allgemeinverbindlich)*, e. g. the whole industry, rather than just the members of the association. The means by which such regulations become generally binding is of secondary importance.

----

[10] Such anti-inflation efforts can have demonstrated consequences on capitalist profitability. For some preliminary evidence on this point see Jacek, 1983 a: 20–22. The quotation is by George Fleischman, President, 'The Government Wage and Price Restraint Program,' a letter sent to GPMC CEO's and Presidents, August 12, 1982.

In examining the actual relationship of resources to the development of private interest government outputs, we first must identify the components of this type of development. Whatever indicators we use they must involve the wielding of authority. There would seem to be four levels of private interest government outputs. The first involves coercive relations with members. The BIA may place demands on its members by asking them to perform certain actions such as signing public statements, refusing to collaborate with state agencies or engaging in lockouts. As well the organization may reprimand, fine, suspend or expel members for acting contrary to association policy. Second, the BIA may be represented on a para-state body that wields public authority in such areas as social security, regional development, industrial policy, standardization of products, prices and wages. Third, the association itself may administer, directly or through its subsidiaries, public policy programs in policy areas such as regional development, industrial policy, vocational training, quality control and price controls. Finally, a BIA may be involved in producing 'monopoly' or 'authoritative' goods such as commercial arbitration, enforcement of quality standards, certification and licensing, registration of patents, negotiation of binding agreements on minimum wages and conditions, negotiation of binding agreements with customer and supplier organizations on prices, supplies and conditions, enforcement of health and safety contracts, and control of members on such things as competitive practices and hiring and firing practices. We are concerned with the intensity of this monopoly activity and the proportion or organizational effort spent on the provision of monopoly goods.

The measurement of diversified and dependable resources involves at least four properties of BIA resource dependence, formalization of membership obligations in dues payments, stability of BIA income, trends in organizational bureaucratization and state recognition. Dependency on members should reduce the likelihood of private interest government while payments and staff given by the state to the BIA should increase the incidence of this form of private government. Overall resource dependence should not be related to this phenomenon. As the BIA is able to extract forcefully financial resources from its members, it should increase its private interest government outputs. It is able to do this by imposing special levies on its members, by taking members to court if they do not pay their dues and special levies and expelling them for the same reasons. Third, the stability of BIA finances should be related to the type of outputs discussed above. Finally, the intensity to which the association is given state access and recognition, that is, political institutionalization, should lead to more private government activity. Especially important here should be formal consultation in drafting legislation and representation before parliament and parliamentary committees.

In general, three resource measurements, the assessment of special levies on members, the increase in office staff and resources provided by the state are related consistently to the provision of private interest government outputs (see Chart 3.4). It would seem that the ability of the organization to raise funds beyond mere membership dues through special membership levies and grants from state agencies are critical to the organization's ability to free itself from dependence on the usual membership fees and the sale of selective benefits. These special levies and state grants lead to professionalism and private interest government. On the other hand, the sale of goods and services makes the association into more of a business firm and deflects the BIA from developing its own base of authority. Diversified financial resources, i. e. membership levies and state grants, would appear to allow the BIA staff to grow and become more professionalized and thus to take on governmental properties.

Looking at the relationship from the output side it is clear that the provision of monopoly goods is best related to the properties of diversification and dependability of BIA resources. In only two instances out of eleven does the predicted relationship not hold and in both instances the relationship is very weak, less than ten per cent. It seems that the strongest level of private interest government, the actual provision of monopoly or authoritative goods, is the level that is most clearly related to the very resources that should be expected to nurture private interest government.

Reinforcing our findings on the overall presence and importance of private interest government, we find that the intensity of the provision of monopoly goods is most prevalent among associations solely representing all or part of the dairy processing industry subsector compared to other types of food manufacturing BIAs (see Chart 3.5). Food processing associations covering the entire industry or at least more than one subsector are likely not to provide any monopoly goods at all. Rather it is at the subsector level that private interest government grows. Again as our earlier charts show, private interest government, this time in the form of above average provision of monopoly goods is more likely in the meat processing associations than among the fruit and vegetable processing associations.

Conclusion

There are a number of important positive findings that arise out of this chapter. Private interest government especially in what is perhaps its strongest form, that of authoritative monopoly goods develops at the subsectoral base of functionally differentiated business interest associations. The dairy industry is especially prone to this phenomenon for a number of reasons. All of these reasons flow from the characteristics of dairy products and the usual economic structure of the chain of dairy production, especially the characteristics of the primary commodity producers, the dairy farmers. Associations representing the fruit and vegetable processing industry are least likely to have private interest government outputs probably because supplier and customer relations are more difficult to regulate in horticulture compared to food products based on animal husbandry.

More importantly, perhaps, is the relationship between resources and outputs. For a business interest association to develop the properties of a private interest government it must diversify its financial resources. It will remain undeveloped if its sole source of finance is regular membership dues. By demanding that members pay special levies in addition to normal membership dues, the organization can augment its financial resources beyond a narrow base. Most important is the ability of the organization to extract financial resources from the state. By so doing the organization can make itself more insulated from its members and thus develop greater relative autonomy. In turn this resource diversification allows for a growth in office staff to implement private interest government outputs.

This chapter has argued that as business interest associations organizationally develop, these organizations through the staff that operates them evolve a relative autonomy from the membership. Such relative autonomy enables the associations to function as private interest governments. The range and character of such functions assumed by associations fall into at least five general policy areas. In order for associations to assume successfully private interest government in these policy areas, new and diversified resources are necessary, the most crucial being state financial resources. In general a diversification of resources allows the successful assumption of private interest government functions which in turn leads to the provision of still more resources by the state including now a public status. This official status position allows increasing access to state officials, especially formal consultation in drafting legislation and representation before parliament and parliamentary committees, and the legal right to be consulted by state agencies and legislative bodies on specific matters.

In general it is the increasing dependability and most especially the diversification of resources that allows for the growth of private government activity, a tendency borne out by our data which shows almost two-thirds of the predicted resource-output relationships sustained. The resources-private government cycle continues indefinitely, if undisturbed by outside factors, as the BIA uses additional state resources to acquire still more strategic independence from its members and a still greater capacity to interact, influence and take on governmental functions.

It is this governmental policy role, such as the BIAs formal involvement in para-state bodies, which is at the heart of private interest government, 'under which an attempt is made to make associative, self-interested collective action contribute to the achievement of public policy objectives' (Streeck and Schmitter, 1984: 22). Associations which have such public status by being formally involved in para-state bodies, 65 per cent of food associations, are more likely to have stable income and more importantly are more likely to receive state financial aid especially those associations involved in two or more para-state bodies, 36 per cent of the food processing BIAs. On the other hand, the majority of associations not highly involved in para-state bodies are less likely to receive state financial aid of any kind. Associations which develop into private interest governments also are more likely to be given the resource of public status in the traditional pluralistic input process of public policy making such a formal consultation in drafting legislation. As public status for the latter type of input drops, so does para-state involvement.

There is not a clear unequivocal relationship between the structure of associational systems and the involvement of BIAs in private interest government.

Even fragmented, competitive and flat horizontal subsystems may take on a public policy role. Highly centralized, hierarchial systems such as those in Austria and Sweden are most prone to private interest government but at the same time there is almost as much of this phenomenon in British food processing BIAs. Indeed in most systems it is at the level of subsectoral associations that private interest government in the form of the provision of monopoly goods is most likely to occur (see Chart 3.5).

However, an integrated, hierarchical subsystem or better yet food associational system seems important if BIAs are to be important players in industrial structure, particularly in the continual oversight and control of investment/ disinvestment, output prices, and profits, and in labour policy, especially industrial relations. A centralized, well-integrated associational system in the overall food processing industry would seem essential if the state desires to implement an industrial policy for a *filière* or production channel.[11] Such an industry-wide comprehensive corporative-associative system would appear to be better able to produce and implement an effective industrial policy than a state-imposed plan.

For associations 'to engage in long-term strategic thinking about the problems facing their industries' (Coleman and Grant, 1984: 209), resources must be predictable and be from varied sources. The association's staff must be free from quickly responding to the member's immediate concerns-the urgent must not be allowed to displace the important. Instead, the staff must be able to insulate itself from immediate member demands by having dependable, alternative sources of finance and symbolic state support. Indeed, by having such resources the association staff should develop the ability to control member behaviour sufficiently so as to act as a private interest government.

However, a further speculative theoretical question ends this chapter. For how long can associational systems remain heterogeneous yet still contain associations that assume important public policy duties concomitant with receiving state financial resources? Will not the public policy demands of the state lead associational systems or fields and the associations themselves into 'an iron cage' of system and organizational isomorphism (DiMaggio and Powell, 1983: 147–160)? As an association increasingly interacts with the state, receives greater and greater state financial aid and performs more and more state functions, it is likely that the association will assume state organizational properties as its outputs increasingly are governmental ones.

---

[11] For a brief description of this feature of French industrial policy since 1981 see Stoffaës, 1985.

Chart 3.1 Amount[a] and Form of Private Interest Government by Country in the Dairy Industry

Country	Private Interest Government Policy Areas					T O T A L
	Industry Structure	Labour	Supplier/customer Relations	Standards	General Macro/ Intersectoral Economic Policies	
Austria	(2) *Milchwirtschafts-fonds*	(2) *Österreichischer Raiffeisenverband*	(2) *Milchwirtschafts-fonds*	(2) *Milchwirtschafts-fonds*	(2) Paritätische Kommission	(10)
Britain	(2) Dairy Trade Federation / Milk Marketing Board for England and Wales	(2) Dairy Trade Federation /Training Policy Committee	(2) Dairy Trade Federation / Food Manufacturers Federation	(2) Dairy Trade Federation / Food Manufacturers Federation	(1) Food Manufacturers Federation	(9)
Canada	(2) Canadian Milk Supply Management Committee / National Dairy Council	(0)	(2) Canadian Milk Supply Management Committee / National Dairy Council	(1) Canadian Frozen Food Association/ Ontario Dairy Council	(2) National Dairy Council of Canada/ other BIAs	(7)
Netherlands	(2) *Produktschap Zuivel*	(2) BIAs negotiating wage contracts / *Bedrijfscommissie/ Bedrijfsvereniging*	(2) *Produktschap Zuivel / Bond van Friese Coöperatieve Zuivelfabrieken*	(2) *Centraal Orgaan voor Melkhygiëne/ Centraal Orgaan Zuivelhygiëne*	(1) *Bedrijfscommissie voor de Zuivelindustrie*	(9)
Sweden	(2) Price Regulation Associations for Milk and Cheese	(2) *LAF/KFU*	(2) Price Regulation Associations for Milk and Cheese	(2) Swedish Dairies' Association	(2) *Ad hoc* parliamentary commissions and the *remiss* system	(10)

Chart 3.1: Continued

| Country | Private Interest Government Policy Areas | | | | | TOTAL |
	Industry Structure	Labour	Supplier/customer Relations	Standards	General Macro/Intersectoral Economic Policies	
Switzerland	(2) SMKV/SGWH/SESK/ZVSM	(1) Vereinigung Schweiz Lebensmittelfabrikanten, Gruppe 'Milch'	(2) ZVSM/SMKV	(2) Zentralverband Schweizerischer Milchproduzenten	(2) Special Commission on Milk	(9)
West Germany	(1) Landesvereinigungen der Milchwirtschaft	(1) Bundesinstitut für Berufsbildung	(1) Centrale Marketinggesellschaft der Deutschen Agrarwirtschaft	(2) Bund für Lebensmittelrecht und Lebensmittelkunde	(2) Deutscher Raiffeisenverband	(7)
Total Amount	(13)	(10)	(13)	(13)	(12)	(61)

ª0 = private interest government not present, 1 = private interest government of minor importance, and 2 = private interest government important.

Chart 3.2 Amount[a] and Form of Private Interest Government by Country in the Meat Processing Industry

| Country | Private Interest Government Policy Areas | | | | | TOTAL |
	Industry Structure	Labour	Supplier/customer Relations	Standards	General Macro/ Intersectoral Economic Policies	
Austria	(2) *Vieh- und Fleischkommission*	(2) *Österreichischer Raiffeisenverband*	(2) *Vieh- und Fleischkommission*	(2) *Vieh- und Fleischkommission*	(2) *Paritätische Kommission*	(10)
Britain	(0)	(2) Meat Industry Training Organization	(2) Food Manufacturers Federation	(2) Food Manufacturers Federation/ Food and Drink Industries Council	(1) Food Manufacturers Federation	(7)
Canada	(0)	(0)	(1) Canadian Chicken Marketing Agency/ Canadian Turkey Marketing Agency	(1) Canadian Meat Council / Canadian Frozen Food Association	(2) Canadian Poultry & Egg Processors Council / Canadian Meat Council	(4)
Netherlands	(2) *Produktschap Vee en Vlees*	(2) BIAs negotiating wage contracts/ *Bedrijfsvereniging/ Bedrijfscommissie*	(2) *Produktschap Vee en Vlees*	(1) *Vleeswaren Kontrole Bureau*	(0)	(7)
Sweden	(2) Price Regulation Association for Meat	(2) *LAF/KFO*	(2) The Swedish Meat Trade Association	(1) The Swedish Poultry Association/ The Swedish Meat Trade Association	(2) *Ad hoc* parliamentary commissions and the *remiss* system	(9)

Chart 3.2: Continued

Country	Private Interest Government Policy Areas					TOTAL
	Industry Structure	Labour	Supplier/customer Relations	Standards	General Macro/ Intersectoral Economic Policies	
Switzerland	(1) *VSM/VSF*	(1) *Verb. Schweiz. Fleischfabrikanten/ VSM*	(0)	(0)	(2) *Schweizerische Genossenschaft für Schlachtvieh- und Fleischversorgung*	(4)
West Germany	(1) *Deutscher Fleischerverband*	(1) *DFV, Bundesverband der Fleischwarenindustrie*	(1) *Centrale Marketinggesellschaft der Deutschen Agrarwirtschaft*	(2) *Bund für Lebensmittelrecht und Lebensmittelkunde*	(1) *DFV/BVFI*	(6)
Total Amount	(8)	(10)	(10)	(9)	(10)	(47)

[a]0 = private interest government not present, 1 = private interest government of minor importance, and 2 = private interest government important.

Chart 3.3 Amount[a] and Form of Private Interest Government by Country in the Fruit and Vegetable Processing Industry

| Country | Private Interest Government Policy Areas | | | | | TOTAL |
	Industry Structures	Labour	Supplier/Customer Relations	Standards	General Macro/Intersectoral Economic Policies	
Austria	(0)	(2) *Österreichischer Raiffeisenverband*	(0)	(0)	(2) *Paritätische Kommission*	(4)
Britain	(1) Campden Food Preservation Research Association	(2) Food Manufacturers Council for Industrial Training	(1) Food Manufacturers Federation	(2) Food Manufacturers Federation/Food and Drink Industries Council	(1) Food Manufacturers Federation	(7)
Canada	(1) Canadian Food Processors Association	(1) Canadian Food Processors Association/Ontario Food Processors Association	(2) Canadian Food Processors Association/Ontario Food Processors Association	(1) Canadian Frozen Food Association/Canadian Food Processors Association	(2) Canadian Food Processors Association	(7)
Netherlands	(1) *Produktschap Groente en Fruit*	(2) BIAs negotiating wage contracts/*Bedrijfsvereniging/Bedrijfscommissie*	(0)	(1) *Kwaliteits-Controle Bureau voor Groenten en Fruit*	(0)	(4)
Sweden	(1) Price Regulation Association for Vegetable Oil	(2) *LAF/KFO*	(0)	(0)	(2) *Ad hoc* parliamentary commissions and the *remiss* system	(5)

Chart 3.3: Continued

| Country | Private Interest Government Policy Areas | | | | | TOTAL |
	Industry Structures	Labour	Supplier/Customer Relations	Standards	General Macro/Intersectoral Economic Policies	
Switzerland	(0)	(1) Swiss Fruit Association	(2) Swiss Fruit Association/Swiss Vegetables Union	(2) Swiss Fruit Association/Swiss Vegetables Union	(2) Special Commissions on Fruits and Vegetables	(7)
West Germany	(1) *Forschungskreis der Deutschen Ernährungsindustrie*	(1) *Arbeitgebervereinigung Nahrung und Genuß*	(1) *Centrale Marketinggesellschaft der Deutschen Agrarwirtschaft*	(2) *Bund für Lebensmittelrecht und Lebensmittelkunde*	(1) *Bundesverband der Obst- und Gemüseverarbeitenden Industrie*	(6)
Total Amount	(5)	(11)	(6)	(8)	(10)	(40)

[a]0 = private interest government not present, 1 = private interest government of minor importance, and 2 = private interest government important.

Chart 3.4 Nature of Relationships between Private Interest Government Outputs and Types of Resources in the Processing Industry (p = predicted relationship, np = opposite of predicted relationship, gamma coefficients)

Outputs	Types of Resources					
	Resource Dependence on Members	Increase in Office Staff	Resource Dependence Overall	Stability of BIA Income	Formal Consultation in Legislation	Intensity of State Access
Intensity of Institutionalization	Direct .024 (NP)	Direct .336 (P)	Direct .562 (NP)	Direct .155 (P)	Direct .319 (P)	Direct .349 (P)
Intensity of Public Policy Administration	Indirect -.346 (P)	Direct .274 (P)	Direct .237 (NP)	Indirect -.021 (NP)	Direct .068 (P)	Direct .064 (P)
Provision of Monopoly Goods	Indirect -.193 (P)	Direct .323 (P)	Direct .065 (NP)	Direct .178 (P)	Indirect -.081 (NP)	Direct .011 (P)
Proportion of Organizational Effort Spent On the Provision of Monopoly Goods	Direct .217 (NP)	Direct .220 (P)	Indirect -.035 (P)	Direct .427 (P)	Indirect -.194 (NP)	Indirect -.093 (NP)
Intensity of Member Sanctioning	Direct .181 (NP)	Direct .291 (P)	None 0 (NP)	Direct 1.0 (P)	Direct .123 (P)	Direct .188 (P)

Chart 3.4: Continued

| Outputs | Resource Dependence on Members | Increase in Office Staff | Types of Resources | | Formal Consultation in Legislation | Intensity of State Access |
			Resource Dependence Overall	Stability of BIA Income		
Demands Placed on Members by the BIA	Direct .129 (NP)	Direct .519 (P)	Direct .434 (NP)	Indirect −.041 (NP)	Direct −.048 (P)	Direct .208 (P)

| Outputs | Resource Dependence On State | Legal Right To Be Consulted By State | Types of Resources | | Formal Consultation in Legislation | |
			Members Taken to Court	Explusion of Members	Special Levy in Last Five Years?	
Intensity of Institutionalization	Direct .400 (P)	Direct .426 (P)	Indirect −.018 (NP)	Direct .536 (P)	Direct .288 (P)	
Intensity of Public Policy Administration	Direct .619 (P)	Direct .275 (P)	Indirect −1.000 (NP)	Indirect −.038 (NP)	Direct .088 (P)	
Provision of Monopoly Goods	Direct .185 (P)	Direct .121 (P)	Direct .238 (P)	Direct .424 (P)	Direct .398 (P)	

Chart 3.4: Continued

Outputs	Resource Dependence On State	Legal Right To Be Consulted By State	Types of Resources Members Taken to Court	Explusion of Members	Special Levy in Last Five Years?
Proportion of Organizational Effort Spent On the Provision of Monopoly Goods	Direct .038 (P)	Indirect -.012 (NP)	Indirect -.037 (NP)	Direct .434 (P)	Direct .520 (P)
Intensity of Member Sanctioning	Direct .132 (P)	Indirect -.235 (NP)	Indirect -1.000 (NP)	Direct .668 (P)	Direct .174 (P)
Demands Placed on Members by the BIA	Direct .213 (P)	Indirect -.280 (NP)	Indirect -1.000 (NP)	Indirect -1.000 (NP)	Direct .835 (P)

Chart 3.5 Provision of Monopoly Goods By Type of Food Processing Industry

Provision of Monopoly Goods	Food Processing Industry As A Whole	Dairy Processing Industry Subsector	Meat Processing Industry Subsector	Fruit and Vegetable Processing Industry Subsector	Total
None	53 (10)	26 (08)	27 (06)	38 (03)	34 (27)
Low	16 (03)	09 (03)	27 (06)	00 (00)	15 (12)
Average	16 (03)	26 (08)	09 (02)	50 (04)	21 (17)
High	05 (01)	26 (08)	33 (07)	12 (01)	21 (17)
Very High	10 (02)	13 (04)	04 (01)	00 (00)	09 (07)
Total	24 (19)	39 (31)	27 (22)	10 (08)	100 (80)

Chapter 4

Sector Structure, Interests and Associative Action in the Food Processing Industry

FRANS VAN WAARDEN

1. Introduction

The possibilities for associative action of capital depend on two broad categories of environment of associations:

a- the structural characteristics of the member firms and the economic and social relations existing between them. In the Research Design for this project they have been labelled 'logic of membership variables' as they influence the 'logic of exchange' between the associations and their members.

b- the characteristics and activities of, and the relations with, interlocutors such as the state, the so called 'logic of influence' variables which influence the logic of exchange between associations and outside third parties.

In this chapter, the influence of the sector structure on the structuring of business interests in patterns of associability as well as on the functioning of created associations will be investigated, by comparing seven countries on these variables.

As will become clear in the course of this chapter, it is very difficult to separate both categories of variables. The sector structure may contain similarities and differences between firms. These will, however, in most cases only lead to common interests — the basis for collective action — under certain conditions deriving from characteristics and activities of the interlocutors. Firms producing different products will only then have a motive for common or separate collective action, when state policy regarding e. g. international trade or quality control affects them in the same, or different way. Differences such as those between high and low labour intensive firms will only become a relevant basis for collective action under the condition of aggressive wage demands by powerful, well organized trade unions. This implies that 'sector structure variables' are not identical with 'logic of membership variables' just as 'logic of influence variables' are not congruent with state/trade union characteristics. The latter not only influence the logic of exchange with interlocutors but indirectly also the logic of exchange between associations and their members.

Given this close relationship between the two categories of variables, the starting point in this chapter will be the sector structure. State or trade union characteristics will be discussed here only in relation to this.

The sector structure may create first of all *problems* for collective action. Prisoner dilemma-type problems will be enhanced by the presence of large numbers of firms in certain sectors and by internal competition, i. e. homogeneous characteristics of firms. Structural heterogeneity of firms on the other hand may provide for insufficient common interests to organize around. It will make it difficult for more comprehensive associations to generate general group interests, not too far removed from individual firm interests, which will be capable of binding members to the association. Heterogeneity may even create contradictory interests, calling for separate interest organization. High concentration may also pose problems for organization. The more powerful resources of large firms provide these with the attractive alternative of individual improvement of their position over collective improvement, thus reducing their willingness to engage in collective action.

On the other hand, the sector structure could also contain factors, *contributing to* more comprehensive and well-knit organizations. Internal competition may be divisive; it might however also provide a motive for organization to regulate and reduce competition. Conflicts with other market-parties, e. g. foreign competitors, suppliers or customers may also provide a motive for close cooperation. The presence of many small firms may create a need for organizations providing collective services, which small firms cannot supply themselves. Finally, the sector structure may contain primary relations between firms, e. g. on the basis of internal supplies, regional concentration or a collective social identity (family relationships, common ownership structure, common ideology), which will contribute to social control and thus for a check on 'free ridership'.

Both categories, factors limiting and factors contributing to associative action, will be investigated. Under the first category, competition and structural heterogeneity will be discussed (section 2 and 3); under the second category, the presence and strength of opponents on markers (section 4) and factors contributing to social cohesion (section 5).

2. Internal Competition

An important factor contributing to strong competition is significant overproduction, present in most countries. The European Community for example has a 10 per cent surplus of dairy products, piled up in the butter- and milkpowder mountains. On the *demand side,* overproduction is due to problems of saturation on the domestic markets. Consumption of basic foodstuffs such as milk, cheese, bacon, sausages and canned peas cannot be increased endlessly. There is a limit to the human stomach and the number of stomachs in Europe does not increase any more. Sometimes, specific cultural changes add up to the problems. Bacon consumption in the U. K. has, for example, shown a long term decline owing to the decreased popularity of the traditional British breakfast. In particular, industries which are solely oriented towards the domestic market show a very low growth rate. Other strongly export-oriented industries, such as those in the Netherlands, have been able to grow at a higher pace, but increased financial problems in third countries create difficulties for further expansion on foreign markets.

On the *supply side*, rationalization and increased use of economies-of-scale, especially in the dairy industry (where this has been possible because liquids can be processed in a closed circuit) have contributed to overcapacity. In the fruit- and vegetable processing industry on the other hand, overcapacity has been the result of low capital intensity and the resultant low entry barriers to the industry. One Dutch association official commented: 'anyone can start with a few drums of sauerkraut in his backyard'. The same low entry barriers cause overcapacity in the significant small artisan sectors in the meat processing industry in Germany and Switzerland (see below). In the dairy industry there is furthermore the pressure of the increasing milk supply coming from farmers, at least in those countries where many dairies are operated by farmer-cooperatives (Germany, the Netherlands, Sweden, Switzerland). Many such cooperatives are obliged to accept all the milk from their members for processing and have to find ways to get rid of their dairy products. In EC-countries surplus milk can of course be disposed of by processing it into the intervention products butter and skim milk powder, which can be handed in at the EC-intervention bureaus at fixed minimum prices. Other countries such as Sweden, Austria and Switzerland have developed similar policies in their efforts to become self-sufficient in food production and to guarantee farmers an income. But this same intervention policy is a further factor contributing to overproduction.

Recently, measures have been taken by the EC to curb the flow of milk and meat through the introduction of the co-responsibility levy. Farmers, producing more milk than in former years are fined. They have to pay a levy on their surplus milk. In the Netherlands this levy is used for subsidies for farm rationalization and mechanization, thus contributing to more overcapacity, a paradox indeed.

Overcapacity has become more costly, due to the increased capital-intensity, especially in the dairy industry. This provides an extra motive for fierce competition. Furthermore, the high concentration of the retail trade in most countries (see below) has increased competition. The demand side can make optimal use of the present overcapacity and competition, thus putting the profit margins of the FPI under constant pressure.

Thus competition among FPI-firms is reasonably high. A good indicator for this is the profit margin, which is in most countries below the national average in our three FPI-sectors (see appendix). In all countries this is the case in the fruit- and vegetable processing industry. In dairy and meat processing only Canada and the Netherlands show an above-average score.

There are however a number of other factors which temper competition. A first one is state regulation of supply and price of dairy- and meat products (for details see the chapter by Coleman in this volume). The same EC-policy, which is responsible for overproduction, reduces the competition which would result from this. It is only a minimal reduction, though. Dairy firms and slaughterhouses can hand in surplus production at minimum intervention prices, but a good profit can only be had by selling produce at a higher price on the market and in the form of products with a higher value added, such as non-commodity cheeses, milk products or hams. Competition therefore is especially fierce on the markets for such products.

The existence of formal cartels sometimes reduces competition in markets for such high added-value products. In Sweden they are of a statutory nature. The farmer coops exploiting dairies work together in the Swedish Dairy Association SMR, before 1967 the sole regulator of the price of dairy products before they go to retailers. In the new system, introduced in that year, the farmer coops are important participants in a newly established statutory price regulating association. A similar arrangement exists in the Swedish meat processing industry, although the Farmers Meat Marketing Association, SCAN, does not have a monopoly of sales. There are also private meat processing firms, not affiliated to this association of producer cooperatives.

In the Netherlands cartels exist for pickled onions, consumption milk, coffee cream and cheese. The latter is relatively unstable. The fierce competition in this high added value product leads to a regular break-up of the agreement, which, however, is renewed again and again in the meetings every fortnight. Holland also contains an international cartel for condensed milk. In the Association of Conserved Milk the world producers of evaporated milk have found one another commercially. Said our informant: 'In third world countries, where the largest part of the sales go to, tenders are invited for. The association here is now used to make deals not to bother one another too much. This is possible, because not too many firms are involved. But those firms do supply 60 per cent of the world trade. In addition, multinational firms like Nestlé and Carnation, who are responsible for the remaining 40 per cent, are present through their Dutch subsidiaries'.

In countries like Germany or the U. K. cartels either do not exist or are secret, as the authorities do not condone commercial collusion. In Britain, recently a number of alleged cartels at the retail end of the dairy business have been discovered and are under investigation by the Office of Fair Trading.

In other cases competition is reduced, because firms sell their products through collective sales and export associations. Farmer cooperatives in Sweden, Switzerland and the Netherlands do so. In Sweden, there is only one such collective purchase, sales, export and storage association. Hence competition is here absent. The Dutch cooperatives are organized in three regional collective sales and export associations. What there is in competition (especially in cheese) takes place between these three collective sales associations.

Informal commercial collusion is probably fostered by the oligopolistic market structure in some sectors in some countries. In the British, Swedish and Dutch dairy industries, four firms account for more than 60 per cent of the total production value. In Britain the largest dairy manufacturer is the Milk Marketing Board, which dominates the butter and cheese markets. In meat processing, the four largest firms together have a production share of more than 50 per cent in Austria and Sweden. An almost monopolistic market structure exists in the Swedish dairy industry, where the single largest firm is good for 63 per cent of the dairy production. Under such conditions competition will practically be absent.

Finally, it should be noted that the market for final products is also ordered by the various binding rules regarding minimum quality norms for both raw materials (milk, carcasses) and final products, set by the state (see the chapter by De Vroom in this volume).

Considering all these factors, which either intensify or limit competition, internal competition is probably the least intense, if not absent, in the Swedish, Dutch and Austrian dairy- and meat processing industries. In Sweden the market is strongly state regulated, there is a high degree of concentration and all farmer-cooperatives organize their commercial activities collectively. The Dutch owe their ordered markets to the combination of EC-regulations, the presence of cartels, collective sales and export associations, the high degree of concentration and the strong dependence on export markets. In Austria, finally, strong regulation by the Kammernsystem is involved. Competition will be the strongest in the U. K., Canada and the FRG, with their liberal tradition of legal bans on cartels (in West Germany of course owing to the postwar influences of Anglo-Saxon occupiers) and generally in the fruit- and vegetable processing industry.

Internal competition may not only exist on the market for final products, but also on the labour market and the *market for raw materials*. Competition on the labour market has not been a problem for some years now, owing to the high unemployment rates. However, the situation on the raw materials markets is different. In some countries there does not really exist such a market. In Sweden and the Netherlands for example, about 90 per cent of the milk is processed by farmer-cooperatives. There is no market relationship here between producer and processor of raw materials. Cooperatives are by their constitution required to accept all the milk from their member-farmers. On the other hand, the farmer is obliged to deliver all the milk which he does not use himself to his cooperative. Nevertheless, there may be competition. Cooperatives, e. g. in neighbouring regions, may compete for members-farmers-suppliers. Such has indeed been the case in the Netherlands in the past. Dairy cooperatives, wanting to increase efficiency (and a higher milk price for their members) by exploiting economies-of-scale required more milk suppliers. Thus they lured farmers away from neighbouring cooperatives, among others by offering them a (temporary) higher milk price for poorer quality milk. These 'border conflicts' have been intense and lead to heavy price undercutting and too high a price for bad quality milk, resulting in further deterioration of milk quality, product quality, reputation and export sales. In addition these conflicts threatened collective action in regional dairy associations. Several cooperatives left their association because of such conflicts.

In the course of history, dairy associations have acted to put an end to this competition between factories for farmers. They have agreed on binding rules on quality determination of milk as the basis for the price and on payment schemes.

One regional association of cooperatives, the one in Friesland, succeeded even in establishing a system of binding determination of 'supply territories', i. e. which farmer should supply which factory — although it took more than thirty years of discussion before the farmers were willing to relinquish their freedom of choice of cooperative.

Generally, in these farmer-cooperatives, prices for raw materials are not directly based on supply and demand, nor on negotiations between cooperatives and individual farmers, but on the quality of the milk (which determines a basic price) and on the profits the cooperative makes. Profits are namely handed back to farmer-owners by giving them at the end of the year an extra final payment for their milk, so that profits appear in the books as costs of raw materials (for tax purposes).

In England and Canada there is also not a market for raw materials in the dairy industry (and in Canada for the fruit- and vegetable processing industry as well), but for different reasons. Price and/or supply is here regulated by a monopoly contract between two partners. All farmers are obliged to deliver their produce to marketing boards, which determine price and allocation to different products by negotiations with (associations of) processors.

In Switzerland we find a combination of both cases. Farmers have to deliver all their milk to the closest local farmer-cooperative, which partly processes this milk in milk treatment plants and butter factories of its own and partly sells the milk to others, such as private dairies and independent artisanal cheesemakers, on the basis of a series of national, regional and local contracts between (associations of) milk selling cooperatives and (associations of) milk buyers. In the first case, the milk supplier is the owner of the milk processing plant, just like the farmer-cooperatives in Sweden and the Netherlands. In the second case, the national and regional associations of coops function as milk marketing boards, just like the ones in Canada and the U. K. This system still allows for competition for milk between private dairies, cheesemakers and milk processing coops. However, this is further reduced by the regulation of the allocation of milk over different products and firms in the central allocation program *(Milchverarbeitungsprogramm)*, made up by the national association of coops ZVSM under its statutory powers. The price of raw milk is furthermore determined by the state (the *Bundesrat*) in consultation with the ZVSM (Farago, Ruf and Wieder, 1984: 239 ff.).

Such forms of regulation of the raw materials market do not, however, exist in West Germany. This country hence shows the most competition on the raw materials market.

What are the *consequences of competition for associational activity* in the FPI-industry? It is of course very difficult to say whether the presence of competition has prevented the establishment of associations, which otherwise would have been formed. Our research focus has been existing associations, so that empty spaces of associative activity were not easily discovered. Nevertheless, the impression is that very few sections of these industries are unorganized. Have we then perhaps found cases where existing associations broke apart or had to reduce activity because of the fierce competition between their members? One would expect to find such phenomena in the less regulated sectors of fruit- and vegetable processing and — to a lesser extent — in the meat processing industry and in those countries with generally more competition, the U. K., Canada and West Germany.

The few cases of dissolution of associations or reduction of activity have indeed been found in the British and West German fruit- and vegetable industries. The British Fruit- and Vegetable Canners Association was dissolved in 1980; the West German *Bundesverband der Obst- und Gemüseverarbeitenden Industrie* reduced its activity in 1978, abolished regional subunits and reduced operating costs by a staff and office sharing arrangement with 2 other associations. However, several factors may be responsible here. These sectors showed a severe decline — just as in other countries — which by itself was a reason for reduction of associative activity. Similar associations in other countries, such as the Netherlands, also tried to reduce operating costs by entering in new staff sharing arrangements, in reaction to a loss of members, due to the decline of the industry. But the decline, of course, also increased competition and conflict among the remaining members, thus diminishing their motivation to generate the necessary resources for continued existence of their associations, especially when the association was incapable of tackling the then central problem of market ordering. As was noted, especially in the liberal countries, the U. K. and West Germany, associations have difficulty engaging in cartel-like activities.

Apart from these two, no other cases of dissolution of associations are known. Competition must, however, have limited existing associations in the development of new activities, especially in the field of monopoly goods, or may have frustrated such attempts. Such was the case with the Association of Dutch Meat Products, VNV. Its attempt to develop new quality control norms was frustrated by competition among its members. A similar situation was found among Swiss producers of air dried meat *(Bündnerfleisch)*. Here too producers were unable to reach agreement over quality regulations.

Competition may put limits to associative activity, but it may also stimulate associability. Associations can be created in response to competition or existing associations may try to regulate it.

In liberal countries, where cartels are generally illegal and where there is relatively little state regulation of markets, such attempts don't seem to have been successful. The British Fruit- and Vegetable Canners Association was dissolved, partly because it could not respond to the need for rationalization of the market (Grant, 1983 b: 81); the German *Bundesfachverband der Marktmolkereien* 'attempted in vain to establish rules of competition among its members in the mid 1970's' (Hilbert, 1982: 17).

In the countries where the state has a more lenient attitude to cartels and/or is itself very much involved in market regulation — especially in the dairy industry — associations seem to involve themselves much more in commercial activities. In these low-competition countries (Sweden, the Netherlands, Switzerland, Austria) the low degree of competition was partly a result of associative activity, as was pointed out. Contrary to German and British experiences, Dutch attempts to establish rules of competition were much more successful. The

associations for coffee cream and for consumption milk were established as
cartels for the domestic market. The association for evaporated milk functions as
such and the Dutch National Cooperative Dairy Union FNZ has a special
committee for 'production control of cheese', where every fortnight price
agreements are attempted. Regional cooperative dairy associations have created
rules on ordering the raw materials market by delineating 'supply territories' as
was mentioned earlier. Swiss associations have done the same. The collective
purchases, sales and export activities of the Swedish Dairy Association SMR, the
Swiss National Cooperative Association ZVSM and of the Dutch collective dairy
sales associations have reduced competition also. Associations furthermore have
played an important role in initiating statutory regulation of markets (e. g. in
Switzerland and the Netherlands, where present state regulations emerged out of
formerly private agreements), are involved in its implementation (the Swiss
ZVSM, the Austrian *Kammern*), or participate on the board of statutory bodies,
implementing market regulation (e. g. the Swiss association of producers of hard
cheese SMKV, which participates in the *Käseunion* or the Dutch FNZ and
VVZM, which participate in the statutory trade association for the dairy
industry).

The response of associations to competition seems hence to depend on
characteristics of the state, such as the legal rules on cartels and the degree of
state involvement in market regulation (which in turn is a function of association
activity in the past in many cases). These are the variables which have been
identified in the research design as variables affecting only the 'logic of influence'. Where such 'state conditions' are favourable, associations seem to develop
much more market-regulatory activities and are consequently — because of the
resultant reduction of competition — less troubled by internal divisions resulting
out of fierce competition. In general, this is especially the case in the dairy
industry, where state market regulation is much more developed than in the
other two sectors.

3. Heterogeneity

3.1 Products

One factor, which also reduces competition is the strong market segmentation. This is a result of the high degree of product heterogeneity in the food
processing industry. This product heterogeneity is one of the most conspicuous
characteristics of the industry.

First of all, it is not really possible to speak of thé food processing industry.
Instead, there is a dairy industry, a brewery sector, a meat processing branch, a
milling sector and a fruit- and vegetable processing industry. These sectors do
not have much in common and not many economic relations exist between them.
Their most important common characteristic is that they process organic material which is produced in the agricultural sector. On most other criteria they
differ.

This is reflected in the associational patterns in all our countries, with the exception of Austria. In almost all countries there are separate associational systems for the dairy, the meat and the fruit and vegetable processing industries. Between the associations in the same branch several institutionalized linkages exist. Between the different branch-systems however there are few interorganizational lines of coordination. Several countries don't even have a peak association for the whole food processing industry (see chapter 2). Only Austria is an exception, as pointed out earlier (see also chapter 2). The industry in that country is organized in sector-unspecific *Kammern* (Chambers of Commerce and Industry), but, as this is a nationwide statutory structure, the associational system is more determined by macro-political factors than by the structure of the food processing industry.

Each sector of the FPI also displays internally a high product heterogeneity. The only thing the sectors have in common is the source of their raw material, milk, meat or fruit and vegetables. It is on the basis of this that they are defined after all. The most heterogeneous sector probably is the fruit and vegetables processing industry. Products here can be distinguished on the basis of raw material (type of fruit or vegetable), on the basis of substance of the product (complete fruit, pulp, syrup, juice), conservation method (sterilization, salting, sugaring, pickling, drying, freezing), packaging methods (tin, glass, carton) and degree of processing (only basic items such as canned tomatoes or formulated products such as soups, juices and sauces). The most important products in most countries are jams and jellies, apple sauce, canned vegetables, fruit juices and frozen products.

Next in heterogeneity comes the meat processing industry with distinctions on the basis of raw materials (cows, pigs, horses, poultry, rabbits, etc.), degree of processing (carcasses, whole sides, cuts, cured cuts, seasoned combinations such as sausages), main or side products (tripe, lard), conservation methods (open pack products, salting and curing, canning, drying).

The dairy industry is probably the least differentiated by product. It can roughly be divided into six groups: white products (milk and milk products like yoghurts and desserts), yellow products (butter and cheese), dry products (milkpowder), evaporated milk, processed wastes such as molten cheese and cheesespread and finally ice cream. The latter is in many countries (U. K., West Germany, the Netherlands) not really considered part of the dairy industry, even though it is included in this sector by the different statistical agencies. Ice cream is to a large extent made of vegetable fats rather than milk fats in many countries and hence does not share the same raw material as other dairy products.

The product differences are important, because they imply differences on many other criteria such as perishable — non-perishable nature, markets, labour intensity, growth and profitability. Consumption milk is more perishable than cheese, therefore proximity to markets is important for the first product. As a result, consumption milk is usually produced for the domestic, or even the local market, whereas cheese is in most countries an important export product. Even though the food processing industry generally is not so labour intensive (it is especially raw materials intensive; in West Germany for example raw materials make up 69 per cent of the production value), there are differences in labour intensity. The production of consumption milk is twice as labour intensive as the production of milk powder. Also, the growth rates for the different products vary. Milk consumption is everywhere stagnant. Growth in the dairy industry must be realized in milk products like yoghurts and desserts or in certain kinds of cheese. Similarly, in the generally declining fruit and vegetable processing industry canned preserves are becoming less popular, whereas frozen products and TV-dinners show a high growth rate. Given these differences in growth, the degree of competition on the markets for the diverse products will vary and so will strategies of competition and marketing. For bulk products like fresh milk, butter, milkpowder or meat cuts it is difficult to build up a brand image. Therefore competition tends to be based on price. For more processed and refined products such as desserts, cheese, bacon, soups and sausages a brand name can be created, based on distinct quality. Henceforth competition is possible on quality, product image and product innovation (new milk drinks, new sausages).

Because all these distinctions often coincide with the product difference, firms derive specific interests from their product orientation. Labour intensive firms will be more concerned about creating a front against high wage demands and strong trade unions than less labour intensive firms. Firms with a high added value, i. e. relatively low costs of raw materials, tend to have other interests vis-a-vis the supplying farmers than firms with a low added value. Declining sectors may attach importance to rationalization of the market; growth sectors on the other hand are likely to have a stake in developing new sales chains or in changes in existing quality legislation when it hampers the development of new products. Finally and most importantly, state regulations will affect firms which differ on such criteria in distinct ways. Hence they will have other — if not contradictory — interests regarding international trade policy, development aid, price and quality regulation, fair trade legislation, subsidies, etc.

All these interest may form the basis for separate organization, the more so since the degree of regulation in the FPI is often high. The product heterogeneity hence has created a highly differentiated pattern of associations in the FPI.

Paradoxically, the sector with probably the highest product-heterogeneity, the fruit and vegetable processing industry, shows the least differentiation. The average number of first order associations on the basis of product in this sector in our eight countries is 4.1. The respective data for the dairy and the meat processing industry are 6.9 and 7.8. The low score of the fruit and vegetable processing industry is probably due to an intervening factor, the relatively small size of the sector, compared to the others. This argument is supported by the fact that the country with the largest fruit and vegetable sector, Germany, also has the highest number of associations.

The product heterogeneity in the fruit and vegetable processing industry is however reflected in a strong intra-organizational differentiation. The fruit and vegetable processing industry in Britain is, since the dissolution of the canners association, mainly organized in a general FPI-association, the Food and Drink

Federation. This association has 5 serviced member associations for different branches of the fruit and vegetable industry: for pickles and sauces, preserves, soups, table jellies and soft drinks. Similarly, the German *Bundesverband der Obst- und Gemüseverarbeitenden Industrie* has seven product committees. The equivalent Dutch association has twenty-four product sections, which are highly autonomous. They are even allowed to be affiliated — as a section — to a higher order association.

In the fruit and vegetable processing industry, the distinction growth — nongrowth product has been a basis for separate organization. The German *Bundesverband der Obst- und Gemüseverarbeitenden Industrie* basically organizes the declining branches. A growth branch, fruit juices, seceded from this association and formed a new *Verband der Deutschen Fruchtsaftindustrie*. Another growth branch, frozen products, is separately organized in the U. K., Canada, the Netherlands and Switzerland. Separate interest organization has been deemed necessary, because the so called 'cold chain' poses a number of special technical problems as well as problems with quality regulations.

In the dairy industry the largest number of associations is found in Britain. The manufacturers of cheese, milk powder, butter, condensed milk, tinned cream, goat milk products and ice cream are separately organized in altogether twenty product specific associations. The least differentiation is found in Sweden and Austria, where only two first order associations exist, which both cover the whole dairy industry.

Britain is also the country with the highest number of product specific associations in the meat processing industry. Separate associations exist for bacon, small bacon, lard, natural sausages, tripe dressing, poultry, turkey, ducks, rabbits and waterfowl. As far as the stage of production is concerned abattoir owners and butchers have their own associations. The lowest number again is found in Austria (no product specific associations) and in Sweden and Switzerland.

Can these variations between countries in differentiation of associational systems by product be explained by differences in sector structure? With a few exceptions this is not likely. Product heterogeneity will not be much less in Sweden, Switzerland or Austria, countries with few product-defined associations, than in countries with many product associations. Some specific differentiations though may be the result of sector characteristics. The existence of separate associations for ice cream has everything to do with the fact that these firms use vegetable fats as raw material and hence are not really being part of the dairy industry. Similarly, the associations for frozen foods owe their existence to specific problems associated with this technique of conservation. Furthermore, the overrepresentation of a product in some countries also has consequences for the number and type of associations found. Thus the presence of four associations for cheese in Switzerland (out of a total of five product-specific associations) is obviously related to the dominance of cheese in the Swiss dairy industry: 46 per cent of all milk is transformed into cheese in this country.

Apart from these examples, 'state variables' are probably more important. Austria for one, owes its extremely low degree of product differentiation to the statutory nature of its associations. In other countries sector differences only become important bases for separate organization of interests in so far as they lead to differential influences on firms by state regulations. A good illustration of this is provided by Sweden, where differences in state intervention have created a protected sector, guarded against foreign competition through import controls and a competitive, unprotected sector. The protected sector contains the slaughtering and meat packing factories and the dairy industry. Fruit and vegetable canning belongs to the unprotected sector.

The influence of state regulation on the importance of the sector structure for the associational system is illustrated by the example of the dairy industry. This branch has the highest number of product specific associations, even though it shows the least product heterogeneity. The explanation must be the intense regulation of this sector, which makes structural differences more relevant for separate organization. The high degree of regulation is in turn related to the sector structure. It is the result of the importance of the industry for public health and for the farmers income and related to the perishable nature of the raw material. Thus it is difficult to separate the influence of state regulation and sector structure on the associational system.

In the end the difference in number of product-specific associations between, on the one hand, Sweden, Switzerland and Austria and on the other hand West Germany and the U. K. seems to show the strongest relationship to country size and hence to size of industry. Intermediate size countries like the Netherlands and Canada have intermediate numbers of product specific associations.

The different countries, in summary, have in common a differentiated pattern of associability on the basis of product (with the exception of Austria), a reflection of product heterogeneity interwined with state regulation. They differ somewhat in the degree and pattern of differentiation. The difference in *degree* can primarily be explained by size-differences of the countries involved. Differences in *pattern* are related to the overrepresentation of certain branches in some countries.

Product heterogeneity is thus responsible for a high degree of associational differentiation. The same factor has not contributed to a complementary integration. Other factors, yet to be discussed, are responsible for that.

One might however expect that blurring of sector borders, e. g. as the result of product diversification by firms and mergers across sectors, could lead to less differentiation or at least some coordination. This does not seem to have happened. There are some cases, where associations have recently broadened their domains, possibly in response to such product diversification. The German *Milchindustrie Verband,* originally an association of evaporated milk manufacturers, opened membership in the early seventies to producers of all dairy products. The equivalent Dutch Associations of Condensed Milk did also enlarge its domain, although not so widely. It decided to include milkpowder producers, partly indeed because it concerned the same firms, but partly also in adaptation to the domain of the international association Assilec, to which it is affiliated.

The presence of firms in different FPI-sectors such as Unilever, Labatt (Canada) or Wessanen (Netherlands) has not lead to closer relationships between associations. Similarly, the fact that the large dairy cooperatives, e. g. in the Netherlands, produce all the different dairy products has not (yet) lead to mergers of product-specific associations. Most of these large firms have a decentralized internal structure. The different product divisions carry on their activities relatively autonomously, including those they undertake as members of associations. What's more, officials of Unilever assured us in an interview that they considered the present differentiated pattern of interest representation as very functional. Some interests could best be represented by a small group of concerned firms directly linked to specialized state and semi-state agencies.

3.2 Region

Regional differentiation between and within associations is also found, albeit much less. Switzerland has regional associations of artisans (butchers, cheese processors) and regional *Milchverbände,* associations of farmer-owned cooperatives, which operate dairy factories. Similar regional associations of cooperatives exist in the Netherlands. Britain has a separate poultry association for Ulster and has Dairy Trade Federations in Northern Ireland and Scotland with product specific affiliates for these regions. West Germany knows regional *Handwerkkammern and Fleischinnungen* (guilds) for the artisan butchers. In Canada 17 of the 24 first order associations found in all three sectors have regionally defined domains. They organize western poultry processors or Quebec vegetable canners. Only Austria and Sweden lack regionally specialized associations.

Of course regional differentiation requires something of the sector structure: the industries must be physically dispersed over different regions. The existence of regional associations in the dairy industry in Switzerland and the Netherlands is the result of the territorial dispersion of the dairy industry over the countryside. This has followed the distribution of farmers because of past difficulties with transporting fresh milk without loss of quality. However, dispersion may be a necessary condition for regional differentiation; it is not a sufficient condition. In other countries, dispersion has not lead to the establishment of regional dairy associations. Similarly, the presence of regional associations of butchers in West Germany and Switzerland requires the territorial distribution of butchers, a result of the fact that they serve local markets. But again, this can not be a sufficient explanation.

For the remainder, regional differentiation must be explained by logic of influence variables. The organization of the state and hence the character and possible differences in state regulation form the basis for separate organization by region. This explains why regional associations are found in countries with a federal political structure: Switzerland, Canada and West Germany, or in a union-state like the United Kingdom. Only the Dutch regional dairy associations form an exception. Their presence is related to their (former) function: servicing the local dairy cooperatives. Finally, not surprising, the presence of regional associations is also related to geographic size of the country, given the presence of such associations in Canada, West Germany and the U. K.

3.3 Firm Size

Differences in firm size are very significant in most countries, with the possible exception of Sweden — where very large firms dominate — and Switzerland — where most meat and the majority of dairy firms are small artisan businesses. In all other countries, the size ranges from multinationals such as Unilever to small artisan butchers. These size differences are very large in the meat processing industry, in ice cream production and in some countries in cheese production. The dairy and the fruit and vegetable processing industry are more industrialized, thereby reducing the range in firm size: the small artisan shops fall away. These, by the way, present a special case, because not only size, but also different production methods are involved in the difference. Therefore first a word on the industrial firms.

Concentration is the highest in Sweden. The share of the four largest firms in output of dairy, meat and fruit and vegetable processing is 99, 82 and 87 percent. The first two sectors are dominated by farmer-owned cooperatives, which create special difficulties of firm definition. The regional associations (of local farmer-owned cooperatives) can best be considered the equivalent of a firm. They are associations, but also operate plants and as such are firms. The largest dairy association/firm is the cooperative in middle and southern Sweden, the *Mjölk-centralen Arla*, with a share of 60–65 percent of the total production of various milk products. In meat, the largest firm is AB Kronfägel, with a market share of 30 percent in poultry meat processing. These regional associations/firms are joined together in national marketing associations (which in turn form the Federation of Swedish Farmers), thus increasing their grip on the market further. These associations too, the meat marketing association SCAN and the dairy marketing association SMR, can be considered the equivalent of a firm, namely a holding with regional subsidiaries. In this case, firm and interest association are congruent, as SCAN and SMR also function as interest associations. If these are taken as firm units, the dairy industry shows a monopoly market structure. The SMR has namely almost a complete monopoly of dairy production. In meat, the cooperative influence is somewhat less extreme. SCAN has a market share of 80 percent in slaughtering, 54 percent in cutting and 32 percent in the meat packing industry.

In the Swedish fruit and vegetable processing industry proprietary firms dominate, but here too concentration is high. The four largest producers Findus (Nestlé), Nova (Unilever), Felix (Volvo) and the consumer coop KF account, as stated, for 87 percent of the production.

Concentration is also high in the British and Dutch dairy industries and in the Austrian fruit and vegetable processing industry. In these countries the four largest firms take care of at least 45 percent of output. This is an average figure. In some subbranches such as ice cream, frozen foods or jams concentration is higher; in others, such as canning or cheese making it is lower. Similarly, some regions may have a strong oligopoly. The four largest red meat processors in Western Canada account for 85 percent of production in that part of the country.

A high degree of concentration however does, by itself, not seem to have many consequences for the associational system, except where concentration is so high as in Sweden. Here firm and interest association merge. What is important is the range in firm size, i. e. the presence of very small firms next to very large ones. Size differences are expected to be important for associations as firms of different size have usually different expectations regarding their associations. Large firms are primarily interested in the possibility of more neutral interest representation through associations and sometimes in commercial agreements. Small firms have a need for services and information, which they cannot provide themselves because of their small size.

Notwithstanding the great range in firm size in most sectors, only in a few cases have FPI-firms organized on the size criterion. These cases are found in Britain (in all three sectors) and in the Dutch meat processing industry. Elsewhere large and small firms have been able to work together in the same associations, thanks to their different interests: large firms seem to be sponsoring services by associations used by small members, in order to create as high a density ratio as possible in the pursuit of external interest representation.

The existence of a high degree of concentration may not have many consequences for the pattern of associative action, a change such as an increase in degree of concentration does sometimes have a significant impact. A case in point is the Dutch dairy industry. Formerly, the about 500 small dairy coops were organized in provincial associations, which in turn formed the national federation of dairy cooperatives FNZ. In the sixties these coops merged gradually into about four large regional cooperatives in order to rationalize production and apply economies-of-scale. In time, the domain of some of these new coops came to be congruent with that of some regional associations. Thus these associations became redundant. In some areas they were dissolved altogether and the new firms became a direct member of the national federation FNZ. In other areas associations still remained in existence, but were divested of their extensive service facilities. Their personnel — in one case over 200 persons — were taken over by the newly formed firms in those regions. Thus voluntary interorganizational coordination was replaced by compulsory intra-organizational coordination. Horizontal lines of cooperation changed into vertical hierarchic lines.

There is a specific size difference which has led to separate organization, but this overlaps with another difference, that, already mentioned, between industrial and artisan processing methods. This difference is important for associative action, because it generates different interests. The technical problems of both types of firms are different, they supply different markets and there are usually different state regulations for both categories. For example, German butchers are statutorily required to join *Handwerkkammern* and are subject to a specific set of rules. The industry is not. Dutch butchers too have to join the statutory trade association created for them and to follow its guidelines and regulations. Butchers are found in most countries, but the importance of their meat processing activities — as distinct from retail trade — differs. In West Germany, where over 50 per cent of meat products are produced by butchers, they do offer a large variety of meats, made by themselves. The same is the case in Switzerland and the Netherlands, where they too take a large share of the market for meat products. In Britain and Canada, by contrast, they produce a smaller range of products and are primarily retailers, salesmen rather than artisans. The greater part of their activities hence falls in the ISIC group 620 for retail trade. Other artisan firms are found in ice cream production (Ice creameries of Italian origin in Britain and the Netherlands) and in the production of Swiss cheeses.

Butchers have organizations of their own in all countries. However, in Britain and Canada they cannot really be considered part of the meat processing industry. Hence their organizations do not belong to the associational system in meat processing in these countries.

Thus, unlike regional differentiation of associational systems, size differentiation and differentiation on the related criterion of production techniques, has been primarily a response to the sector structure.

3.4 Ownership Structure

Another characteristic of the sector structure, firm ownership, has also influenced differentiation of associative activity. Sweden and Switzerland probably show the greatest variation in property structure. FPI-plants in these countries are owned and operated by farmer cooperatives, consumer cooperatives, domestic owned proprietary firms, foreign owned private firms and — in Sweden — also by state enterprises. In Switzerland, an additional distinction can be made between actual producer cooperatives (small local cooperatives of artisan cheesemakers) and farmer cooperatives (larger regional associations of farmers which operate milk and butter factories).

Farmer cooperatives are the most important owners of dairy factories in Sweden (where they process 100 percent of the milk), the Netherlands (90 percent), West Germany (80 percent) and probably in Switzerland. In Canada they only dominate the dairy industry in Quebec, Saskatchewan and B. C. In the important dairy province of Ontario, the opposite relation exists: private dairy firms own dairy farms, hence called 'corporate farms'.

In meat processing, farmer coops only dominate in Sweden. Elsewhere (Switzerland, the Netherlands, West Germany, Canada, the U. K.) they own a minority of plants. In fruit and vegetable processing, farmer coops exist only in Switzerland (for potato products, fruit juice, wines).

The distinction farmer coop — private firm produces important conflicting interests. Cooperatives are tied to the agrarian sector. The raw material is for them not a cost of production, which should be kept as low as possible. Instead, they strive to make as high a price as possible for milk and meat. Profits are handed over to the farmer-owners in the form of a higher price for the raw material they supply. Private firms, however, are buyers of raw materials and try to reduce the price as much as possible — especially since raw materials make up two-thirds of the production costs generally in the FPI. Here there is a market relationship, which is absent in the case of cooperatives. The differences in operation of both types of firms may have become somewhat less as the cooperatives have grown larger, as the influence of the professional management has increased and as normal business objectives such as profits for investments have become more important. Nevertheless, the relationship of the cooperative to its supplier of raw materials remains different.

Also coops must be organized in a different way, as they usually have no control over the supply of milk. They are obliged to accept all milk, offered to them by their members. The positive side of this is that their supply is more safeguarded than that of private firms, which run the risk of not getting enough on the market and hence being left with expensive unused capacity.

The tie to the raw materials furthermore makes it more difficult for coops to diversify outside of their sector of origin. The owners are mainly interested in the processing of their products. Private firms are free to diversify as much as they want. As a result, most large private firms are indeed active in many sectors of the FPI and even outside this industry. Coops usually stick to the branch they originate from.

Given this difference, both types of firms have different interests vis-à-vis the trade and agricultural policy of the state. Private firms are opposed to protection of the domestic agricultural sector, e.g. by import restrictions. They are interested in free imports of raw materials, as this decreases their dependence on domestic suppliers and may force prices down. Of course they are also opposed to statutory (minimum) prices of milk and meat. Thus Unilever complains about the Common Agricultural Policy of the EC, about 'the political belief that the primary producer of food must alone have special treatment' (Grant, 1983 b: 12). Such opinions will not be heard from farmer cooperatives.

Usually farmer coops and private firms also have different interests in tax matters. Coops try to avoid taxation by hiding profits in higher prices for raw materials. Tax agencies, alert to this, need a norm for basic raw materials prices (the extra payment on top of this can then be considered profit) and may find this in the price private firms pay for their milk or meat. Hence coops have an interest in high raw materials prices for private firms, a direct conflict of interests.

Such interests have been distinct enough for private firms and farmer coops to organize separately. An additional reason for this was that farmer-owners in some countries had a special need for associations. Associations with knowledgeable staff were required to assist the farmer-governors of coops in controlling the management of their factories. Associations took it upon themselves to audit their annual accounts, to advise them on investments and to select candidates for the function of factory director. Thus the regional associations of coops in the Netherlands grew to significant size, in two cases to more than 200 employees (for industries with only 1,500 to 2,000 employees).

Separate associations for producer coops and private firms exist where both types of firms are present and where coops dominate: in Switzerland, Sweden, the Netherlands and Canada (Quebec). They are absent in the U.K. and Austria. In West Germany, cooperative interests are represented by the sector unspecific *Deutsche Raiffeisenverband,* to which all coops by law are required to be affiliated (in order to have their annual accounts audited).

Consumer coops, active in the FPI, exist in Switzerland, Sweden and the U. K. Swedish consumer coops take care of 12 percent of meat cutting and 22 percent of packed meat production. In Britain, the retail cooperatives, acting through the Cooperative Wholesale Society, account for the processing of 25 percent of the milk supply. The large Swiss coops, COOP and MIGROS, have their own plants in all three FPI-sectors. MIGROS is good for 54 percent of the fruit juice production, 46 percent of yoghurt and 39 percent of butter production.

Swedish consumer coops are separately organized in an employers' association KFO. In Britain too, an association of consumer coops exists in the dairy industry, the Cooperative Milk Trade Association, which organizes the retail coops and their wholesaler with its dairy processing plants. Swiss coops however are not separately organized. Their small number — two — and their individual political influence owing to their size, provides them with alternatives for formal collective interest representation (Farago et al., 1983: 116).

Foreign owned companies are important in the Canadian, Swiss and U. K. fruit- and vegetable processing industry. In Canada, they account for 70 percent of the value added, in Sweden they are good for 63 percent of total sales. In Britain foreign firms are especially important in the canned soup branch (98 percent of sales) and that of canned fruit (59 percent). Nowhere has this lead to separate organization of foreign and domestically owned firms. However, in Canada 'the problems of foreign ownership and the different objectives sometimes held by foreign and domestic firms are important contributing factors to the weak integration of the associational system in the Canadian food processing industry' (Coleman, 1984: 14).

4. The Presence of Opponents

The existence of opponents on the different markets and their strength and organization is likely to stimulate associative activity. This could lead to further differentiation, but also to integration of existing patterns of association. The need for collective front forming against opponents or for institutionalized consultations and negotiations with others may induce firms to create new associations, thus increasing associational differentiation. The same motives could however also lead to closer cooperation between associations, either hierarchic or horizontal, in that way improving integration. They also may bring members to strengthen their associations, to vest them with more resources or to agree on new mutual binding rules, thus bringing organizational development to a higher level.

The food processing industry is confronted with many such opponents: trade unions, foreign competitors, competition from fresh produce, retailers, suppliers and the state. The influence of trade unions, the state and retailers on associative action in the FPI-industry is the subject of separate chapters in this volume. Therefore only the other categories mentioned will be discussed here.

4.1 Foreign Competition

Foreign competition is especially important to the Dutch FPI. In the Netherlands 43 percent of domestic production in the dairy industry is exported (and when consumption milk, which is mainly sold on the domestic market, is not counted, 83 percent). In meat processing this figure is 55 percent and in fruit and vegetable processing 45 percent. Import penetration is also high: 27 percent of the domestic market for dairy products, 25 percent for meat products and 43 percent for fruit and vegetable products. More than any other country the Netherlands is integrated in international trade and subject to foreign competition, both on the domestic markets and on markets abroad.

All the other countries remain below a 10 percent export ratio. The domestic market share of imports in fruit and vegetable processing (a less regulated market in the EC and an 'unprotected sector' in Sweden) is high in all countries: it varies between 23 percent (U. K.) and 43 percent (the Netherlands). The U. K. has relatively high import penetration ratios in the other sectors too: 27 percent in meat processing and 13 percent in dairy market supply. Britain has always been a food importing country, ever since its industrial revolution. Dutch and Danish economies have for a long time been based on exports of agricultural products to the industrialized European heartland Britain. 60 percent of the important bacon and ham consumption is still satisfied by imports: 40 percent from Denmark and 12 percent from the Netherlands. Most countries, however, are more or less insulated from the international market. In politically neutral countries like Sweden, Switzerland and Austria this is due to the state policy for self sufficiency in food production, although this is not always 100 percent successful. Even Switzerland has never been completely self sufficient in food production and imports — of all products — a lot of cheese.

Notwithstanding the importance of foreign competition in some countries, there are only a few cases known where firms have organized around their interests derived from foreign competition. The Dutch dairy industry has an association for butter concentrates, which are mainly exported to India and Arabic countries. This association is solely concerned with export activities. It discusses tenders elsewhere in the world and lobbies with the EC and the Dutch Ministry of Development Aid to increase the share of butter concentrates in foreign aid. This type of organization for export interests, however, is not so much directed against foreign competitors in the dairy industry as against competition by other food products for inclusion in development aid. Front forming against foreign competitors has not really been deemed necessary. Foreign competition is considered more a challenge than a threat by the Dutch FPI. This industry is highly competitive — as is indicated by its high export ratio — and does not need to fear foreign competition very much. There is however one organization for such purposes, but it is not specific to the FPI. That is the national peak association 'Central Organ of Economic Relations Abroad', to which the large FPI-exporters are associated.

4.2 Suppliers

More than e.g. organization of labour, organization of suppliers forms a threat to the industry, as the FPI is not so much labour intensive as well as raw materials intensive. Raw materials make up 69 percent of the production value (in West Germany), whereas labour costs come only to 13 percent of production value.

Of course where processing is done by farmer-owned cooperatives, this does not lead to conflicts between producers and processors of raw materials as both are more or less the same. However, it is different in those countries and sectors where such processing cooperatives do not exist ánd where milk producers have organized themselves. Such is the case in the U.K., Canada, Sweden and Switzerland, where fresh milk is sold through marketing boards. Here the industry is confronted with a monopoly supplier.

What's more, such a monopoly supplier may also turn into a competitor, thus threatening private processors from two sides. A good illustration is formed by the developments in the western part of the Netherlands in the postwar years. Up until the war, the dairy industry in this urbanized part of the country was dominated by private milk treatment plants (quite distinct from other areas where coops dominated), producing consumption milk for the urban citizens. After the war, the farmers here organized themselves in a marketing board, explicitly set up after the example of the British Milk Marketing Board. This board, the CMC, started in due time also to take over private plants, a programme, financed by a compulsory levy by the board on the milk. The private plants reacted in defence. First they organized themselves in a voluntary association, but later on they formed a holding, the Melkunie. Hierarchic coordination could give the firms more strength versus the organized suppliers than horizontal coordination. However, in the end they lost the battle. In 1968 the CMC bought all the shares of the Melkunie, with the result that the western part of the country is now also dominated by farmer coops. A similar development can be observed in Britain, where the Milk Marketing Board has already amassed a sizeable share in dairy production by buying up plants belonging to private firms.

The threat of organized suppliers is even greater to the small Swiss cheese-makers. They are surrounded on all sides by organizations of suppliers and have become competely dependent on them. The farmer coops not only supply them with raw material; they also own the premises where the cheesemakers carry on their activities and they buy their cheeses for their wholesale organization.

In those countries where (still) marketing boards exist, i.e. in Canada, the U.K., Sweden and Switzerland, processors have organized themselves according to their interests as buyers of raw material. In these countries it has been a major determinant of the structure and function of interest associations. Thus in Britain, the high degree of integration of the otherwise strongly differentiated associational system in the dairy industry is due to this factor. The whole British dairy industry has formed the Dairy Trade Federation, which conducts, on behalf of the processing industry, the negotiations with the monopoly supplier, the Milk Marketing Board through an institutionalized channel, The Joint

Committee, where allocation and price of milk supplies are determined. Relations are generally good, although there have been strains in the early 1980s. The partners in the negotiations cooperate also in other activities such as training and education, research and product quality control. The Marketing Board even supplies the DTF with its income. Rather than by member contributions, the DTF is financed by a levy on the milk, collected by the MMB. Thanks to this arrangement, the DTF is one of the best resourced associations in Britain.

In Canada relations are not always so friendly. Here some processors have also organized themselves politically. The Grocery Products Manufacturers Association (dominated by US-owned firms) has tried to break the monopoly of the marketing boards by lobbying against levies on imported raw materials, however thus far in vain.

Similar conflicts exist in Sweden between the organization of the cooperative meat processors SCAN and the organization of private meat processors KF (formed on the basis of such conflicts). SCAN namely functions also as a marketing board for meat. Its members are required to deliver all their animals to its slaughterhouses. Private firms are dependent on SCAN-slaughterhouses for their raw materials. KR has in vain tried to break this near monopoly of SCAN. As a result relations are rather troubled. Private slaughterhouses, which experience the strongest competition, have even organized themselves separately within KR in order to coordinate their activities against SCAN.

Swiss cheesemakers have also organized themselves, both as partner in negotiations with coops in statutory bodies such as the *Käseunion* and for political action.

4.3 Competition from Fresh Produce

Sometimes suppliers are also direct competitors. Fresh farm produce, mainly in the fruit and vegetable sector, competes with conserved produce. Canned vegetables function often only as second class alternatives to fresh vegetables. This type of competition may form an important threat. Producers of fresh fruit and vegetables, e. g. in the Netherlands, are strongly organized. In Holland they form the Central Bureaus of Horticulture, which also operate the large auction halls for fruit and vegetables. They have significant funds for collective advertising and marketing of fresh produce. Nevertheless, the producers have not separately organized themselves on this issue (and neither in other countries). The general association for the fruit and vegetable processing industry does, however, find a task in opposing these organizations of horticulturalists on a number of issues.

5. Social Cohesion

Cooperation in interest representation could also be stimulated by social ties or common identities and beliefs among firms. Such ties and identities may be derived from structural conditions such as the existence of commercial relations,

territorial concentration overlaid with regional sentiments or a common ownership structure.

Some of these variables have already been discussed under heterogeneity. That
is no coincidence. Structural factors contributing to social cohesion are the
complement, or sometimes the reverse, of those creating heterogeneous interests. A wide variety in types of ownership structure may result in a differentiated
pattern of associations. The logical complement is that a lack of such a variety
may make it easier for businessmen to have their interests represented by a single
association.

The relationship between heterogeneity and level of organizational development is however a little more complicated. Whereas such a heterogeneity may
result in a differentiated and fragmented pattern of associations and hence a
weakly developed associational system, it may strengthen individual associations. Heterogeneity implies first of all that the group of e. g. producer cooperatives is smaller than would be the case when the whole industry was made up of
producer coops. Strong social ties are more likely to develop in a small group
than a large group. Secondly, heterogeneity implies the presence of groups with
different structures and possibly different interests, who may become opponents
for one another. Just as the existence of 'external enemies' such as suppliers or
foreign competitors may foster associative action, so may the presence of
'internal enemies' within the sector, such as a group of firms with a different
ownership structure. This is even more likely where special subgroups have an
identity of their own, which sets them apart from others. Such an identity may
be derived from a common ideology — in the case of ownership — or common
culture — in the case of regional groups.

What now is the situation with regard to these factors contributing to social
cohesion in the sectors and countries under study?

5.1 Interdependence

As stated, social connections may first of all stem from commercial relations
within the sector. An indicator for such relations is the importance of customer-
supplier relations or the interdependence in the branch. Businessmen will get to
know one another through such relations and this acquaintance by itself may
contribute to cooperation in associations. In addition, they may develop common interests out of this relation. Even though suppliers and customers have, of
course, contradictory interests when it comes to prices, their interests may run
parallel as far as quality or assured supply/sale is concerned.

As may be seen from tables 4.1–4.3 in the appendix, interdependence is almost
everywhere high and especially in the meat processing and the dairy industry. In
meat processing, which is basically a gradual process of disassembly, there is a
chain of processors, starting with slaughtering houses producing whole sides of
beef or pork through firms, which reduce these to special cuts to retailer-
butchers who do the final cutting and producers of formulated products and
processors of wastes, such as lard or offal. Sometimes these different stages of

production are found in a single firm. More often however, they are handled by separate firms which stand in commercial relationships to one another.

In the dairy industry such a chain of consecutive processes is absent (Milk is not first transformed into butter, before one makes cheese out of it). Internal sector supplies are high here for other reasons. The high scores in Sweden, Switzerland and Britain are the result of the fact that fresh milk first passes through the hands of producer cooperatives/marketing boards, which have a monopoly in marketing the raw material but also process a part of it themselves. These are hence special supplier-customer relations: the suppliers supply not their own final product but part of their raw material. In addition, there is considerable buying and selling of product between dairy processors, who want to enlarge the product assortment they market. Because of the increase in the scale of production and the specialization this requires, most dairies are not capable of producing the full range of products themselves, especially in cheeses and milk products (yoghurts, desserts, milk drinks). Thus, e. g. in the Netherlands, there is only one firm in the country which produces 'kwark', a kind of cottage cheese, and which supplies all its competitors with this product.

The customer-supplier relations mentioned are of a different nature, have different consequences for the interests of the partners and hence for their cooperation in associative action.

The first type of relation of supplier-customer of intermediate products, found in the meat disassembly chain, does not have clear cut consequences for the pattern of associations. In some countries, slaughtering houses, specialized meat cutters and meat packers are organized in the same association(s) (Canada, Sweden); in other countries they form separate associations (Switzerland, West Germany, the U. K., the Netherlands). However, one might conclude from this difference that slaughterers and meat processors have organized separately in those countries where the chain of meat processing is longer, where more specialized and formulated products are produced and thus where heterogeneity is greater.

The second type of dairy producer coops supplying a part of their own raw material to competitors, shows a more distinct consequence. Here the interests are so different that suppliers and customers have organized separately, as mentioned in par. 4.2.

Finally, in the type where firms, engaged in more or less the same stages of production, buy final products from one another to widen their assortment, supplier-customer relations seem to moderate competitive conflicts and contribute to cooperation.

Thus it could be concluded that, where customer-supplier relations exist between otherwise different firms (in different stages of production), the interests of the partners in the relationship are so different that they organize separately. Where internal supplies take place between firms in the same stage of production, interdependence adds to the factor which already enhances cooperation, namely homogeneity. A general conclusion could be that the variable heterogeneity is more powerful than the variable interdependence.

5.2 Territorial Closeness and Regional Identity

The regional concentration of the branches of the food processing industry under study is generally not very high. Exceptions are the Canadian dairy and fruit and vegetable processing industries (concentrated in Ontario and dairy also in Quebec) and the Swedish fruit and vegetable processing industry, situated in the southern part around Malmö (see indicator in tables 4.1–4.3). The FP-industry is, just as its major suppliers, the farmers, dispersed over the country-side.

One would generally expect that social cohesion cannot be very high, given this high degree of dispersion. Firms are located far apart and not all of them share in the same regional sentiments. Even though this may be true for the sectors as a whole, it does not necessarily hold for regional subgroups. The territorial dispersion has led to a weakening of the system through regional differentiation. But because of this, individual regional associations may be strengthened by social cohesion due to regional sentiments. Such is indeed the case. The regional associations in the Dutch dairy industry belong to the most tightly organized voluntary associations imagineable. The same could probably be said for the German associations of butchers and the Swiss regional associations of artisans. The strength of these associations is of course primarily due to other factors, such as the small size of the firms, their need for central services by associations or state protection and support in the case of the German *Handwerksverbände*. Nevertheless the dispersal has prompted the regional pattern of organization and has provided for relatively small associations and closer member-association ties. In a number of cases such associations have also benefitted from regional sentiments to keep their membership together, have it accept the authority of the association as well as get it to vest the association with resources. The Frisian dairy association, the strongest regional one in the Netherlands, has profited from the existence of a particular Frisian identity, derived from a distinct culture and language as well as from longstanding conflicts of economic interests with other parts of the country. Friesland has always had an agrarian economy, whereas the dominant western part of the country has made money with international trade and industry. It is very likely that the same will be the case in associations in certain Swiss cantons or German *Kreise* or *Länder*, Bavaria for example.

5.3 Ownership Structure

Just as with territorial dispersion, heterogeneity of ownership structure may not only lead to differentiation of the associational system but also to strengthening of individual associations. Especially the presence of plants owned by consumer coops and farmers coops is important in this respect.

In the case of consumer coops, this is because they nurse a specific ideology, resulting from their ties with the labour movement and because they all have relations with the same central cooperative wholesale organization. In Sweden this has lead to separate interest organization of consumer coops, but probably also to strengthening of this association, the more so since they are often treated in a hostile manner by other firms. Swedish capitalist run enterprises have declined to cooperate with firms owned by consumer coops because of their ties with the trade unions. They tended to give in too easily to union demands.

Farmer coops may not adhere so much to a common political ideology. However, their conflicts of interests — and those of farmers — with the proprietary industry and wholesale firms (especially in the past) have stimulated social cohesion. In addition, their common ties to the agricultural world with its associations, culture, etc. enhances feelings of togetherness, which may be used to overcome other contradictions. If not, the powerful associations of farmers may sponsor associative activity of the cooperative industry. In a number of countries they not only took the initiatives to setting up cooperatives, but also helped to establish associations of cooperatives and in later years mediated and aided in the solution of problems and conflicts within such associations.

6. Conclusion

What can now be a general conclusion as to the influence of the sector structure in the food processing industry on the associative action of business? Which factors are important and do they stimulate or inhibit the development of strong associations and of tightly knit associational systems?

Competition, first of all, does not seem to be such an important factor in this industry, certainly much less so than, for example, in the construction industry. Although there is overcapacity in the FPI, the competition which could result from this is weakened by state intervention. This is especially the case in the dairy industry. Thus competition could not often form a motive for, but neither is it a barrier to, organizational development.

The existence of opponents in the economic environment plays already a more important role, especially the pressure emanating from large retail chains. Therefore, this is treated in a separate chapter (Chapter 9).

The most important characteristic of the FPI and also most influential in explaining the pattern of association is certainly its heterogeneity. This industry is much more heterogeneous than the other industries studied in the international project on business interest associations, such as the chemical industry or the construction industry. Firms in the food processing industry differ on many variables: product, processing method, source of raw materials, markets, marketing strategies, labour intensity, size and especially ownership structure. One of the most important distinctions certainly is that between farmer-owned cooperatives and proprietary firms. These differences produce a wide variety of interests and are responsible for the high degree of differentiation and the relatively weak integration of the associational systems.

However, since they may produce small homogeneous subgroups within the industry, this same factor, heterogeneity, also enhances social cohesion in some subsectors and thus strengthens individual associations within the system, especially the regional associations of cooperatives, which profit both from regional identities, ties to the agricultural world and sometimes a common cooperative ideology.

As is generally the case, the logic of membership variables exert primarily pressures for differentiation and fragmentation, for a weakly developed associational system. Such is the case with the influence of the factor heterogeneity. Pressures for integration come in the case of the FPI primarily from logic of influence variables, discussed in other chapters, and from the macro-social structure.

Another important conclusion is that the sector structure is not the main variable, explaining the logic of membership and through this associative action. Decisive as variables are government regulation and government organization, which were in the Research Design supposed to affect only the 'logic of influence'. There will be few industries which are more heavily regulated than the food processing industry. Supply of raw materials, sales, prices, product quality, labour, all are more or less influenced if not determined by state intervention. Patterns of association and variations in strength of associations are primarily dependent on differential treatment of different subsectors by regulation. Therefore, even the most important sector characteristic, heterogeneity, exerts its influence on associative action only because it is influenced by state intervention. Whether or not structural differences in the industry will become important bases for different interests depends to a large extent on the way in which they are affected by regulation. Therefore, even though variables regarding state characteristics are more important in explaining the level of organizational development, they are so in combination with sector structure variables. It is impossible to separate the two. That fact justifies consideration of the sector structure.

Table 4.1 Summary Sector Variables Dairy Industry

Variables	D	GB	A	CH	S	NL	C
Number							
— number of establishments 1980	817	715	277	1,842	119	158	456
— number of establishments 1965	1,413	868	175	2,237	279	499	1,413
Internal Competition							
— overcapacity	yes	major	—	yes	yes	minor	yes
— existence of licensed cartels	yes	no	no	no	yes	yes	no
Growth							
— average yearly growth rate (1970–80)	3.4	0.7	2.8	2.1	1.8	4.0	0.008
— stability growth (coeff. of var. of rates)	62.5	464	182	151	—	51	575
Profitability							
— relative prof. compared to other sectors	lower	lower	—	lower	lower	higher	higher
External Competition							
— domestic market share of imports	− 10	13	3	—	0.001	27	10
— export as pct. of domestic output	11	8	10	—	1.5	43	11
Equality							
— pct. total output largest firm	4	27	17	—	63	21	—
— pct. total output 4 largest firms	13	60	39	—	99	67	36
— pct. employment largest firm	3	32	17	—	61	20	—
— pct. employment 4 largest firms	9	66	30	—	83	63	34
Interdependence							
— pct. sales within the sector of total sales	—	—	—	—	100	8	37
— significant customer-supplier relations?	no	yes	—	yes	yes	yes	yes
Social Cohesion							
— pct. firms in domestic ownership	—	high	—	—	100	98	88
— pct. capital in domestic ownership	—	—	—	—	100	95	62
— pct. family firms	—	high	32	70	0	5	20
— pct. cooperatives	70	—	—	—	—	—	—
— pct. cooperatives in processing of milk	80	—	—	—	93	89	—
— territorial concentration index[1]	—	14	74	147	75	114	170

[1] Index for territorial concentration is the coefficient of variation of the range of percentages of employment in the dairy industry in the total employment by region (county, province, land, canton).

Table 4.2 Summary Sector Variables Meat Processing Industry

Variables	D	GB	A	CH	S	NL	C
Number							
— number of establishments 1980	29,000[1]	1,304[2]	3,130[1]	4,079[1]	189[2]	503[2]	637[2]
— number of establishments 1965	41,000[1]	29,564[1]	4,684[1]	4,987[1]	233[2]	—	549[2]
Internal Competition							
— overcapacity	yes	yes	—	yes	yes	major	major
— existence of licensed cartels	no	yes	no	—	—	no	no
Growth							
— average yearly growth rate (1970–80)	4.5	—	9.8	2.6	1.8	2.3	3.8
— stability growth (coeff. of var. of rates)	—	—	94	123	—	65	71
Profitability							
— relative prof. compared to other sectors	lower	lower	—	lower	lower	higher	higher
External Competition							
— domestic market share of imports	20	27	5	—	4	25	6
— export as pct. of domestic output	3	5	2	—	3	55	8
Equality							
— pct. total output largest firm	7	8	1	—	32	15	—
— pct. total output 4 largest firms	20	12	5	—	82	40	45
— pct. employment largest firm	6	12	2	—	13	13	—
— pct. employment 4 largest firms	18	16	5	—	49	37	37
Interdependence							
— pct. sales within the sector of total sales	—	—	—	—	—	11	41
— significant customer-supplier relations?	yes	no	—	yes	yes	yes	yes
Social Cohesion							
— pct. firms in domestic ownership	95	high	—	—	98	90	94
— pct. capital in domestic ownership	95	high	—	—	98	—	83
— pct. family firms	95	low	98	77	± 10	60	22
— pct. cooperatives	—	—	—	—	—	—	—
— territorial concentration index[3]	—	32	68	99	—	28	124

[1] Includes butchers. The subsequent data in the columns for this country refers to the industry including butchers.

[2] Excluding butchers. Further data in this column also is excluding butchers.

[3] Index for territorial concentration is the coefficient of variation of the range of percentages of employment in the meat processing industry in total employment by regions (county, province, land, canton).

Table 4.3 Summary Sector Variables Fruit and Vegetable Processing Industry

Variables	D	GB	A	CH	S	NL	C
Number							
— number of establishments 1980	542	209	128	163	43	101	232
— number of establishments 1965	1,004	349	265	231	46	98	313
Internal Competition							
— overcapacity	yes	yes	—	minor	no	minor	yes
— existence of licensed cartels	yes	no	no	no	—	minor	no
Growth							
— average yearly growth rate (1970–80)	2.3	—	− 2.2	—	9.0	0.2	2.0
— stability growth (coeff. of var. of rates)	155	—	438	—	—	3,100	158
Profitability							
— relative prof. compared to other sectors	lower	lower	—	lower	lower	lower	lower
External Competition							
— domestic market share of imports	36	23	30	—	37	43	28
— export as pct. of domestic output	7	7	2	—	6	45	6
Equality							
— pct. total output largest firm	10 −	15	25	—	35	—	—
— pct. total output 4 largest firms	23	26	54	—	87	—	42
— pct. employment largest firm	10 −	15	30	—	32	26	—
— pct. employment 4 largest firms	17	30	46	—	71	45	39
Interdependence							
— pct. sales within the sector of total sales	—	—	—	—	—	4	26
— significant customer-supplier relations?	no	no	—	yes	yes	no	yes
Social Cohesion							
— pct. firms in domestic ownership	95	—	—	—	—	90	73
— pct. capital in domestic ownership	—	—	—	—	37	80	35
— pct. family firms	1	5	98	37	5	70	6
— pct. cooperatives	—	—	—	—	—	—	—
— territorial concentration index[1]	—	37	48	150	272	97	156

[1] Index for territorial concentration is the coefficient of variation of the range of percentages of employment in the fruit and vegetable processing industry in the total employment by region (county, province, land, canton).

Frans van Waarden

Table 4.4 Relative Size of the Different FPI-Sectors
         (Annual sales in mln. dollars and employment, 1980.)

Country	Meat processing		Dairy industry		Fruit + vegetables	
	sales	empl.	sales	empl.	sales	empl.
Canada	6,780	45,214	3,683	26,028	1,330	17,570
United Kingdom[1]	7,122	96,200	9,538	52,100	1,936	26,800
Sweden	2,855	19,585	1,697	10,019	595	6,496
The Netherlands	3,945	21,300	5,390	22,360	880	7,500
West Germany[1]	24,629	145,879	11,260	48,322	2,747	23,300
Switzerland[2]	—	24,832	—	10,935	—	7,245

[1] Figure for meat processing includes butchers; [2] data for 1975.

Chapter 5

The Effect of State Institutions on Associative Action in the Food Processing Industry

VICTOR PESTOFF

The aim of this chapter is to analyze the effects of state structures on the capacity of associations to coordinate the behavior and actions of their members as well as their capacity to gain sufficient independence from these members to function as intermediaries between them and the state.

The first section introduces a discussion of the effect of state structures on associations' capacity to coordinate their behavior and actions as well as on their capacity to gain sufficient independence vis-à-vis their members to function as intermediaries between members and the state. The two next sections examine the capacity of BIAs to coordinate the behavior and actions of their members at greater length in the light of two factors: the constitutional character of the regime and the degree of decentralization of policy-making and implementation related to the FPI. The following section considers the capacity of BIAs to gain autonomy in relation to two additional factors, the relative independence of the bureaucracy from the food processing industry and the kinds of state structures available for the implementation of policy. The impact of membership in the EEC will be dealt with in a separate section.

A. Introduction

The relation between BIAs and the state is given special attention in this project on associative action of business interests. There is, of course, wide variation in state structures, from the one extreme of a liberal state, with minimal formal associative action by business interests, to the other extreme of an actively interventionist state with public coordination of organization intermediation and promotion of organizational properties conducive to the control of their functions. Any number of intermediate positions may, of course, exist. Most empirical illustrations are, however, expected to be found in the middle, somewhere between these two extremes (see Schmitter and Streeck, 1981, section III 3, for details).

Laski argues that every state is a territorial society divided into government and subjects, where the latter are submitted, if necessary, by compulsion to certain legal imperatives or rules made and enforced by those individuals comprising the government (1931 & 1951). Easton maintains that a political system consists of those interactions through which values are authoritatively allocated for society (1965). Streeck and Schmitter suggest that the ideal typical state bureaucracy is one in which decisions to allocate are made through 'public policies' that are enforced, with the ultimate backing of the state's monopoly on legitimate coercion, by civil servants striving to satisfy their dominant career interests (1984).

According to these and similar definitions, the state is not a monolithic institution with a single will, but rather segmented in character with a composite will of alternatively conflicting and cooperating parts. This general term can be used to denote a wide range of phenomena, including variation in the constitutional character of regimes and the degree of centralization in policy-making and implementation. It readily applies to all the nations which are members of the United Nations, but not as readily to supranational bodies like the European Community. Although the latter has certain state-like properties, such as being able to make binding decisions which supersede those of its member states in previously agreed-upon areas, it in no way replaces the decision-making of individual member states in other areas. The EEC will therefore be regarded as a supranational organization with state-like properties in the present context.

In examining the impact of intervention, it is not necessary, however, to conceive of the degree of centralization of state structures as positively and linearly related to the degree of centralization of associative action. Although 'pressure group' literature argues that groups often copy the structure of the authorities they wish to influence, I feel such a view is too simple and unidimensional. It is just as conceivable that BIAs might sometimes pattern their organizations to compensate for the structure of the state, rather than to mirror them. Under certain circumstances, non-corresponding structures may facilitate their aims and provide greater rather than less influence (Schmitter and Streeck, 1981).

Furthermore, there are numerous factors which influence the degree of centralization of business interest associations, not merely state structure. Coleman and Grant refer to three different factors contributing to the regional differentiation of BIAs in Canada and the United Kingdom (1984). These are government structure, industrial structure and collective bargaining structure. Each of these three factors is multidimensional and several indicators are provided for them. The forces represented by these indicators do not always pull or push organizations in the same direction. Only the first of these factors will be treated here, while the other two are the subject of other chapters in this book. Thus it is possible that certain features of government structure in any given country may encourage centralization in BIAs, while others may discourage it and yet others may promote neither centralization nor decentralization in BIAs.

It is also important to keep in mind that, while these various factors may be conceived as vectors going in different directions, our main interest is in the impact of various aspects of state institutions on associative action in the food processing industry and on the organizational development of the FPI.

The reason why the state is attributed such primary importance in terms of organizational development is its ability to reward or punish its specialized interlocutors for acquiring organizational properties which increase the probability of satisfying its policy interests and constraints. Exchange relationships or transactions between BIAs and the state may be both direct and indirect. Direct transactions involve toleration, recognition, encouragement of specific BIAs, subsidizing their existence and/or activities, control of their activities, etc. The indirect impact of exchange relations with the state is conditioned by transactions between the state and individual member firms. Such transactions take the form of subsidization, taxation, purchases and perhaps even ownership. They also influence the needs and interests of actual or potential members and thereby determine their demands on, and expectations of, BIAs.

Granted, BIAs cannot survive and develop without extracting resources from both state agencies and member firms. But this fact has no implications whatever for the nature of such exchange relations. It cannot be maintained, *a priori*, that they are contradictory or not, but simply that the pursuit of different goals complicates the choice of strategies available to BIAs.

Table 5.1 Number of BIAs at the subsectoral and peak levels of the food processing industry

Country	Meat	Dairy	F & V*	Peak FPI	Whole FPI**
Austria	3	2	3	3	3
Canada	11	9	6	0	26
W. Germany***	474	21	12	2	509
Netherlands	11	14	3	na	na
Sweden	6	2	3	3	8
Switzerland	6	7	6	4	20
United Kingdom	19	26	14	2	61

na = Not available.
* F & V = Fruit and vegetable canning industry.
** Some BIAs are not subsector-specific and are therefore included in several subsectors. Others are product-unspecific and do not represent the interests of a given subsector. In Sweden, for example, the Employers' Association of Swedish Food Processors and the Federation of Swedish Food Industries are both found in each of the subsectors as well as under the heading 'Peak FPI'. Product-unspecific associations like the frozen food associations found in Canada, Britain or Switzerland, or trade mark associations found in West Germany and Switzerland, represent a particular function common to several or all subsectors and even other industries. The total figures for all three subsectors and peak associations may therefore not correspond to a simple addition of these columns.
*** 450 local and 11 regional coops in meat plus 12 regional coops in dairy.
Source: Organization of Business Interests Project Data Bank.

Overview of the Associations

The number of business interest associations in the food processing industry open for direct membership and of peak organizations differs from subsector to subsector and among countries. Table 5.1 above presents this information.

Austria and Sweden have the smallest number of BIAs in the food processing industry, while West Germany has the greatest number. If local handicraft and regional coops were eliminated from the meat and dairy subsectors, the German figures would fall in between the Canadian and British figures. After such adjustments, the average number of BIAs in the meat and dairy subsectors are almost the same as the fruit and vegetable subsector. On the whole there is a high degree of small, product-specific and relatively specialized BIAs at the subsectoral level in most countries. Austria and Sweden are the main exceptions. At the peak level there is much less variation. The number of peak associations ranges from two to four, with the exception of Canada, where no peak association exists for the FPI.

Ideally governments should prefer to deal with a small number of associations representing comprehensive domains in which interests are aggregated at as high a level as possible (Grant, 1983 b). This, of course, assumes a far-sighted government with no conflicting responsibilities. The food processing industry, sandwiched as it is between well-organized producers and increasingly centralized wholesale and retail trades, is truly not in an ideal situation. Government encouragement of and even financial support for organizational development are frequently characteristic of agricultural policy. During the Great Depression marketing boards were set up for product after product in various countries. Prices and quotas cannot, however, be negotiated with individual farmers or a myriad of local producer organizations, even if they make no conflicting demands. In Sweden, for example, public regulation schemes were approved in 1932 on condition that national product-specific farmers' organizations be set up to negotiate for the entire dairy industry, meat industry, etc. Corresponding national producer cooperatives were established in these industries the same year (Pestoff, 1981). Similar evidence is found elsewhere in the present project. However, the existence of well-organized producers or wholesalers and retailers is likely to impede the organizational development of the industry trapped in between them.

There are, however, two institutional constraints BIAs must face in their transactions with the state, neither of which they can hope to influence very much. These constraining factors determine the focus of their exchange relationship with the state, and reflect the institutional structure of public policy-making. These are, first of all, the constitutional nature of the regime and, secondly, the degree to which the state structures for policy-making and implementation are organized on a sectoral or subsectoral basis.

Both constitutional and state structures reflect greater or lesser degrees of centralization. The constitutional nature of a regime expresses the level of territorial centralization and ranges from federal to unitary states. State structures express the level of functional centralization and range from a single agency to a myriad of competing agencies. Variations in the degree of decentralization will provide the starting point for examining the effect of these structures on the organizational development of BIAs in the food processing industry.

B. Constitutional Structures and Territorial Differentiation

The constitutional division of powers and territorial decentralization will probably influence the way in which business interests are organized. The devolution of responsibilities by the central or national government in federal systems, either of the functional type such as in Austria or West Germany or the jurisdictional type, as in Canada and Switzerland, or in a union state like the United Kingdom, should affect the organizational structures of BIAs in a fashion not witnessed in a unitary state. In the case of functional federalism, policy-making is centralized and given over primarily to the national government, while the administration and implementation of policy is conferred on subnational units. In the case of jurisdictional federalism, subnational units have significant policy-making and administrative responsibilities which they undertake auton-omously from the central government. A 'union state' (Rokkan and Urwin, 1983) is one that primarily has a centralized, unitary constitution but still retains certain areas where administration is decentralized as a result of its historical pattern of formation. Thus in the U. K., Scotland and Northern Ireland maintain significant administrative autonomy. Sweden and the Netherlands are examples of strictly unitary states.

Well-articulated regional structures in associations might be expected to be more imperative in federal or union state systems than in a unitary state. The division and decentralization of responsibilities between two or more levels of government may well lead to a similar division within the relevant BIAs. In a well-developed system, each level of a BIA will have its particular focus of exchange relations, e. g. central or peak organizations will focus on the national government, regional associations on the provincial, state or canton govern-ments and local branches on local or municipal governments. In a less well-developed system there may be numerous missing links in these organizational structures. Central or regional structures may be undeveloped or non-existent. This will of course affect the overall capacity of a sector and its subsectors to coordinate their activities at various levels and to manage the diversity or heterogeneity of the sector.

Table 5.2 Percentages of BIAs that are territorially differentiated

Country	Meat	Dairy	F & V
Austria	0	0	0
Canada	63.7	77.8	50.0
W. Germany	98.1	71.4	41.7
Netherlands	0	28.6	0
Sweden	16.7	50.0	0
Switzerland*	16.7	28.6	33.3
United Kingdom	10.5	23.1	7.1

* Corrected Figures.
Source: Organization of Business Interests Project Data Bank.

Table 5.2 presents figures concerning the percentages of BIAs differentiated by territory. These figures merely indicate the proportion of territorially subdivided BIAs. They say nothing about which organizations are geographically subdivided, nor about their importance. Thus a country with several narrow product-specific BIAs may score low since only the major BIA in a given subsector is a confederation of independent regional associations. The narrow product-specific BIAs may have too few members to operate anything more than a letterbox association in the capital city.

A relatively clear pattern emerges from the data when Austria is excluded, because its highly concentrated system of associations is statutorily determined. The remaining three federal states show an overall higher degree of territorial differentiation than do either of the unitary states or the union state. The unitary states are the only ones which are not territorially differentiated in all three subsectors, while the union state takes an intermediate position.

Differences in regional systems of supply management can, moreover, serve to illustrate the impact of constitutional structures. Regional variation in supply management systems in the U.K. dairy industry '... provide a powerful incentive for the presence of independent dairy trade federations in each part of the country', according to Grant (1983 c). Concurrent jurisdiction over agriculture between federal and provincial levels in Canada '... gives both levels ... a hand in the food processing industry', according to Coleman (1984, p. 14). Thus we find independent regional dairy councils alongside the National Dairy Council. But this territorial division of powers provides little incentive for further horizontal and/or vertical integration of the association system of the whole food processing industry.

C. Decentralization in Policy-making

It is necessary, however, to go beyond such general variables concerning the nature of the constitutional regime in order to explore the form and content of policy-making at the sectoral or subsectoral level. How centralized or decentralized is policy-making in the whole FPI or in the dairy industry, with regard to both the formulation and the implementation of policy? In addition, consideration must be paid to the relative centralization of the administration in a functional sense. Is the regulation of the FPI or its subsectors of a general or a specific nature? Is there a single agency associated with more general matters or are various agencies responsible for more specific questions? To what extent do their areas of competence overlap and to what extent do they compete with each other? To what extent are food policy and policy formulation concerning the FPI considered an extension of agricultural or industrial policy, or perhaps both? At the ministerial level, does the FPI find its main 'sponsoring agency' in an agricultural or industrial department or ministry?

Table 5.3 lists the names of the Ministries or Departments responsible for the food processing industry in the seven countries under study here. As we see, the concept 'food' appears explicitly in only two of them, W. Germany and the

Table 5.3 Ministry or Department Responsible for the Food Processing Industry

Country	Ministry or Department
Austria	Agriculture & Forestry
Canada	Agriculture
W. Germany	Food, Agriculture & Forestry
Netherlands	Agriculture & Fishery
Sweden	Agriculture
Switzerland	Agriculture
United Kingdom	Agriculture, Fisheries & Food

United Kingdom. In all the rest there is no direct reference to food, but rather to agriculture. It would thus appear that food, food policy and the promotion of the interests of the food processing industry is traditionally seen as an extension of agricultural policy rather than something separate from agriculture.

Although the notion of sponsorship differs from country to country, the existence of a single 'sponsoring agency' with general and specific responsibilities will facilitate and simplify the structural development of BIAs in the FPI. The existence of several competing agencies for various subsectors of the FPI will promote organizational diversity and complexity. It will also tax the capacity of BIAs to coordinate their behavior and actions. It is highly likely that diversity in public structures and functions will facilitate direct contacts between the largest member firms and relevant public authorities. The greater the coordination problems faced by a BIA, the greater the likelihood that one or a few resourceful members will find it advantageous to go it alone, thus further magnifying the coordination problems of a BIA.

The state can be expected to demonstrate varying patterns in terms of the number of national agencies necessary to govern a given sector or subsector. A greater number of national agencies might be interpreted as an indicator of decentralization. However, consideration must also be given to whether a single predominant agency exists. The data collected by the project permit us to establish variations in the pattern of relations between different subsectors of the FPI and the state. Table 5.4 demonstrates that more national agencies are set up on average to govern the meat slaughtering and packing industry and fewer to govern the fruit and vegetable canning industry than the dairy industry. This holds true even at the national level in most countries. The Netherlands and Sweden have the greatest number of agencies, while there is only one for each subsector in Switzerland. However, with few exceptions, there is a single predominant national agency in each subsector. Thus these figures may bear greater witness to variations in the functional specialization of these subsectors than to their functional decentralization. The meat industry in Austria, the dairy industry in Canada and the fruit and vegetable industry in both countries lack a single predominant national agency. This may, if mandates overlap, encourage bureaucratic competition, something which is detrimental to organizational development (Coleman, 1984).

Table 5.4 Number of National Agencies in Three Subsectors of the Food Processing
Industry

Country	Meat	Dairy	F & V
Austria	3*	1	0*
Canada	3	2*	6*
W. Germany	4	5	5
Netherlands	11	5	1
Sweden	7	7	3
Switzerland	1	1	1
United Kingdom	3	2	2
Average	4.6	3.3	2.6

* No single predominant agency exists.
Source: Organization of Business Interests Project Data Bank.

Agencies not only vary in numbers, but also in terms of the functions they are
designed to fulfill or the products they are supposed to promote. They can be
organized along product lines or according to various functions corresponding
to different policy goals. The risk of overlapping responsibilities and competition between agencies is greater where functional rather than product divisions
exist. This picture can, of course, be complicated by the existence of several
levels, as in a federal system. Where the division of responsibilities between the
central and provincial governments is clear, no competition need occur. If,
however, their responsibilities overlap, the degree of decentralization in the
bureaucracy will probably hinder integration of the association system.

The most centralized situation is found in the unitary state where a single
predominant agency, the Swedish Agricultural Marketing Board, has sole
responsibility for most or all subsectors and for most or all important policy
matters. Here we find a highly integrated associational system consisting mainly
of very few, broad product-unspecific associations, almost all of which are
affiliated to peak associations. The latter cooperate extensively (Pestoff, 1983).
Even the existence of several agencies, organized along product lines, results in a
high degree of centralization. Thus we find three product-specific divisions in
the Swiss Office of Agriculture — a Department of Meat, another for Milk and a
third for Fruit and Vegetables. When, in addition, there are three levels involved,
as in the milk subsector, including a regional programme commission in each
canton, then such decentralization promotes the formation of confederal
organizations, as opposed to the unitary patterns found in the more centralized
fruit and vegetable subsector (Farago, 1984). In the meat sector, there are
additional agencies involved in the regulation of this industry. They are the
offices for veterinary service, price control and household economy. Here, too,
a more decentralized organizational network exists.

The existence of several agencies with overlapping responsibilities which
compete with each other in one or more policy areas may encourage the
emergence of several associations, each competing with one another. Coleman

finds that state structures in Canada produce such a situation in the food processing sector. He feels that 'the bureaucratic conflict that arises from this situation appears to lead to a lack of integration in the associational system' (1984: 36). The existence of competition among agencies fosters clientelism between them and given associations, since each agency will seek supporters in the form of 'client associations' *(ibid.)*. Different associations from the same sector may ally themselves with different agencies. For example, in one main policy area in Canada, e. g. protecting consumers against health hazards, there is competition between the Food Product Inspection Branch at the department of Agriculture and the Food Directorate of the Health Protection Branch at the Department of Health and Welfare. This example prompts Coleman to argue that 'such developments will constitute a significant deterrent to achieving integration in the associational system'. Without integration, the industry will not be a significant participant in the formulation of longer-run and more general policy for the sector *(ibid.,* p. 38). The absence of a central or peak association in the FPI underscores this lack of integration in Canada.

The proportion of BIAs which are differentiated by product is an indicator of their structural orientations as well as the extent of their domains. BIAs can have either task-oriented or product-specific structures or a mix of both. They can also be narrowly product-specific at the sub- or even subsubsectoral level, or they may encompass several subsectors in their domains. Although a high degree of product differentiation excludes task orientation in terms of structures, it also argues for broader domains. Table 5.5 presents the data on product differentiation in BIAs in the food processing industry.

Table 5.5 Percentage of BIAs Differentiated by Product

Country	Meat	Dairy	F & V
Austria	0	0	0
Canada	81.8	88.9	100
West Germany	1.3	4.8	58.3
Netherlands	72.7	42.9	33.3
Sweden	83.3	100.0	66.7
Switzerland	83.3	71.4	66.7
United Kingdom	73.7	76.9	85.7

Source: Organization of Business Interests Project Data Bank.

No product differentiation is found in Austrian BIAs, and almost none exists in either the meat or dairy subsectors in W. Germany. In the remainder of sectors and countries nearly every second BIA or more expresses some product differentiation.

The extreme product hetereogeneity characterizing the FPI appears to account for much of the abundance of BIAs found in these subsectors (see Table 5.1). Grant maintains that in a highly product-heterogeneous industry we should expect the internal differentiation of associations to be on the basis of product rather than territory (1983 b). Comparing Tables 5.2 and 5.5, we note that product differentiation is greater than territorial differentiation in most countries and subsectors. It should, however, be borne in mind that many of the BIAs in both the meat and dairy industries are an expression of external rather than internal differentiation on the basis of product. Thus in the Swiss meat sector, alongside three broad organizations (the Associations of Swiss Manufacturers of Meat Products, Swiss Butchers and Swiss Slaughterers), there are several very narrowly defined independent product-specific associations. There is an Association of Swiss Manufacturers of Air-Dried Meat, another for Salami and a third for Horse-Butchers. This type of product differentiation precludes extensive territorial differentiation among members, and it also results in a low level of organizational development.

We thus find that, in terms of bureaucratic centralization, when taking all three subsectors as a whole, there is a highly fragmented pattern which varies from one subsector to another and which often reflects the high level of product heterogeneity characteristic of the FPI. The low degree of centralization noted for this sector as a whole in most countries often coexists with a high degree of subsector centralization, as is the case in West Germany and in certain subsectors elsewhere. The net result is that, as Grant noted for the U. K., the characteristics of the state in the food processing sector reinforce rather than counteract the fragmenting effects of the logic of membership variables. There are, however, differences between subsectors. These very differences in turn constitute a major hindrance to the development of a more encompassing association system for the whole sector. The pressures from the state are of a diffuse rather than uniform nature and they fail to counteract the heterogeneity of the product market.

D. Effects of State Institutions an Associational Autonomy

There is a second important area in which state forms and functions are likely to have a major impact on the associative action of business interests. This impact is related to the capacity of BIAs to gain sufficient autonomy vis-à-vis their members to function as intermediaries between them and the state. In the context of organizational development discussed by Schmitter and Streeck (1981), organizational autonomy can be conceived of in terms of the inputs and outputs of BIAs. An organization's survival and growth require a minimum supply of resources (inputs). It also requires the capacity to determine its goals and a minimum of independence to select the means and strategies necessary to pursue its goals (outputs). The greater the stability in inputs, the greater the likelihood that a BIA will develop long-range objectives. Thus there are two types of autonomy, i. e. resource and strategic autonomy. They are, however, related to one another.

Organizations strive to protect themselves from uncertainty and rapid changes in their environments. The greater the autonomy of a BIA, the less any single environment is able to dominate its inputs and determine its behavior. Low resource autonomy implies that financial and manpower inputs are made on a voluntary basis. Resource autonomy can, however, be increased in one of three ways, according to Schmitter and Streeck: (a) by formalizing the supply obligations of members and insuring the professionalization of the staff; (b) by selling goods and services to both members and non-members, and (c) by turning to 'sponsoring environments' for support. The state is the most likely 'sponsoring environment' for most BIAs. It commands a variety of resources, in addition to the financial ones, that can be used to support BIAs. Thus there are three ways of gaining resource autonomy and reducing dependence upon members, and they can be summarized by the terms professionalization, formalization and institutionalization.

Strategic autonomy, by contrast, is related to the outputs of BIAs. An organization which depends upon its members for most of its resources will most likely have short-term goals which are determined by direct member demands and support. Through professionalization, formalization and institutionalization, it can acquire the capacity to reject it members' short-term demands and thereby develop a more long-term perspective — its strategic autonomy. Only when it becomes unresponsive to the demands of some of its constituents, and only when it develops the capacity of discretion to represent the interests of its members selectively or in a more general sense, can a BIA achieve strategic autonomy. This can only be obtained if a BIA responds to environments other than its members. The state can provide BIAs with resources such as recognition and licensing, monopoly representation, etc., all of which enhance their strategic autonomy.

The impact of state institutions on organizational autonomy in the FPI will be explored below by considering two main facets of autonomy, namely relative autonomy of the bureaucracy vis-à-vis the FPI and the kinds of state structures used for implementing policy. The first factor will be examined by two types of indicators, first how dependent is (are) the sectoral or subsectoral agency or agencies on the industry in general for obtaining the information necessary for formulating policy? And, secondly, how dependent is (are) the respective agency or agencies on the industry for self-discipline in terms of compliance with regulatory policy in particular?

The role of the state (other than as owners) in terms of governing an industry can be conceived of as falling into one of three general categories: that of a regulator, a mediator or a promoter. All of these categories involve a variety of activities, each of which may be implemented by one or more state agencies. State regulation in the food processing industry can include the regulation of prices, profits, investments, health and safety, competitive practices, etc. The state may also promote the interests of the industry by allocating public funds for research and development, etc.

If the state has an agency and a set of programs designed to deal more or less explicitly and exclusively with a sector, this will naturally affect structures of relevant BIAs. If there is, on the one hand, a single predominant agency which is too resourceful and autonomous, it may anticipate the needs of the sector so well as to exclude the development of organizational autonomy in relevant BIAs. If, on the other hand, an industry faces a myriad of overlapping and competing state agencies, then incentives for developing centralized, hierarchical organizational properties will be weak. Middle-range administrative resources and autonomy will lead to the need on the part of the bureaucracy to collaborate with a single, comprehensive, highly dense and resourceful BIA to provide the agency with information and to insure self-discipline in the implementation of policy (Schmitter and Streeck, 1981).

Bureaucratic dependence on BIAs is also related to the second factor in our analysis, namely the kinds of state structures used for the implementation of policy. Here, we must of course keep in mind whether the various policies are general, sectoral or subsectoral. We must not lose sight of whether the administration of public policy is concentrated in the central bureaucracy rather than delegated to para-state structures with association representation or perhaps to the associations themselves, as private interest governments. Certainly, the general inclination of states to adopt one or the other of these implementation strategies will affect the autonomy of BIAs. A lower degree of state-centered administration implies a greater role attributed to BIAs and greater autonomy for them.

Public authorities at national or regional levels may allocate various funds for special programs to a sector or subsector and may even channel them through BIAs, thereby using them directly as instruments of policy implementation. This is common in terms of marketing schemes for agriculture and food processing. Such payments or subsidies may become important 'monopoly goods' for BIAs, inducing presumptive members to join even where subsidies cannot legally be denied to non-members. Public funds for specific programs may even pay a substantial proportion of overhead expenses for BIAs and provide them with the resource autonomy necessary for developing professionalism and organizational autonomy. Research and development funds are another example of such programmes.

1. The Information Needs of the State

The greater the bureaucracy's information needs and dependence on the industry for self-discipline in terms of compliance with regulations, the higher the probability that methods will be found for ensuring the permanent and formal participation of the relevant sectoral and/or subsectoral BIAs. Both the information needs of the bureaucracy and its dependence upon the FPI for self-discipline in terms of compliance with regulation policy are, of course, variable qualities. The need for information and compliance will depend upon the nature of the policy and the extent of regulation. Is the regulation general and categorical, or is it subsector-specific and detailed in nature? It has been argued that the more general regulation is, the greater the likelihood is that it will be carried out under the auspices of the state. State regulation will normally involve the whole food processing industry and not just a single subsector or a specific product. Conversely, the narrower and more specific regulation is, the more probable it is that private interests will be charged with fulfilling it (van Waarden, 1984).

The establishment of institutionalized forums is a traditional method of insuring a permanent and formal dialogue between an industry and the bureaucracy. By 'institutionalized forum' we mean a body of functional representation, normally with associational participation, that deals exclusively and especially with the (sub)sector. Formulation of long-term general policy for the sector will be greatly facilitated by the existence of institutionalized forums which not only permit the respective subsectors to enter into a dialogue with the state, but also grant the relevant BIAs public recognition and incorporation into public policy-making. Such forums also encourage BIAs to develop a greater capacity to contribute to the formulation of long-term goals for the industry. Thus it could be argued that they facilitate organizational development. The information needs of the bureaucracy vary from subsector to subsector in the food processing industry. Institutionalized forums exist in most subsectors and countries, with the exception of the meat industry in W. Germany and the fruit and vegetable industry in Austria and West Germany.

Table 5.6 Number of Institutionalized Forums

Country	Meat	Dairy	F & V
Austria	1	1	0
Canada	8*	2	3*
West Germany	0*	1	0*
Netherlands	8*	7	1
Sweden	3	3	2
Switzerland	2	4	2
United Kingdom	1	1	1
Average	3.3	2.7	1.3

* No single predominant institutionalized forum exists.
Source: Organization of Business Interests Project Data Bank.

According to Table 5.6, the average number of institutionalized forums is greatest in the meat industry and smallest in the fruit and vegetable industry. The dairy industry invariably includes a predominant forum in all countries, while no single forum dominates in either the meat or fruit and vegetable industries of three countries. In W. Germany no forum exists for either of these subsectors while in Canada, where a number of such forums exist, no single one dominates.

This suggests that the bureaucracy's information needs are more general in the dairy industry, while they are more extensive, but perhaps more specific, in the meat industry. The lack of a single predominant forum complicates the choice of strategies available to BIAs in countries where several forums exist. The existence of a single predominant forum should more readily promote the strategic autonomy of BIAs in the dairy industry in all countries. However, given the variation among subsectors, the development of an organizational network for the entire FPI will be retarded.

A similar pattern is found when considering the dependence of the bureaucracy on the FPI for compliance with regulation policy. This emerges clearly
from a comparison of the various subsectors under study. Milk market boards
exist in almost all of the countries included here, while other commodity market
boards also exist in some countries. These boards normally manage the prices
and supply of agricultural produce. Commodity market boards invariably mean
institutionalized access to the state since relevant BIAs are ensured permanent
representation, usually in tripartite structures.

It is important to realize that a state bureaucracy cannot envision, let alone
fulfil, detailed regulation of prices and supply without the full support of the
parties concerned. Its information needs and dependence upon self-discipline are
quite simply unequivocal. Without the active participation of BIAs and the
farmers, such detailed regulation is doomed to failure. In fact in Sweden, as
mentioned above, the state promised to establish a legally binding regulatory
system once the necessary BIAs had been created. The founding of a BIA was a
precondition for such detailed regulation. The Swedish state was also willing
actively to promote their establishment, and help finance their activities during
several decades (Pestoff, 1981). Such active support insures that its information
needs and dependence upon self-discipline will be met. Eight market boards exist
in Sweden, formally as 'economic associations', which in effect are quasi-public
bodies. They include products like dairy produce, meat, potatoes, cereals, etc.,
but not fruits or vegetables (Pestoff, 1983). In Austria, the compulsory chamber
system permits the milk marketing boards to determine all important parameters
of the dairy industry, including prices, production volume, profits, investments
and even wages (Traxler, 1984). The milk marketing board can quite simply
legally compel all member firms to provide it with all information requested for
its clearing system (ibid.).

Milk market boards are found at the provincial level in Canada, rather than at
the federal level. Meat market boards also exist at the provincial level to fix prices
and allocate quotas to farmers and processors (Coleman, 1984). However, both
the farmers and the retailers are so well organized that 'it is a waste of time for
the provincial bureaucracy to try to get information from the food processing
industry' (ibid.). Thus when the bureaucracy can meet its needs from alternative
sources it is unlikely to promote the development of strategic autonomy by BIAs
in the food processing industry. The state will instead engage in exchange
relations with BIAs outside the food processing industry, providing them with
scarce public resources. The results in terms of the resource autonomy of the
Canadian food processing industry is that 85 per cent of their resources are
provided by membership dues, they lack permanent staffs and must rely upon
voluntary participation (ibid.).

In Switzerland there are, in addition to milk market boards at both the
cantonal and federal levels, federal market boards for the two economically most
important dairy products, i. e. cheese and butter. There is also a market board
for meat, another for fruits and a third for vegetables. In the Netherlands,
statutory commodity boards exist for various products such as dairy, fish,
livestock and meat, fruits and vegetables, poultry and eggs, etc. (van Waarden,

1983). Their autonomous powers in terms of regulating imports and exports have been curtailed since 1964 and turned over to the supranational bodies specified by the Treaty of Rome.

Other types of regulation exist beside that of prices. Data are available for seven additional types or areas of regulation, all of which will require greater or lesser cooperation and compliance by the food processing industry. They are state regulation of profits, investments, health and safety, environmental effects, products and competitive practices. Environmental effects of the FPI are not regulated in any of the countries or subsectors included here. Profits are not regulated in either the meat or fruit and vegetable subsectors of any country. In addition, neither investments nor competitive practices are regulated in the fruit and vegetable subsectors of any country. Rather than providing detailed information concerning all types of regulation in every country, the information has been summarized in terms of the number of areas regulated or the frequency of regulation for each subsector and country. Table 5.7 below presents this information.

Table 5.7 Number of Areas Regulated

Country	Meat	Dairy	F & V
Austria	3	6	3
Canada	1	2	2
West Germany	2	3	2
Netherlands	2	4	2
Sweden	4	4	2
Switzerland	2	4	0
United Kingdom	2	4	1
Average	2.3	3.9	1.7

Source: Organization of Business Interests Project Data Bank.

The average figures indicate that the dairy subsector is the most highly regulated, while the fruit and vegetable industry is the least regulated. This in turn means that the bureaucracy's dependency in general on the dairy industry is greater than either of the two subsectors in terms of compliance with regulatory policy. This implies that the bureaucracy should have a greater interest in promoting the strategic autonomy of the dairy industry than that of the meat or fruit and vegetable industries. This interest, however, is limited to organizational development at the subsectoral level and does not extend to the sectoral level due to the variation among subsectors.

Finally, the state in its role as a promoter can also affect the development of resource and strategic autonomy in concerned BIAs. Public funds and grants for research and development (R&D) can provide an important stimulus both to an industry and to the relevant BIAs. The latter can play a role in formulating the needs of a particular sector or subsector for R&D as well as in channelling public funds to concerned firms in the industry.

No public funds whatsoever are available for any of these subsectors in Austria. Only insignificant public R & D funds are available in Canada, West Germany and the Netherlands in all three subsectors. Switzerland is the only country which makes a significant contribution of public funds to R & D in all three subsectors. Both the United Kingdom and Sweden make a significant contribution to the fruit and vegetable sectors, while the meat industry also receives significant funds in the United Kingdom. Thus only in a limited number of countries are BIAs in the FPI encouraged to aggregate and articulate the needs of the industry for public R & D funds. The extent to which BIAs are actually involved in channelling such funds is not obvious from the data at hand. However, it seems unlikely that R & D operations contribute to the promotion of resource or strategic autonomy in BIAs in these subsectors outside Switzerland and the United Kingdom.

2. Implementation Structures

The structures employed to implement public policy vary with the nature of the policy involved. 'Where the information capacity of the state bureaucracy is low or where the compliance problems faced by the bureaucracy are high, the bureaucracy will seek to give associations a share in the decision-making in exchange for either information or securing compliance from their members or both', according to Coleman (1984). It was argued earlier that the more specific the nature of the regulation and the narrower its scope, the greater would be the need to formally coopt the respective BIAs into the implementation structures. Regulation can be divided into various categories, depending upon the degree of self-regulation by the industry concerned and state intervention. For our purposes, three categories will suffice. They are state-sanctioned private self-regulation (also called private interest government), tripartite public structures (also known as para- or quasi-state regulation) and regulation by public authorities or central administrative agencies.

Supply management and price regulation are narrow in their scope and specific in their nature. This far exceeds the information capacity of the state bureaucracy and greatly outweighs its normal compliance problems. The BIAs concerned must be given an active role in the relevant market boards, if such boards are to have a ghost of a chance to implement such schemes. These market boards normally take one of two forms, in accordance with the above categories. Responsibility for this type of regulation can be statutorily relinquished to the interest groups concerned, or quasi-public tripartite structures can be established. Austria and the Netherlands appear to have opted for the former solution, at least for their milk market boards. In Austria, four universal rather than sector-specific interest organizations compose the milk market board. Although Traxler sees this as a condition for self-regulation (1984), experience from Sweden runs counter to this (Pestoff, 1983). Statutory commodity boards in the Netherlands fall under the classification of state-assisted private regulation (van Waarden, 1984).

Tripartite structures provide the basis of market boards in the rest of the countries studied here. These legally-defined structures result in agreements that are formally binding on members. The parties to such structures are normally farmers, the state and processors (plus sometimes the consumers) of agricultural produce. The milk and meat market boards found at the provincial — although not national — level in Canada are composed of farmers, the state and producers. In Switzerland milk commissions exist at the canton level, while market boards for cheese, butter, meat, fruit and vegetables exist only at the federal level (Farago, 1982). All interest groups concerned are included in the milk commissions and meat market board, while only the relevant BIAs representing private interests are represented on the fruit and vegetable boards (*ibid.*). 'All concerned interests' refers here to wholesalers, retailers and consumers in addition to farmers, processors and bureaucrats from the Department of Milk or Meat.

In the U. K., it is only in the dairy sector (of the subsectors studied) that we find market boards. Thus the U. K. has the distinction of probably having the most limited application of tripartite structures of all the food processing systems studied here (Grant, 1983 b).

Finally, in Sweden there are eight quasi-public price regulation associations for agricultural products and another for fish. These market boards cover about 60 per cent of all agricultural produce and foodstuffs consumed in Sweden. They have functioned continually since the early 1930s. Their focus is price regulation rather than supply management, although the latter is increasingly becoming a major problem. Today, all nine of them have tripartite corporate structures, but during the first 35 years, until 1967, the board for dairy products and that for potatoes were officially run by and from the respective producer cooperative branch organizations. They usually have nine members, three of whom are nominated by the farmers and the food processing industry. Normally they include one from the cooperative peak organization, LRF, and two from the relevant producer cooperative branch organization.

The allocation of public funds for market boards is not documented in a systematic fashion in the available data. The Dairy Trade Federation receives a levy on the milk subject to the domain of the U. K. milk market boards. Presumably similar schemes exist in other countries. The statutory nature of quasi-public structures of market boards found in all countries indicates that the binding decisions they make also include the right to extract funds related to the financing of their own activities. In Sweden certain levies are imposed in connection with the delivery of the raw materials to the marketing board or branch producer cooperative. The joint budgets of market boards were 576 MSEK in 1981/82. An additional 3 140 MSEK of public funds were spent as 'food subsidies' the same year in order to curtail food price increases. These funds are administered by the market boards and distributed to member firms of the respective BIAs. Such public funding becomes a 'monopoly good' for the BIAs represented on these market boards.

The Swedish producer cooperatives are involved in the implementation of a wide variety of public programs, including 'replacement farmers' and agricultural occupational health services, etc. The Federation of Swedish Farmers,

LRF, received 90 MSEK from public funds for these and other services in 1982. This amounted to 12 per cent of LRF's total budget, while membership dues earned a mere 8 per cent (Pestoff, 1983).

Thus formal representation of BIAs in the structures employed to implement public policy promotes both the resource and strategic autonomy of BIAs. However, providing representation for narrow product-specific interests in market boards promotes autonomy of BIAs on a product-specific basis, since subsectoral BIAs are given resources such as recognition and monopoly representation, and even permitted to provide monopoly goods. This proves detrimental to the development of organizations for the whole FPI. Moreover, by inviting BIA representation in such matters, and excluding it from broader areas of a more general or uniform character, it reinforces the fragmenting effects of the logic of membership variables. Once again, state structures constitute a major hindrance to the development of a more encompassing associational system for the whole food processing sector.

Obviously the more national in level and the broader in scope institutionalized forums and implement structures are, the greater the incentive for higher and more hierarchic modes of interest intermediation. Conversely, the more regional in level and the narrower in scope either is, the smaller the incentive for higher and more hierarchic modes of interest intermediation. Product-specific bodies tend to 'freeze' the fragmented structures of organized intermediation by ensuring participation for the narrow but existing BIAs and raising the costs for the organizational development of the whole FPI. Thus the FPI speaks with a multitude of voices and finds it difficult obtaining attention for its often conflicting demands. This becomes strikingly obvious when the din by the FPI's subsectoral BIAs is compared to the orchestrated interests of producers or the wholesale or retail trades, when they are well organized.

E. Supranational Institutions — the EEC

Only three of the seven countries studied here are full members of the European Economic Community (EEC). Two of them, the Netherlands and West Germany, were among the original six to sign the Treaty of Rome in 1957, while the United Kingdom joined nearly 15 years later. Austria, Sweden and Switzerland opted to remain in the European Free Trade Association (EFTA) after the United Kingdom left to join the EEC. Canada, for obvious reasons, has never belonged to either of these European organizations.

There are numerous views about what the EEC is, might become or should be. Broadly speaking, it has been argued that the EEC is either a supranational organization, a state or a supranational organization with state-like properties. This is not an appropriate forum for weighing these various perspectives. Rather we will simply note that in the following the EEC will be considered a supranational organization with state-like properties.

Ideally, in a study of the impact of EEC membership, not only should consideration be given to the before-after effects found in the FPI BIAs in the

UK, but non-members should be compared with both old and new members during the last 20 years. However, such an ambitious comparison rapidly approaches the point of resulting in a single country in each category, e. g. member of EEC, member of EFTA, switched from EFTA to EEC, non-member of both. Nor does the space available justify such an ambitious undertaking. Instead the more concise and fruitful before-after method will be employed, combined with pair-wise comparisons between old and new EEC and EEC and non-EEC. Availability of data will also determine the presentation.

There is ample evidence from the UK project to show that EEC membership has led to major changes at the sectoral and subsectoral levels. Grant states that the EEC will not normally take note of individual companies, but only representative UK bodies like BIAs in lobby campaigns (1983 b: 90–91). In the United Kingdom, the government is open to lobbying both by individual companies as well as BIAs. Nevertheless, the Food and Drink Industry Council would not have been formed if Britain had not joined the EEC. Neither would the independent dairy trade associations in England & Wales, Scotland and N. Ireland have joined hands to form the U. K. Dairy Trade Federation, were it not for their need to facilitate EEC representation. Prior to EEC membership and the subsequent change in UK agriculture support policy to a more interventionist system, the need for a concerted food and drink lobby focusing on agricultural policy was simply not recognized by the British FPI. This newly-won recognition also facilitated the establishment of the FDIC. In West Germany, however, BIA spokesmen see the EEC as having little major influence.

Grant explains this contrast in terms of the state of disarray in 1973 of existing organizational structures in the UK FPI. Existing BIAs simply could not cope with the new responsibilities imposed by EEC membership. In particular, the absence of a sector-wide association would have excluded UK participation at the European association level. Furthermore, in the dairy industry arrangements had to be made in order to coordinate EEC policy between the three regional federations and the milk marketing boards (W. G. correspondence 29. 08. 85).

The EEC's preference for dealing with BIAs rather than individual firms, new policies and the subsequent new responsibilities, plus the necessity of being represented in European-level associations, all worked to greatly enhance the importance of associations to their members. Furthermore, as a result of these and similar developments, the relevant BIAs indirectly obtained 'monopoly goods', which augmented their authority even more. This not only improves BIAs' resource autonomy, but appears also to augment their strategic authority, by increasing their capacity to take a long-term perspective (Coleman and Grant, 1984: 225). As a result of EEC membership, strategic thinking on the long-term developments of the industry in Europe became a necessity for BIAs in the U. K., something which is not necessarily true for BIAs in non-EEC countries, as the Canadian case so clearly illustrates *(ibid.)*. The acquisition of this capacity through the professionalization of its staff also improves a BIA's position vis-a-vis its own national government. Furthermore, the technicalities of some EEC policy may even outstrip the capacity of national governments, which then will have to turn to relevant BIAs for help. Grant documents such developments in the U. K. He concludes that this significantly increases the opportunities for BIAs to act as intermediaries between their members and the government.

Another factor that Grant draws attention to is the development of new tensions between agriculture and the FPI as a result of EEC membership. Given the higher priority attributed by the Community to producers compared with processors, the need for more effective representations of processors at the Community level was recognized and accepted. Furthermore, EEC agricultural tariffs could potentially have a divisive effect in British FPIs. Those processors using EEC raw materials such as milk were not subject to import duties, while producers who largely imported their raw materials from outside the EEC paid such duties. The need for dealing with these new tensions furthered the development of new and more encompassing BIAs in the UK food processing industry.

Thus on a number of counts EEC membership appears to have made a substantial impact on the organizational properties of the BIAs in the United Kingdom. Sparse evidence from older EEC members and non-EEC members suggests that such broad changes were absent elsewhere. In West Germany no impact is traceable. In non-EEC countries few changes are to be found. In Sweden, for example, the mould was set in the early 1930s at the time when various product market boards were established. Organizations were represented on them from the outset. A democratization of these market boards in 1967 by including 'consumer' representatives was an extension of Swedish consumer policy and had no impact on the organizational development of the FPI.

In Canada even fewer changes in the organizational development of the FPI can be found. Given the low level of organizational development, it is not surprising still to find the FPI in disarray there. The Canadian FPI is fragmented and uncoordinated and its BIAs lack vertical integration brought on by hierarchically ordered systems. They also demonstrate a dearth of extensive horizontal ties among associations (Coleman and Grant, 1984: 223). Thus, in contrast, the UK membership in the EEC represents a considerable impetus for organizational development.

European Community Level Organizations in the FPI (Wyn Grant)

A major problem that the FPI faces in organizing at the European Community level is the relative indifference of the Community to what is the EEC's largest industry in terms of its share of gross manufacturing output. (FDIC, 1982, p. 41). As was pointed out in the introduction, food processing is not a 'glamorous' industry and, within the EEC, it is overshadowed by agriculture, which has a lower output but employs three times as many people (Harris, 1984, p. 3). Indeed, it has been argued that 'The Commission's unspoken but, nevertheless, implicit attitude to the Community's food industries is that they are the mechanism whereby the CAP is operated' (Harris, 1984, p. 8). Such an attitude is reflected in the relatively sparse administrative resources devoted by the Commission to the FPI, compared with the presence of a whole directorate-general for agriculture. As Swinbank and Burns note, 'Within the Commission the division of responsibilities between the Directorate-General for Agriculture (DG I), with its large staff, and the Foodstuffs Division, within the Directorate-General for Industrial Affairs and the Internal Market (DG III), with its very limited numbers of staff, might well strike the observer as unbalanced' (Swinbank and Burns, 1984, p. 166.) As far as DG 6 is concerned, there is no proper consultation with the food processing industry before proposals are put to the Management Committees.

The heterogeneity of the food processing industry is reflected in the existence of a considerable number of product-specific organizations at the European level: for example, CIMSCEEE (the European Sauces Association), CIMCEE (the European Mustard Association), the European Chip and Snack Association, and the Fédération Européenne de l'Industrie des Aliment pour Animaux Familiers (FEDIAF). Product areas which have not organized at a European level have expressed concern about their position: for example, the spice trade has been unable to make progress on securing amendments to the EEC Labelling Directive in the absence of a European-wide organization. Nevertheless, most product areas of the industry are covered by a European-level federation. Research by de Vroom shows that food, beverages and tobacco had the largest number of European-level business interest associations (sixty-five) of any two digit sector apart from metal products, machinery and equipment. Associations in food, beverages and tobacco accounted for one quarter of all the sector specific associations detected. (See de Vroom, 1985 a, p. 11.)

The general representative organization for the food industry at the EEC level, the Confederation des Industries Agricoles et Alimentaires (CIAA) could not be said to be a particularly strong body, especially when compared with the organization representing agricultural interests (COPA). Formed in 1959, CIAA functioned for many years as a committee of the European employers' organization, UNICE, only becoming an independent organization under Belgian law in 1982, although it continued to operate from UNICE's headquarters. However, the establishment of CLOB (Comité de Liaison avec les Organisations par Branche) is intended to bring about closer liaison between CIAA as a whole and the branch organizations. CLOB brings together the major branch associations in a quarterly meeting.

Although there has been some progress, it has not been easy to develop a political unity of purpose between European food manufacturers. For many years the Italians were outside the organization. At the first meeting of the Standing Committee of the independent organization, the British chairman called for 'a readiness on the part of each delegation to concede a little here and there and not to stay adamant in the defence to the last syllable of a position obviously unacceptable to the Committee as a whole.' (FDIC Bulletin, Number 21, p. 7). One consequence of the difficulty of finding agreement, and of the weakness of the organization, is that national organizations make considerable use of separate representations to the Commission on their own behalf. Quoting from a FDIC secretariat note, Stocker states:

There is no doubt that the national members of CIAA maintain their informal liaison with the Commission, particularly, but by no means exclusively, with those in the Cabinets of Commissioners and the directorate-generals of like nationality. FDIC maintains some direct links with Commission staff, indeed the latter have on occasion requested it, but it has been reluctant to detract from the authority of CIAA. On the other hand, CIAA is not always able to reach agreement, particularly on trading matters, so that if an organization feels it is insufficient to leave matters entirely in the hands of its national officials (who establish their own priorities) it has no other alternative than to have unofficial contact with the Commission. (Stocker, 1983, p.244).

The lack of interest of the Commission in the industry, the way in which its product heterogeneity is reflected in its representational arrangements, and the relative weakness of the European umbrella organization, all interact with one another to limit the effectiveness of the industry's impact on the development of Community policy at the European level. However, this lack of political displacement is in part compensated for by the attempts of national associations to influence the stances of national governments on the development of Community policy. It should also be noted that national associations in those countries which are not EEC members have to take some account of the impact of developments in the CAP and other EEC policies on their own activities and seek to exert influence, where appropriate, on their governments' negotiations with the EEC on trade agreements and other matters.

F. Summary and Conclusions

The aim of this chapter was to analyze the impact of state forms and functions on the organizational development of business interest associations in the food processing industry. This was to be achieved by examining the effect of state structures on the capacity of associations to coordinate their behavior and actions, as well as their capacity to gain sufficient autonomy vis-à-vis their members to function as intermediaries between members and the state. The capacity to coordinate the behavior and actions of their members was to be studied in the light of two factors: the constitutional character of the regime and the degree of decentralization of policy-making and implementation in the FPI.

The constitutional structures determine the degree of territorial decentralization in public policy-making in different countries. Territorial decentralization appears to have a more limited impact on the capacity of BIAs to coordinate their behavior and actions of their members than does the degree of functional decentralization in terms of state structures. There are numerous national agencies in each subsector and different agencies exist for different roles and functions. This functional decentralization is important in such a highly heterogeneous industry. State structures are diverse rather than uniform in character. It is therefore difficult for the logic of influence variables to overcome the fundamental heterogeneity caused by the logic of membership variables, owing to the diversity of state structures. The development of the various subsectors' capacity to coordinate the behavior and activities of their members is restricted to a particular subsector. The development of organizational capacity for coordination takes place on a narrow product-specific basis, resulting in a fragmented organizational pattern. Thus we find that the functional decentralization and ensuing product-related nature of state structures encourages subsectoral fragmentation of the BIAs and 'freezes' the existing pattern of narrow subsectoral BIAs in the FPI. This, in turn, becomes a major hindrance to the development of a more encompassing associational system for the whole FPI in most countries.

The capacity of business interest associations to gain autonomy vis-à-vis their members was considered in relation to two additional factors, the relative dependence of the public bureaucracy on the FPI for obtaining the information necessary for its policy functions and self-discipline in terms of compliance with regulation, plus the kinds of state structures available for policy implementation. The information needs of the state and its dependence on the industry for self-discipline were found to be related to the type of regulation in question. The narrower and more detailed such regulation is, the greater the bureaucracy's needs and its dependence on the industry.

The information needs of the state appear greater in the dairy subsector than in the other two. This also appears to be the most regulated subsector and one where market boards are usually found. The state's dependence on the subsector for self-discipline is therefore greater. Commodity market boards provide an example of narrow and detailed regulation. Where the information capacity of the state is low, or where the compliance problems it faces are high, it will seek to give associations a share in decision-making and policy implementation in exchange for obtaining information and/or securing compliance from their members. Thus the narrower the regulation, the more permanent a role attributed to BIAs. Commodity market boards tend either to be quasi-state and tripartite in their composition or, in some countries, simply private interest governments.

Once again the characteristics of the state reinforce rather than counteract the fragmenting effect of the logic of membership variables. BIAs are encouraged to represent narrow product-specific interests in detailed market boards. Thus implementation structures constitute a hindrance to the development of a more encompassing associational system for the whole sector.

Finally the impact of supranational institutions could most clearly be illustrated by examining the development of organizational structures and capacities following British membership in the EEC. A number of factors stemming from this membership worked to greatly enhance the importance of BIAs to their members in the FPI. Subsectoral factionalization could be overcome and a sector-wide BIA be established. When compared to other countries, both older EEC members and non-members, the British FPI demonstrates significant changes and major developments in its organizational network unparalleled elsewhere.

Thus in concluding it can be maintained that the state appears to play an important, in fact highly important, role in terms of the development of organizational properties and structures of business interest associations. Just how great the impact of state institutions is will depend upon the degree of heterogeneity of the industry in question. A highly heterogeneous branch like the food processing industry requires significant impetus from the state if it is to overcome the fractionalization and low level of organizational development inherent in the logic of membership. This is, however, not generally the case in most states studied here. The functional decentralization of state structures hinders rather than promotes organizational development. Such diverse state structures render it difficult, if not impossible, to overcome the fundamental heterogeneity of this industry. In fact functional decentralization and product-specific state bodies promote and 'freeze' a fragmented organizational pattern.

The information needs of the state are greatest where the regulation in question is narrow and detailed, i.e. for regulating specific commodities like milk, meat, etc. Representation on product-specific, narrow subsectoral boards is exchanged for information and self-compliance on the part of the industry. BIAs in the FPI are thus able to gain autonomy vis-a-vis their members only in a limited sense. Restricting their inputs and participation to narrow product-specific matters inhibits rather than promotes the organizational development of the FPI. Narrow state structures make it difficult to overcome the fundamental heterogeneity of this industry. In fact by limiting representation to product-specific bodies the state thwarts any efforts toward more encompassing BIAs for the whole FPI by 'freezing' the existing fragmented structures of organized intermediation.

Chapter 6

The Effect of Trade Unions
and Collective Bargaining Systems
on the Organizational Development
of Business Interest Representation

Josef Hilbert and Helmut Voelzkow

Introduction

Business firms operate and compete on four markets: the capital market, the consumer market, the input market and the labour market. With regard to all four markets, but especially in relation to influencing the legal and political conditions of this competition on consumer, input and labour markets, business firms of the same market section cooperate in the form of associational organizations. The present literature on collective action of employers, however, mainly focusses on conflicts relating to social policy and collective bargaining issues. Aspects of the labour market are clearly in the centre of discussion.

The emphasis on the organization of industrial relations is justified by the fact that two very unequal forces meet on the labour market. Capital owners need not sell their goods by any means at a specific date on specific terms and in the long run can switch to other types of investment. Workers, by contrast, are constantly obliged to sell their labour and can hardly secure their living otherwise — if one leaves social welfare payments out of consideration.

In order to counteract the 'natural' predominance of capital, workers depend on collective action, whether directly in the form of strikes or strike threats, or indirectly by exerting influence on the state which then feels compelled to consider workers' interests. To parry the political pressure exerted by labour, capital finds itself compelled to take collective action on a plant-wide or company-wide and, if necessary, even on an industry-wide basis. Given these considerations, the labour market and industrial relations constitute a quasi 'natural' field for conflicts and cooperation among the organized interests of particular groups in society.

Yet the analysis of the collective action of employers cannot be limited to the events on the labour market, i.e. the direct conflicts between organized capital and organized labour. When workers unionise, they acquire political power and under certain conditions can use the state as a tool to promote their interests. Labour unions then also have an influence on the conditions under which the business firms are acting on the capital, consumer, and input markets. Because the power of labour union action lies in the fact that unions can 'shift from markets to politics' (Korpi 1983: 76), highly interdependent relations develop between collective action of labour and capital, on the one hand, and the intervention of state agencies which set up regulations for the capital, labour, consumer, and input markets on which business firms operate, on the other hand.

Concerning business interests associations (BIAs), a distinction is generally made between employers' associations (EAs) and trade associations (TAs). In most cases, however, the respective tasks and functions are performed by one and the same association. Nonetheless, in some countries we also find autonomous employers' associations existing alongside trade associations. These differences in the structure of organized interest representation hitherto have hardly been analysed. By comparing the organization of business interests in the food processing industries (FPIs) of the seven countries investigated within the context of the BIA-Project, in the following discussion an attempt is made to shed some light on the causes underlying the differentiation, or non-differentiation respectively, between employers' associations and trade associations. This is based on the assumption that the interdependencies which exist between the input, consumer and labour markets and which are affected by the collective conflicts between labour and capital, can be referred to as independent variables.

We start with a description of the representation of employers' interests in the different food processing industries (Section 1). We then treat the structure of the labour force and the labour unions (Section 2). The third Section focusses on the outcomes of the clash between organized capital and organized labour as well as on the influence which labour unions exert on state institutions and sector-specific regulations.

The Structure of Employers' Interests Representation

As already applied to the surveys of associational structures, economic structures and governmental regulations, the epithet 'heterogeneous' also characterizes quite well the collective activities of the food processing industry in the domain of social policy and collective bargaining. As the different country studies show,[1] this holds first for the national level when the three subsectors

---

[1] Almost all of the information used and given in the following is based (if not indicated otherwise) either on the six different food-processing sector-reports written in the context of the BIA-Project (Coleman 1984, Farago et al. 1984, Grant 1983 b, Hilbert 1983, Pestoff 1983, Traxler 1983 b) or was collected by means of an additional questionnaire circulated among BIA-Project participants. Nevertheless, the full responsibility for all mistakes, misunderstandings, and misinterpretations remains with the authors. Last but not least, we are very thankful and obliged to all those participating in the BIA-Project-Food-Processing-Sector team for having contributed to an understanding of capital-labour relations in this particular sector of industry.

Table 6.1: Existence of Employers' Interests Associations (EA)[1]

type of EA	A	CDN	CH	countries D	GB	NL	S
Peaks-TAs with a Labour Committee	N	N	N	N	N[2]	N	N
Independent EAs existing	N	N	N	Y	_[2]	Y	Y
Employers' interests representation by subsector BIA	Y	N	Y	Y	Y	Y	Y

[1] N = No, do(es) not exist. Y = Yes, do(es) exist.
[2] GB seems to be something of an intermediate case between Sweden and Germany and the other countries; for details, see the comments in this chapter.

under study are compared. We find firms, groups of firms or entire sectors managing completely without collective action in the representation of employers' interests (Canada) as well as firms, groups of firms or entire sectors operating within associational systems and collective bargaining systems acting industry-wide, i. e. for the food processing industry as a whole (Sweden, Germany). If one considers the three subsectors which have been closely investigated as a whole and regards them as typical of the entire food processing industry, the same variance of course can be observed in international comparison. As Table 6.1 shows, two patterns however prevail.

Most frequently associational systems occur in which sub-sector-specific associations work primarily as trade associations and only incidentally, i. e. without much commitment and expenditure, perform the function of representing employers' interests. In Austria and in Great Britain, the trade associations are aided in their activities by central organizations of trade associations which, apart from their main functions, are also concerned with coordinating the employers' interests represented by their member associations.

However, the coordination efforts in the countries mentioned are of only limited efficacy. In Great Britain, several associations deal with employers' interest representation and bargaining. The FMIG (Food Manufacturers Industrial Group) which deals with collective bargaining is an FMF (Food Manufacturers' Federation) affiliate with a separate subscription. However, the FMF also has industrial relations committees which are not confined to FMIG members. Furthermore it is possible to belong to the FMIG without being a member of its peak association, the FMF. The Bacon and Meat Manufacturers' Association (BMMA) has a specialized affiliate dealing with employers' organization matters; but nevertheless the employers' side of the bargaining body in this industry is serviced by the BMMA itself. Some important associations of the sector, in particular the new Food and Drink Federation, more or less stay away from this area. In general, organizations like the FMF are more effective in areas such as industrial relations law and dealing with the impact of strikes in other industries than they are in collective bargaining questions which are highly decentralized. The structure, of course, causes a lot of problems in relation to the 'non-conforming member' practice, i. e. the coverage and liability of agreements. In Austria, whilst all subsector-specific trade associations are affiliated to the chamber system, specific coordination efforts among the different subsectors of food processing concerning collective bargaining issues are not being undertaken (Traxler 1983 b: 53 ff.).

The case is somewhat different in Sweden and in the Federal Republic of Germany. In these two countries, there exist employers' associations which (a) cover the entire food processing industry and (b) constitute autonomous organizations acting independently in the respective central organizations of trade associations.

The German *Arbeitgebervereinigung Nahrung und Genuß* (ANG) is an association of associations to which are affiliated both trade associations (at the subsector level) which operate nation-wide and also perform the functions of an employers' association, as well as regional employers' associations of the food processing industry. In Sweden, by contrast, the individual business firms are directly affiliated to the LAF, the employers' association of food processors in Sweden. The density ratio of the ANG is about 80 percent (Hilbert 1983: 218), that of the LAF about 87 through 88 percent (Pestoff 1983: 29). The remaining 12 through 13 percent of the Swedish business firms in the food processing industry are consumer cooperatives which cannot become members of an employers' association on account of their common origins with the labour unions. Together with other consumer cooperative firms, they have however established an association of their own, the KFO. KFO's agreements in food processing normally follow in detail the terms set by the collective agreements negotiated by the LAF. The function of the German ANG mainly consists in coordinating the activities of its member associations. Its most important aim is to prevent collective agreements which might serve as a point of reference for all subsequent claims in other bargaining areas. As to the LAF, the individual product-sections, in which employers of different subsectors are organized, negotiate directly with the labour unions.

The situation in the Netherlands also displays distinctive features. Here, the employers' interests in many food processing firms are represented by an autonomous employers' association. According to its constitution, its domain is manufacturing industry as a whole but in fact it is dominated by chemical and food processing firms. However, the *Algemene Werkgevers Vereniging* (AWV) neither participates in collective bargaining activities of the food processing industries, nor is it responsible for the food processing industry as a whole. Its main activity is service and advisory functions and about 70 percent of its total organizational effort is spent on this. The wage negotiations are always carried out by representatives of TAs, but next to them at the negotiating table sit experts from AWV. Thus their experience and the reliance of the sector associations on this experience makes the AWV capable of significant informal coordination.

A first explanation for the limited efforts to represent employers' interests in the different food processing industries is easy to find. In the business firms of this sector, labour intensity is rather low as compared to the firms in other sectors of the economy. Moreover, the firms are confronted with grave problems (e. g. retail pressure, regulated raw-material markets), the solution to which ranks higher for the development of the branches and firms than collective wage contracts which perhaps might have turned out a little bit lower with the help of an autonomous sectorwide employers' association. Moreover, because in the food processing industry the representation of employers' interests is not so necessary as in industries with a higher labour intensity, initiatives for coordinating employers' interests find it especially difficult to overcome the heterogeneity of the sector in terms of organization. Relatively independent product-specific subsectors, strong artisanal traditions, the upstream growth of producer cooperatives and the downstream growth of consumer cooperatives and retail chains — all this hence may serve as an explanation for the fact that in relation to an issue which has no dominant importance for the food processing industry anyway, associational action does not take place. (These issues are discussed further in the next chapter by Rainbird.)

Such an explanation however implies that the associational structures outlined for Sweden and Germany would have to be ascribed to national idiosyncracies. This could be substantiated by pointing to the fact that these countries generally are also countries in which the division between employers' associations and trade associations prevails on a wide scale. For theoretical and empirical reasons, however, we do not want to content ourselves with such an explanation. When recourse is made to historical or national idiosyncracies, in theoretical terms, the question always remains as to the factors accounting for these very idiosyncracies in the first place. In empirical terms, it is astonishing that in the Federal Republic of Germany there existed no autonomous employers' association of the food processing industry until 1977 and that such an organization was not established until the responsible labour union scored its first successes with a changed collective bargaining policy which mingled qualitative (e. g. working conditions) and quantitative (e. g. wages) demands.

Schmitter and Streeck (1981: 107) suppose that the division in trade associations and employers' associations 'is more likely to occur in politics or sectors where the interaction between business associations and organized labour is particularly intensive and broad in scope'. In order to test this hypothesis, and — as the case may be — to further specify it, the following section deals with the structure of the labour force (see also the chapter by Rainbird) and the specific features of union organization and strategy. In this section we encounter a first set of independent variables by means of which we want to find out the causes underlying the differentiation into employers' associations and trade associations.

The Labour Force and Labour Unions in Food Processing

As has been mentioned already, labour costs in food processing are extremely low. On an average, they amount to about 15 percent of the total manufacturing costs. Wages tend to be lower than the respective national average. It is generally the case that the wage level is closer to national average earnings, the more modern the equipment of the respective industries. Thus, in the U. K., where the food processing industry shows the highest degree of modernization, average earnings are about 101 percent of the respective national average, whereas in Austria, where small and medium-size enterprises prevail in the food processing industry, wages only amount to 80 percent of the national average earnings. In the British case, a study based on the CBI pay data bank maintained since 1979 suggests that workers in the food industry consistently settle for relatively high pay agreements compared with other sectors (other than chemicals and paper). (*Financial Times*, 11 November 1985.)

The structure of the labour force in the food processing industries under study, by contrast, generally speaking shows no striking peculiarities and approaches the national average values. This holds — provided that reliable data are available at all — for the ratio of skilled and unskilled workers as well as for the extent of seasonal work and part-time work. Only where small and medium-size firms clearly prevail do we obtain another picture. In the meat processing industry of the German-speaking countries with their artisanal traditions, we find a larger proportion of helping family members and firm owners. The level of qualification is especially low in fruit and vegetable processing. Moreover, part-time work and a higher share of female employment are more frequently to be found in this subsector. In Canada, some workers are brought in from the Caribbean to work in the factories at peak season.

The level of employment develops — again in comparison with the corresponding trends in the overall national employment levels — without particular ups and downs. However, in most of the countries investigated, the number of workers employed continuously decreases when seen in absolute terms. With sales remaining constant or even increasing, this reflects a trend towards rationalization, probably triggered off by the fact that other decisive factors ensuring profits cannot be influenced. The raw material markets are regulated to a large extent by political intervention, on the outlets the passing on of costs is ruled out by the ever increasing pressure from retail trade. Regardless of how low labour intensity may be, the attraction of saving labour costs increases against this background. The control of labour costs, however, can rather be achieved by an increased 'efficiency with which labour is used than over the wages paid, since in a competitive environment the food industries tend to have to pay the market rate...' (Ashby 1983: 59).

Within the respective national economies (Switzerland is an exception, cf. Farago et al. 1984: 15 ff.), the food processing industries under study assume a leading position. This holds both for their contribution to GNP and — even though with some modifications — for their share in employment. Nevertheless, this important economic sector is treated rather with neglect on the part of the labour unions. This phenomenon which we find in many countries (A, CDN, CH, GB) can be illustrated in the light of some considerations the central organization of British labour unions made in order to warrant a coordination of different labour unions playing a role in Food and Drink Manufacturing. The TUC considered setting up an industry committee for food and drink but has commented:

> There is a question whether there are sufficient general underlying policy matters distinct to the sector to warrant the establishment of a TUC-committee, given the need for the TUC carefully to choose its priorities. The unions in any case already meet and discuss policy matters for their sector under the auspices of NEDO (National Economic Development Office) ... The narrow basis of food and drink employing about 750,000 people *(sic!)* would not produce sufficient issues for consideration which are distinguishable from those considered by the Economic Committee.

A survey of the number of labour unions which play a major role in the food processing industries under study shows that the situation within this sector does not considerably differ from the general structure of labour union organization in the respective countries.[2] Thus, in Great Britain and the Netherlands — countries with a competitive labour union system and a fragmentation of the labour union movement — we encounter six, or seven respectively, the largest number of labour unions. And in the Federal Republic, in Austria, and in Sweden, we have only two relevant labour union organizations — one which represents both blue- and white-collar workers' interests and one which represents only white-collar interests.

Hence, the organization of workers' interests in the food processing industry shows the highest level of concentration, hierarchization and integration in countries which are generally known for a high degree of union concentration and concertation. The case is slightly different in Canada and Switzerland. In Canada, there is one union pre-eminent, the United Food and Commercial Workers Union, an 'international' union based in the United States (Coleman 1984: 25). In Switzerland, we again find two more or less sector-specific labour unions, each being affiliated to a central sector-unspecific organization acting at the national level. In addition, a *berufsständische* association (i. e. a professional association) is playing a major role in meat processing (Farago et al. 1984: 64 ff.).

In Table 6.2, the variable existence of sector-specific labour unions is defined so that it also includes organizations representing a larger domain (e. g. in addition to food processing also catering, as is the case in Germany) and not only the food processing industry, but which are nevertheless organized according to the principle of the *Industriegewerkschaft*. Labour unions of this type can be found in almost all of the countries under study, except that in Great Britain and

---

[2] Lecher (1981) gives a characterization of different labour unions and different collective bargaining systems in different European countries by evaluating their degree of centralization. Among other countries, his book treats Germany, Great Britain, and the Netherlands. For the other countries dealt with in the BIA-Project, see Traxler (1982), Farago et al. (1984: 62 ff.) (CH), and Coleman (1984: 25) (CDN). For Sweden, cf. footnote 6.

Josef Hilbert and Helmut Voelzkow

Table 6.2: Character of National Labour Movements

special characteristics	A	CDN	CH	countries D	GB	NL	S
Number of major trade unions negotiating collective agreements	2	1	3	2	7	7[1]	2
Sector-specific labour unions[2] existing	Y	Y[3]	Y	Y	Y	Y[1]	Y
Density ratios — generally — sector-specific (percentages)	58 60	? 70–90[5]	33[4] 10–15[5]	38[4] 20–60[6]	51[4] 88[5]	36[4] 40–70[7]	90 90
Competition between labour unions	low	low	low	low	medium[8]	medium	low
Labour militancy[9]	low	low	low	low	medium	medium	low
Importance of demands concerning working conditions[10]	medium	low	low	high	low	low	high

[1] In NL the number of labour unions differs for each subsector of the food processing industry. Altogether, in the three subsectors we studied, seven different unions are involved, two of them are operating specifically for the food processing industry. Three unions are affiliated to the socialist/Catholic trade union federation FNV (Federatie Nederlandse Vakbeweging), four are members of the Protestant federation CNV (Christelijk National Vakverbond).

[2] This classification includes those associations organizing more than food processing but having at least a significant foothold in food processing and dominating labour interest representation in this particular sector of industry. Y = Yes, do exist; N = No, do not exist.

[3] The sector is dominated by a U.S. based union, the United Food and Commercial Workers Union.

[4] See Visser 1984.   [5] These data are only valid for non-office employees.

[6] Meat Processing = 35%; Dairy Industry = 60%; Fruits and Vegetables = 21%.

[7] About 70 percent in dairy products manufacturing and 40 percent in meat processing.

[8] Seen from a national perspective, the labour union competition is low. Thirty-five percent of establishments had more than one union recognized, about the national average. Inter-union problems had occurred in 13 percent of establishments, under half the national average, and the best record of inter-union relationships in any sector apart from metal goods n.e.s. which had an equally good record. If compared to the other countries of our international comparison, inter-unions' competition in Great Britain seems to be intensive.

[9] Qualitative judgments of the authors on the basis of information as to whether the sector is relatively strike-prone in comparison with the national economy as a whole and as to whether strikes are predominantly local, regional or national, official or unofficial, of long or short duration.

in the Netherlands there is no such form of indirect coordination of labour union action through a dominating union. In the U. K., six out of seven labour unions playing a major role in food processing are not sector-based. Moreover, they are not even integrated and coordinated by a committee of the TUC, as is the common practice within other major sectors of the British economy. In the Netherlands, it is true that two central union organizations representing workers from the food processing industry have member associations which are exclusively composed of workers from this sector, but the two central organizations are confessional associations which stand in a competing relationship. Consequently, it can be assumed that also here the level of inter-union concertation is relatively low.

In spite of the, by international comparison, large number of labour unions in the British food processing industry, the competition among the different organizations is relatively low on the national scale. Thirty-three percent of establishments had more than one union recognized above the national average. Inter-union problems had occurred in 13 percent of establishments, which is under half of the national average, and the best record in inter-union relationships in any sector (apart from metal goods n. e. s., which had an equally good record) (Brown ed., 1981).

The case is similar in the other countries of our sample. Only in the Netherlands and in Switzerland did we find a specific competition among individual labour unions: in Switzerland on the part of the union *Verkauf, Handel, Transport und Lebensmittel* (VHTL) — the most powerful union of the sector — vis-a-vis the *Metzgereipersonal-Verband* (MPV), which is a *berufsständische* (i. e. professional) organization specialized in meat processing; in the Netherlands, there is a significant competition between unions of different religions and a domain overlap between general industry unions and a white-collar union. In Germany, Sweden, and Austria, where apart from the sector-specific labour union organizations, we also find white-collar unions, there is no major competition between these two types of labour unions. In these countries, the sector-specific unions are so powerful that the white-collar unions have no other choice but to conclude rider-agreements. In general, the level of competition among the different labour unions is rather low in all of the countries under study. In many cases, however, this is due to labour unions' neglect of the food processing industry rather than to the existence of a comparatively homogeneous and cooperative labour union system.

With the exception of Sweden and the Netherlands, union density in food processing is below the national average values. Moreover, it varies considerably among the different subsectors. The low degree of unionization as well as the great variance can be explained by the heterogeneity of the economic structures. Thus, in the meat processing industries of Sweden and Germany, where artisanal structures prevail (i. e. a large number of small enterprises which are spread all over the country), the degree of unionization is minimal. The centralized

[10] Measured by the question of whether the sector has been the place of major negotiated innovations in labour relations in the past ten years and by qualitative judgments of team members.

production and distribution structure of the German dairy business, by contrast, implies a unionization degree of 60 percent.

Like density ratios, labour militancy is also below the national averages. In many countries, strikes hardly ever occur (e. g. in Sweden, Germany, Austria). In almost all of the countries under study, strikes occur more rarely in the food processing industry as compared to other sectors of the economy. Great Britain seems to be an exception, but

> The industry (Food, Drink and Tobacco) does appear to be relatively strike prone in that incidents per 100,000 manual empoyees have run at about twice the national average. However, although strikes of under one day are particularly common, strikes of over one day do not exceed the national average. (Grant 1983: 23; cf. also Brown 1981: 84).

Dutch employers in the food processing industry are confronted with a very active and (at least) vocally radical *Voedingsbond* FNV, which is by far the most important union of this sector. But several attempts to organize strikes in the past decade failed because they were declared illegal by the courts. They gave the interests of the farmers to have a steady marketing of their continually produced raw materials (e. g. milk) and the interests of the consumers concerning the uninterrupted provision of processed food priority over the workers' interests to go on strike in case of labour market conflicts.

In Sweden, the almost two weeks long general labour conflict in 1980 affected the food processing industry less vehemently than other sectors of the national economy. The consumer cooperatives (i. e. about 12 through 13 percent of the food processing industry) were exempted from the strike — on account of the traditionally good contacts they maintain with the unions (Pestoff 1983: 23). If we recall that wages in food processing tend to be below the respective national averages, the low level of labour militancy might also be explained by the low degree of unionization within this sector and the subsequent neglect this sector is given in union calculations. It must be added, however, that in some subsectors of the food processing industry we find extremely segmented labour markets — on the one side, male skilled workers earning high wages, on the other side women or guest-workers wages are considerably below the national average. Segmentation might also be an obstacle to labour militancy.

Union strategies must balance quantitative (wages) against qualitative (working conditions) demands. In the last decades, the emphasis of union efforts was on the improvement of the financial situation of employees. Due to rationalization processes, however, working conditions and security of employment have come to the fore in recent years. Also, and especially in the food processing industry, which in every country is exposed to increasing pressure in terms of input and output, firms are constrained to push automation and capital intensification ahead. Systematic attention to this process on the part of the unions, however, has so far only been forthcoming in Sweden and Germany. In some subsectors of the food processing industry — for example, in the tobacco and in the brewing business — the German *Gewerkschaft Nahrung, Genuß, Gaststätten* (GNGG) succeeded in achieving innovations in collective bargaining agreements (e. g. additional vacations and free time for shift workers, introduction of gradual retirement age and/or reduced weekly working hours) which met with protests from employers of other branches and from the *Bundesvereinigung der deutschen Arbeitgeberverbände* (Federal Union of German Employers' Associations). In Sweden, a part of these qualitative demands was already settled by an agreement binding for all economic sectors which had been negotiated between the nationwide peak associations of capital (SAF) and labour (LO) and by the 1983 law regulating working hours, respectively.[3] If one considers the countries under study as a whole, from the union perspective there seems to exist a need for qualitative union policies especially in the food processing industries with their specific economic difficulties. However, it will not be easy for the unions to respond to this need. It looks as if only a homogeneous and centralized labour union system would be in a position to deal with the new tasks arising for the unions.

If one summarizes the findings on the organizational structure and the policies of labour unions in the food processing industries of the countries under study, a rather gloomy picture arises with respect to the unions:

1. In most of the countries, we find a heterogeneous labour union system in which the difficulties of coordinating union strategies cannot be overlooked. In every country, the state of the labour union movement in food processing shows the same features which are also characteristic of the state of the respective national labour union movement. The food processing industry ranks, comparatively speaking, at the bottom of union interests. This finds expression in the small number of unions which are exclusively concerned with this sector. Apart from that, coordinating bodies are lacking, which could guide the activities of the different labour union organizations.

2. The present state of the labour union movement in the food processing industry however cannot only be attributed to deficits in union strategies. It mirrors for its part the heterogeneity of the employment structure within this sector in which we find both subsectors where small enterprises with strong artisanal traditions prevail as well as subsectors where multinational concerns with modern, capital-intensive automated production processes dominate. However, attention must also be drawn to the fact that — perhaps with the exception of the Federal Republic, Austria and Sweden — the structures of the labour movement described above are hardly sufficient to effectively protect workers' interests against the consequences of the increasing pressure for rationalization which is exerted on the outlets and the raw material markets as a result of the power relationships governing these markets.

3. The labour unions and the policies they pursue in the food processing industry provide relatively few impulses for the development of business interests' associations in general and the representation of employers' interests in particular. In view of the heterogeneity of the sector, the in general

[3] Particularly with respect to working-time issues, an introductory report was written by Carina Nilsson (1982). A summary of laws adopted by parliament relating to working conditions (e. g. the 1978 Act on Working Environment) and of the general role of the Swedish government in regulating working life is given by Hammarström/Viklund 1980.

comparatively low labour intensity and the absence of coordination efforts and capacity to settle conflicts on the part of the labour unions we cannot expect this to be otherwise.

Organized Labour and Political Decision-Making

The general picture of the organizational structures in the labour union movement provides only a few indications of its having a determining effect on the establishment of employers' associations. However, some exceptions must be considered. In Germany and in Sweden, comparatively homogeneous and cooperative labour unions correspond with separate, sector-encompassing employers' interest associations. Even so, the question is not yet determined as to whether the power of the labour unions constitutes the key variable for explaining the existence of autonomous employers' associations. First, there still would be Austria and Switzerland where we find — even though with some modifications — similar union structures. Secondly, this coincidence furnishes no answer to the question as to under which conditions, in which way and why a homogeneous and cooperative labour union system in the food processing industry contributes to the development of autonomous employers' associations. To answer this question, we will turn in the following section to the outcomes of the encounter between differently structured employees' and employers' organizations.

The configuration of bargaining areas has a bearing on both the labour unions and business interest associations involved and at the same time the structure of the latter has a bearing on the former. When considering the number of sector-specific collective bargaining agreements, the enormous differences among the different countries immediately catch the eye. Whereas in Sweden we only find six collective agreements — two in each subsector under study (one for blue-collar workers, and one for white-collar workers, respectively) — in Canada the number of agreements is considerably greater as bargaining is only conducted at the company- or plant-level. A strong tendency towards company- or plant-level agreements is also to be noted in Great Britain. It is true that in the three subsectors under study 20 multi-firm agreements were counted, but in the entire Food and Drink Industry wages and working conditions are settled merely in 28 percent of all firms by this type of agreement.

In the form of local adjustments to industry wide collective arrangements, this tendency is also to be found in Sweden and the Federal Republic. In these two countries, however, there is no company- or plant-level bargaining. Only in one firm of the German dairy manufacturing industry are agreements concluded at the plant level. In general, however, in the food processing industries collective bargaining systems are heterogenous and decentralized, i. e. collective bargaining is conducted either at the subsector level or at the plant level.

The large number of collective agreements which we find in a heterogeneous collective bargaining system, however, need not necessarily correspond with heterogeneous organizational structures on the side of employers' associations

Table 6.3: Labor Organization and Political Decision-Making

issues	countries						
	A	CDN	CH	D	GB	NL	S
Number of sector-specific wage agreements	50	F[1]	33	33	20[2]	8[3]	6[4]
Average earnings per employee in percentages of employees' earnings on the natural average	80	?	99	98[5]	101[5]	87 (meat) 97 (dairy)	100
"wage-drift"	low	F[1]	15 %	low	F[1]	low	low
Break-through agreements?[6]	N	N	N	Y	N	N	N
Representational bodies dealing with sector-specific labour issues	1[7]	0	0	1[8]	4[9]	16	1[10]
Labour influence on food processing relevant policies	high	low	low	high	low	low	high

[1] Unanswerable; firm-level collective bargaining prevailing.

[2] It should be noted, however, that only about 28 percent of all food and drink firms are covered or at least dominated by multi-firm agreements.

[3] The data for NL are only based on information about meat processing (seven agreements) and dairy products manufacturing (one agreement).

[4] Two per subsector. In addition, there are local adjustments to industry-wide collective agreements.

[5] Food, Drink and Tobacco industry as a whole.

[6] N = No, do not occur; Y = Yes, do occur.

[7] "Paritätische Kommission".

[8] As the case may be, the Federal Institute for Vocational Training Issues ("Bundesinstitut für Berufsbildung", BIBB) establishes sector- and/or job-specific bodies of functional representation. Their main task is to develop new job-outlines.

[9] NEDO and three non-statutory (vocational) training boards.

[10] The Educational Organization of the Food Processing Industry and work environment matters (LUO).

and labour unions. This is shown by the example of the Federal Republic where about 33 collective agreements were counted; these can continue to exist also in a relatively homogeneous system and become a motive for standardization efforts on the part of employers — this at least was one of the concerns of the ANG (sectorwide peak association of employers' interests) established in 1977 (Hilbert 1983).

In most of the countries, the wages and salaries in the food processing industry are below national average earnings. Exceptions are Great Britain and Sweden. Using this indicator, we also find considerable differences between the subsectors under study. Apart from that, the data mirror the weakness of the labour unions and the heterogeneity of the sector. The decentralization is furthermore reflected by a relatively low wage-drift, i. e. the difference between contract wages and actually paid wages. This indicates that contract wages fit actually paid wages and can be interpreted as a proof of the hypothesis of limited centralizing forces within the respective parts of this industry.

That a decentralized collective bargaining system does not automatically imply that centralizing forces are completely absent is shown by some German experiences. Moreover, within heterogeneous economic structures and a heterogeneous system of business interest organizations, the heterogeneity of the collective bargaining system may even turn out to be a chance for cooperative and sector-encompassing labour unions. For it was just in this scenario that the German *Gewerkschaft Nahrung, Genuß, Gaststätten* (GNGG) succeeded in concluding 'break-through agreements' in some subsectors of food processing. Later on and to some extent still today, recourse is and was made to these agreements when labour unions want or wanted to prove that it is possible to realize qualitative demands. Therefore it is not surprising that a further motive for the already repeatedly mentioned establishment of the ANG has been to prevent agreements which might serve as a precedent for subsequent claims. In the present case, the agreements had been neither centrally coordinated on the part of the employers nor had they been examined by the employers as to whether they matched the interests of the sector *as a whole*.

As has already been mentioned in the introduction, the power of a labour union decisively depends on the influence it is able to exert on the governmental policies which are relevant to the sector it is representing. Leaving out of consideration the influence a union has in collective bargaining for wages, its influence can also be identified when considering the institutionalization of labour unions' inter-company co-determination and participation rights. Representational bodies dealing with sector and/or (sector-) labour-specific problems exist in Austria, Germany, Great Britain, the Netherlands, and Sweden. In England, seven labour unions are represented in the Food and Manufacturing Economic Development Committee, a sector-specific subdivision of the National Economic Development Office. An effective labour unions' influence on the political decision-making of the Committee is not only thwarted by its minor importance in terms of economic policy (Grant 1984: 8 f.), but, in addition, is considerably hampered by the coordination problems among the labour unions (Section 2). In Austria, so-called *paritätische Kommissionen* (i. e. joint committees) play a central role in the implementation of specific economic laws. It is only in the manufacture of dairy products, where wage increases are coupled to price movements (Traxler 1983 b: 58), that labour union interests' representatives gain actual significance (ibid.: 33 ff.). The bodies of functional representation in Germany and in Sweden are exclusively concerned with planning and/or implementing measures of professional training policy. Hence, labour unions cannot expect much from institutional representation for increasing their political influence. Consequently, the institutionalization of union co-determination rights in the food processing industries is not conducive to the development and the unity of the employers' associations system. A somewhat different case is the Dutch situation. Here, three sector-specific committees established in accordance with the act of work councils are supervising the implementation of this act. The other representational bodies deal with pension funds, social security, early retirement or are institutionalized fora for collective negotiations. None of these bodies function as a channel for exerting influence towards the government, hence they are of no importance in any political respect (van Waarden 1984: 42). However, there is another important institutionalized channel for influence, the right of the labour unions to take up seats in the statutory trade associations (STA) which exist in all three subsectors that were studied. Labour unions can use their presence on the STAs to gain some influence on government decisions. But due to a lack of success, the radical *Voedingsbond* FNV has kept its seats on the STA-Boards unoccupied for a number of years now.[4]

In addition to institutionalized possibilities of influence, labour unions also use informal channels to influence political decision-making. Thus, for example, the chances for realizing labour union demands increase when Social-Democratic parties determine governmental policy or when large areas of social policy are subject to tripartite negotiation and cooperation. Within such a framework, spill-over effects become possible which facilitate stable and cooperative collective bargaining relations (Schmitter/Streeck 1981: 108 ff.). Such a framework, however, holds only for the national level. Sectoral conditions which would make it easier for sector-based labour unions to influence political-decision making were not specified in the research design of the present project. Nevertheless, the available national sector reports provide a considerable number of indications which permit us to draw a first mosaic-like picture.

An important function of business interest associations is the maintenance and the improvement of the competitiveness of the firms represented. Concerning the realization of this aim, state regulations are of central importance. This especially applies to the associations of the food processing industry, as it is one of those economic sectors which are most strongly affected by state interventions

---

[4] It is possible that the increased commitment in terms of professional training policy, of which there are some indications (Rainbird and Grant 1984, Hilbert 1983: 226 f., Pestoff 1983: 26) in future might strengthen both employers' associations and labour unions. As is shown, for example, by the development of the associational system in the German metal industries (cf. Weber 1983), professional profiles constitute good criteria for defining organizational domains and bargaining areas. It is possible that also in the food processing industry a collective sectorwide identity will be achieved only when sectorwide professional profiles are developed.

(e. g. EEC market regulations; product labelling obligations; nutrition policies). The volume of political regulations increases the need for collective action vis-a-vis the state decision-making institutions. At the same time, however, state institutions depend on support from societal interest groups and thus constitute appropriate addressees also for the unions' efforts towards influencing public policy. This applies especially to measures of food policy, because these in general have also implications in terms of health policy and, moreover, — on account of the strong (substitution) competition of the entire agro business — produce within the sector not only 'winners', but also 'losers', whose opposition must be taken into account.

As state interventions in most cases do not affect the entire food processing industry in the same way, it is not surprising that we find a decentralized fragmented associational system. A centrally coordinated labour union which concludes agreements at the subsector or plant level, thus has the chance to profit from the legislators' orientation to specific groups of products and to specific subsectors. If in exchange for supporting particular subsector-specific interests vis-a-vis the state, unions succeed in achieving breakthrough agreements in a particular subsector, these can be used as precedents in other bargaining areas. In Sweden and Austria, labour union influence on industrial and food policies is dependent on overall national conditions. In Germany, by contrast, we find a centrally coordinated labour union covering the whole food processing industry and having practically no competitors, which tries to achieve single breakthrough agreements in a decentralized collective bargaining system. Where possible and necessary, the willingness to compromise on the employers' side is reinforced by the unions' supporting the political concerns of the branch in question (Hilbert 1983).

Such a union strategy, of course, functions best if capital only has subsector-specific business interest associations which regard themselves primarily as trade associations and thus are representing employers' interests only in addition to their primary functions. If the selective support on the part of the unions, for example, helps to secure outlets, business interest associations, when in doubt, will more readily consent to higher wages or improved working conditions even though negotiations cover only collective bargaining issues. Such a union strategy, however, triggers off reactions on the part of employers. As we have already seen, the most important motive for the establishment of a sector-based employers' peak association in the FRG was the endeavour to prevent union successes which establish precedents for other bargaining areas. Whereas with regard to business interest associations which are both employers' associations and trade associations, the labour unions could profit from their strategy of combining industrial policy matters having implications for competition with collective bargaining issues in decentralized collective bargaining areas, employers now have at their disposal a central committee which is designed to judge, relatively free from implications in terms of competition policy, union policies solely from the viewpoint of collective bargaining policy (Hilbert 1983: 72 ff., 215 ff.).

In Germany, the political influence exerted by a cooperative labour union dominating in the German food processing industry, was conducive to the establishment of an autonomous employers' association. That the union was able to exert such an influence is due to the fact that labour union support constitutes an important resource of legitimation for public-decision makers and sector-specific business interest associations given the highly controversial industrial and food policies. The basis of the union successes and the employers' reactions in the FRG hence was the fact that the unions succeeded in combining collective bargaining issues with industrial policy matters.[5]

In Sweden — the second country in our sample with an autonomous employers' association — the existence of such an organization rather seems to be due to general national development. This also applies to the majority of collective bargaining results, which in the German food processing industry had a 'break-through' character, but in Sweden were achieved at the national level.[6] An industry-wide and centralized system of industrial relations which is relatively free from state interference had already developed in Sweden in the first three decades of this century. As centralized bargaining rounds cannot function if regard must constantly be paid to specific economic problems of single branches, an autonomous representation of employers' interests is the obvious choice. Combining trade association and employers' association functions, by contrast, increases the risk that class-specific and subsector-specific interests are being mixed and thus making the different (sub-)sectors prone to concessions vis-a-vis organized labour. Whereas the Swedish industry-wide agreements in general are explained by the strength of Swedish social democracy, the respective developments in the German food processing industry are to be understood as

[5] In this context, the establishment of a new and independent EA in German food processing is more or less explained as being a rational answer to a collective interest responding to a functional imperative. Seen from the literature on 'free-rider problems' and other collective action problems of businessmen (Olson 1965; Schmitter/Streeck 1981), this kind of explanation is nothing but a prerequisite of a successful collective strategy — i.e. we still have to add how and by whom an identified collective interest is transformed into collective action, into organization. In German food processing, the ANG foundation process was initiated and sponsored by some (economically) leading firms. These firms — almost all without exception multi-plant and multi-national companies producing in different food processing subsectors (e.g. Unilever in margarine, meat processing, dairy products manufacturing, frozen food, etc.) — are forced by the labour force in their companies to accept the most favourable contracts among those being valid for the different subsectors. Therefore, a multi-sector company is particularly hit by the effects described above. While single-subsector firms are not forced to accept and implement the obligations of a prejudging collective agreement until the next contract is bargained, a multi-subsector company has to accept it straightaway. Because of that, the few but multi-subsector firms had a particular interest in avoiding these effects and helped — as a small group in Olson's sense — to establish a new level of coordination.

[6] For a brief account of the Swedish system of industrial relations, see Korpi (1981).

resulting from the possibilities of exerting political influence which a centralized and sector-encompassing union has in this specific sector and policy area.[7]

The situation in the Netherlands does not quite fit in with this picture. Though the labour unions there can use institutionalized channels of influence to play the game of trading off favourable labour conditions for support in technical, industrial and economic policy matters, they did not succeed in achieving significant results. This can surely be taken as proof of the fact that it is not the specific nature of the problems in the food processing industry that affects the chances that labour unions have in any case to influence political decision making. On the other hand, such an objection cannot invalidate the emerging conclusion that it is precisely in the food processing industry that centralized, sector-encompassing labour unions have particularly good chances of obtaining political influence on government decisions. For the level of concertation in the Dutch labour union system is significantly lower than in the German one.

Conclusions

In the majority of the food processing industries under study, labour unions and collective bargaining systems have no significant influence on the development and the structure of the systems of business interests' representation. However, this finding neither is without exception nor can the possibility be excluded that conditions will change in the not-too-distant future. From the perspective of employees, there is an increasing need for a more effective articulation of their interests and there are also promising starting points concerning the realization of this need. If this need is perceived, the probability increases — as is shown by the example of the FRG — that employers will also intensify their efforts towards a concertation of their heterogeneous interests.

The need for a more effective articulation of employees' interests is due to the increased pressure for rationalization in food processing. This pressure, in its turn, is directly attributable to the increased pressure on the outlets and the raw material markets. Starting points for the realization of employees' interests follow from the numerous and usually subsector-specific regulations. The latter

---

[7] It is interesting to note in this context a slight undermining of the centralized bargaining system in Sweden (cf. Bengtsson et al. 1984). Because central negotiations were too long for metal employers, and because losses of output were threatening, which the branch could not afford for reasons of competition, a rapid, employee-friendly, however branch-specific wage agreement was concluded in 1983. Whereas in the German food processing industry the attempt is made to separate sector-specific from class-specific interests through the establishment of autonomous employers' associations, the development in the Swedish metal industry outlined above goes just in the opposite direction: in order to maintain the position of a branch in (international) competition, employers refrain from taking a hard line towards labour unions, but at the same time thus create precedents the realization of which is causing difficulties in other branches.

have a considerable importance in terms of competition policy for the groups and firms affected and require specific legitimation efforts, if only because of their implications in terms of health policy. If the labour unions succeed in achieving favourable collective agreements in exchange for supporting regulations which are favoured by individual branches, they can establish precedents for other subsectors. In order to guard against the rising flood of demands triggered off this way, it is functional and useful from the perspective of employers to establish an autonomous, independent and sector-encompassing employers' association.

These considerations, however, in no way lead to the conclusion that pressure for rationalization automatically entails an effective articulation and organization of employers' interests. The resistance against rationalization on the side of the unions is in no way and *per se* the cause of the corresponding efforts on the side of the employers. On the contrary, from the individual capitalist's perspective it seems more advantageous to first disregard the interests of employees. If necessary, the employer is always left with the possibility to threaten employees with making use of his power to invest and to direct his capital flow into other branches.[8] Employers only depend on collective cooperation with organized labour if they expect better production and distribution conditions to be the result of such a cooperation. This is most likely to happen when one labour union is predominating in the food processing industry and is using manifold formal and informal channels to influence state institutions and, in a heterogeneous collective bargaining system, finds itself confronted with a heterogeneous system of business interests' representation. In such an environment, labour unions are able to score successes through a strategy which deliberately combines collective bargaining issues with industrial policy matters. Thus, pressure for rationalization can only come into consideration as a cause for a more effective representation of employers' interests, if at the same time the state has a need and an interest to cooperate with labour unions and if the latter thus have the possibility to exert well-aimed pressure on particular capital fractions (e. g. subsectors, regional groups).

Provided that this complex interrelationship among the state, organized labour and the structure of business interest representation actually exists, there is an interesting possibility to formulate the theory of collective action somewhat more precisely: Offe/Wiesenthal (1980) speak of fundamental differences in the

---

[8] An interesting illustration in Britain is a firm called Hillsdown Holdings founded by two hoteliers which has been going round buying up bankrupt or near-bankrupt companies, or parts of companies, at very low prices (it is by now the largest meat processing firm). They have been quite ruthless in *cutting* workers' wages. For example, following their acquisition of the Telfers meat processing business, they cut shift premiums, overtime rates etc., to reduce average weekly earnings for hourly paid staff from £120 to £115. The workforce was reduced from 1,270 to 1,000, road transport was sub-contracted and the company pension scheme was scrapped. The unions (the TGWU and the bakers) simply had to accept it. As the TGWU district secretary commented, 'we could be in for a whole lot more'. No associational involvement; no nonsense about qualitative demands; no toleration of the union viewpoint — just unilateral action by the employer.

logic of collective action of capital and labour. Because capitalists can always resort to their power to invest, they do not depend as much on collective interest representation as do labour unions. As we have seen, however, the thesis of an asymmetry between capital and labour only applies in those cases where governmental decision-making bodies do not allow labour unions to influence industrial policies or where the labour unions do not dispose of sufficient power to bring their influence to bear in this special policy field. Actually, this might be the situation in Great Britain in particular. In countries, by contrast, where government cannot afford to neglect labour unions' demands, this not only strengthens the unions but at the same time also adds to the coordination and governing capacities of employers' associations. The opportunity for labour unions to influence public and industrial policy — i. e. 'to shift from markets to politics' (Korpi 1983: 76) — is both a force propelling labour unions to assume governing capacities as well as a force propelling employers in that direction.

To sum up it can be said that — quite in accordance with the innumerable other experiences of the labour movement in its struggle for the improvement of wages and working conditions — the effort for the unity of the labour union movement and for gaining political influence is in the centre of union strategies. In food processing, unity is hampered by the sectors' very heterogeneity. Given the legitimation need for subsector-specific regulations on the part of the state, the labour unions' aim to build up channels of political influence is comparatively easy to achieve. That labour union efforts for a higher level of concertation and coordination repay themselves, is illustrated by the concern of employers in Germany for the successful application of such a collective bargaining concept. This concern found expression in the establishment of an autonomous sector-encompassing employers' association.

Editor's note: Since this chapter was written, there has been a change in the organization of employers' interests in Britain. Following a merger of the Food and Drink Federation and the Food Manufacturers' Federation in January 1986, an information and advisory service to members is provided through the Industrial Relations Section of FDF Services.

Chapter 7

Occupational Structure and Employment in the Food Processing Industry

Helen Rainbird

Introduction

In Chapter 6 it was argued that low levels of unionization and industrial militancy in the food processing industry could be attributed in large part to the existence of a highly segmented labour force. That is to say, that the employment of large numbers of women, members of ethnic minority groups (migrant and/or resident), part-time and seasonal workers in jobs with poorer conditions and wages than those of their male counterparts has contributed in most countries to the absence of strong, unified organization representing the interests of labour in this industry. The consequence of this for business interest associability is that there has been only a limited development of employer organization functions. The aim of this chapter is to examine the empirical evidence for the existence of a segmented labour market through the analysis of occupational data.

Labour market segmentation represents a process of compartmentalization, whereby people who are otherwise comparable receive different rewards and encounter different opportunities for training and career advancement in the labour market. Ryan has distinguished two types of discrimination which occur; that which takes place before entry into the labour market, and that which takes place whilst individuals are active in the labour market (1981: 4). The concern of this chapter is not with the process of premarket discrimination, since this refers to the ways in which some groups entering the labour market are placed at a disadvantage as a result of their education, social class, gender or race. Rather, the concept of labour market segmentation will be examined as it refers to discrimination within the labour market, whereby existing inequalities are reinforced through occupational structures.

As indicated in Chapter 4, the food processing industry is characterized by its heterogeneity, both in products manufactured by the different sub-sectors and in the size of production units and the methods of production employed. The latter range from relatively unchanging artisanal forms of production based on craft skills — found particularly in sectors producing meat products and cheese — to capital-intensive plants introducing new technologies and employing a mix of skilled, semi-skilled and unskilled labour. The degree of concentration of ownership and the coexistence of family and cooperative enterprises alongside

multi-national corporations varies from one country to another and has important implications for the skill composition of the labour force.

The nature of skills used in the process of production is important in defining
wage rates, status and promotion prospects. Jobs which are defined as having a
low skill content are generally less well paid than more highly skilled ones,
though cohesive and militant union organization may effectively reduce differentials (Roberts et al., 1972). Whilst orthodox economic theory maintains that
inequality in the labour market simply reflects existing inequalities in the quality
of labour (that is to say, unskilled labour is low paid because it is worth little)
segmentation theory suggests that the labour market itself 'acquires an active role
in the generation of inequality and low pay' (Ryan, 1981: 6). Therefore, if we
examine why women tend to occupy low paid, unskilled jobs in the food
processing industry, then the explanation would partly rest on women's subordinate position in society and lack of access to the acquisition of skills, and partly
on the fact that low paid, unskilled jobs are considered as being appropriate for
women.

As indicated above, skill is an extremely difficult concept to define, yet crucial
to determining wage rates and the form taken by occupational hierarchies. There
has been considerable debate on the extent to which it denotes real technical
competence which is necessary to the process of production or is 'socially
constructed'. (See Wood, Ed., 1982.) The social construction of skill occurs
through workers acting to maintain a shortage of their skills (for example,
through demarcation agreements, the restriction of apprentice numbers) so that
they can command high wage rates. Management also socially constructs skill in
the interests of maintaining work discipline, through occupational structures and
through differential treatment. Whilst the women and ethnic minority workers
who make up much of the unskilled labour force in the food processing industry
are less likely to have the qualifications to acquire the technical competences
leading to skilled wage rates and status, they are also less able to socially
construct their skills in the same way as their male counterparts (cf. Beechey,
1982). The subordinate position of both these groups in society at large is
reflected in their lower rates of active participation in trade union hierarchies and
workplace organization. Furthermore, male trade unionists may seek to maintain differentials and exclude them from skilled trades (cf. Cockburn, 1983). As a
result, both these groups are less likely to pursue successful collective bargaining
strategies enabling them to socially construct their skills through their control of
the labour process. Where they do have technical competences equivalent in
terms of training to male white workers' skills, they are not recognized as
equivalents through the wages structure. As Phillips and Taylor argue:

> Far from being an objective economic fact, skill is often an ideological category imposed
> on certain types of work by virtue of the sex and power of the workers who perform it
> (1980: 79).

The food processing industry is characterized as a low skill industry with a
highly segmented labour force. This can be attributed, on the one hand, to the
low level of technical skills required to transform materials into finished pro-

ducts. On the other hand, employers also play an active role in shaping the structure of the labour force by showing preference in their recruitment and employment practices. The aim of this chapter is to examine patterns of differentiation in the labour force in food processing in the countries in our sample.

The Data

As might be expected, the analysis of the skill composition of the labour force in an industry is complicated by the interplay of socially constructed skills with technical competence. The classification of occupational structure is confused by a 'host of ambiguities' and job titles, which are often the only guide to skill content, may reflect 'little of the actual work content of the title holder' (Elias, 1985: 1). Moreover, there is evidence that cultural and institutional factors play an important role in determining the level of control workers can exercise over the labour process by virtue of their skills. This has been demonstrated in a comparative study of the introduction of computerized machine tools which found that companies introducing CNC in West Germany were more likely to be training and up-grading skills than companies introducing the same technology in Britain (Hartmann et al., 1983). For this reason, definitional problems of this complex concept are intensified when making comparisons between countries. Furthermore, the frequency and quality of data collection is not standardized. Where data is available across our sample of countries and is useful for comparative purposes, it has been drawn upon. Where it is not available across the full range of the sample, selective references have been made. Generally speaking, occupational data is not of high quality and the inadequacies of the data are compounded by a lack of comparable data sets. Therefore the shortcomings of the source material must be recognized from the outset.

Employment in the Food Processing Industry

The food processing industry is a large sector accounting for substantial employment in all countries. Table 7.1 shows the numbers in employment in each country. In all countries a sizeable proportion of the workforce is composed of women, ranging from approximately 40 per cent in Austria, FRG, Sweden and the UK to nearer 25 per cent in Canada and the Netherlands.

The general trend in employment has been towards a decline in overall levels, with some notable exceptions. Table 7.2 shows how between 1975 and 1982 employment declined in Austria, Italy, the Netherlands, Sweden and the UK. In contrast, Denmark, FRG and Canada experienced a slight growth in employment, whilst Swiss employment in the ISIC category (311–312) increased by almost 40 per cent.

These employment trends have affected men and women differentially. In Table 7.3 it can be seen that women's employment in the UK has declined in proportion to the general reduction in employment (13.1 per cent in the food and drink industry compared to an overall decline of 15.7 per cent in food processing and 13.1 per cent in drinks). As a result, the percentage of the labour force which is female has remained constant at 39 per cent. Sweden has also undergone a decline in the numbers of women employed, and they now form a marginally lower percentage (38 per cent) of the labour force than they did in 1975 (39 per cent). The remaining countries in the table have all experienced increases in female employment. In the case of FRG and Canada it has been substantial (19 and 24 per cent respectively) and has far exceeded increases in total employment. Since the Canadian figures refer to a shorter time span than the remaining countries in the sample, they reflect an even higher absolute rate of growth than the table suggests. The Dutch figures, in contrast, indicate a proportional growth in female employment whilst overall numbers of employees declined. Therefore, Table 7.3 suggests that in the two countries where female employment is lowest, there are moves towards an increasing number of women in the labour force. In the Netherlands there are indications that females are to some extent displacing male employees, whilst in the FRG not only are they displacing men but the expansion of employment in the industry (an increase of 45,000 employees between 1975 and 1982) is entirely accounted for by growing female employment.

It has often been suggested that women find employment in jobs and in sectors which reflect their activities in domestic labour in the home. Therefore, women are frequently to be found in the caring professions and jobs which involve serving, cleaning and food preparation. There are many jobs, for example, secretarial work, which are almost entirely female jobs and few men are employed in this capacity. Women tend to be employed in the service sector and are least well represented in manufacturing industry. Therefore, in order to examine the extent to which food processing has attracted a female labour force, it is necessary to make a comparison between female participation rates in this industry compared to manufacturing and employment as a whole. In Table 7.4 these rates are shown. In all countries for which statistics are available, female employment in food processing exceeds levels in manufacturing in general. In countries, such as the Netherlands, women's participation rates are lower in manufacturing than they are in the labour force as a whole. This reflects women's greater employment in the service sector. Women's higher participation rates in food processing than in manufacturing in general would suggest that women are actively recruited as employees in this sector.

It is not possible here to examine why female participation rates in the labour force vary so much from one country to another. However, since food processing does employ a relatively high proportion of women, this is one indication that segmentation is operating in the labour force. Of course, it could be that in the countries showing lower levels of female employment, that the secondary labour force is made up of other groups which are discriminated against in the labour market. Certainly in Canada many workers of Caribbean origin are employed, and in the Netherlands they are of Moroccan and Turkish origin. However, other countries in the sample, such as Switzerland, are also employers of immigrant labour in their food processing industries and this does not appear to have affected female participation rates.

The mere existence of a large proportion of female workers is not of itself indicative of the operation of a segmented labour market, but of the likelihood of its operation. In order to examine the ways in which women are discriminated against in the labour market in this industry, it is necessary to make a closer examination of occupational and skill structure and to analyse women's position within it. Comparison between countries (the statistics unfortunately are not available for a comprehensive comparative exercise) indicates that there is considerable variation in skill mix from one country to another.

A comparison of the skill structure of the German and Dutch food processing industries demonstrates that the former has a much larger skilled labour force due, undoubtedly, to the *Handwerk* system of craft training (cf. Doran, 1984). Table 7.5 shows that 35 per cent of workers in the German food processing industry are skilled as opposed to only 23.4 per cent in the Netherlands. In the Netherlands the majority of workers are semi-skilled whilst in the FRG there is a greater polarization between skilled and unskilled workers. In both countries the majority of women are unskilled workers. Over 50 per cent of male workers in the FRG are skilled, and though only 26.3 per cent are skilled in the Netherlands, a further 44.5 per cent are semi-skilled. This raises the question of whether higher levels of female employment in the FRG have had the effect of enhancing male worker's skill status and thus increasing differentials.

A breakdown of each of the skill categories by sex composition further reinforces the impression that segmentation is operating. Table 7.6 demonstrates that over 95 per cent of skilled jobs belong to men in both countries. Similar levels pertain to semi-skilled jobs in the Dutch food processing industry, though the proportion is lower in the FRG. In the FRG women form the majority of unskilled workers though in the Netherlands they do not. These figures would seem to support the view that in the absence of high levels of female employment in the Netherlands, immigrant workers may form the secondary labour force.

Further evidence of differences in the social organization of production between countries can be seen in Table 7.7. In this instance the structure of the non-manual labour force in the Netherlands and the FRG is shown. Whilst similar proportions of the labour force make up the categories of top management executives and other senior executives, in the FRG assistants form the greatest proportion of salaried employees whilst it is the clerical category in the Netherlands.

A more sophisticated breakdown of occupational structure, though not directly equivalent to the above data, is available for the UK. This further emphasizes the importance of cultural and institutional factors in shaping the types of skills attributed to the labour force and the way in which they are socially recognized. In Table 7.8 it can be seen that over 40 per cent of employment falls into the unskilled category 'other operatives'. Skilled occupations including engineering craftsmen and technicians account for less than 15 per cent of employees. This contrasts starkly with the 35.8 per cent of skilled workers in the German industry. Clearly, greater investment in training is responsible for this differential (cf. NEDO/MSC, 1984) as well as the greater currency of artisanal forms of production. As in the FRG and the Netherlands, women are greatly under-represented in the skilled categories of labour (Table 7.9). Where they do have skills and predominate in an occupation their skills are not recognized as equivalent to similar male skills through the wages structure.

In the foregoing paragraphs it has been established that women and immigrant workers form a secondary labour force in the food processing industry in a number of countries. Compared to other manufacturing industries women form a relatively large proportion of the labour force, but are generally to be found in jobs which are defined by their low skill content. In the introduction it was suggested that discrimination takes place both before entry and in the labour market. Once in the labour market several types of discrimination operate. Firstly, as outlined above, certain groups of workers will be directed towards particular categories of work which are classified as unskilled. In this, their access to initial training is important in determining their wages and future career development. Secondly, a point which has yet to be developed, is that workers who are discriminated against in the labour market will receive lower wages than others who perform the same or similar jobs. Thirdly, they may, by virtue of their subordinate position in society, be awarded secondary conditions of employment such as part-time or temporary employment. As such, these workers are most likely to lose their jobs in the event of redundancies.

In order to examine these three areas of discrimination it is necessary to consider data which is of only limited availability. Despite this shortcoming, it is possible to make some points of general applicability.

As would be expected, given the general skill level of women's employment in food processing, women's access to training leading to skill recognition is restricted. Table 7.10 shows that women's enrollment in the German *Handwerk* trades appropriate to this sector is considerably lower than men's. The major exception to this rule is in the category of small food traders and processors, where women predominate, suggesting that in occupations most closely linked to retail and thus involving a service element, women predominate.

Data on male and female wage rates for comparable jobs is not widely available and, supposedly, disparities do not exist in countries with Equal Pay legislation. Table 7.11 shows male and female wage rates for a series of occupations in the Canadian food processing industry. It demonstrates that women performing the same jobs as men generally receive a lower wage for the same work, sometimes as little as 55 per cent in the case of fish graders and driver-salespersons. In three noteworthy instances they receive more. Without further information on numbers in employment it is not easy to explain this anomaly, though it could be hypothesized that these are occupations in which few men are employed, thus depressing average male wage rates relative to female's.

Finally, women's dual role as workers and housewives means that they often prefer to work part-time, especially when they are also responsible for child care. Women's characteristic breaks in employment during child-bearing years nearly always result in a decline in employment status on their return to the labour force (Elias and Main, 1982). The lack of availability of more highly skilled jobs on a part-time employment basis means that they are forced to accept low paid, unskilled jobs. Table 7.12 shows that in the four countries for which data is available women work shorter hours than men, whilst in Table 7.13 it can be seen that 16 per cent of the labour force in the UK food processing industry is part-time, of whom the vast majority are women.

Conclusions

This chapter has examined occupational structure in the food processing industry with the aim of discovering if segmentation of the labour force operates. The findings suggest that women and members of ethnic minority groups are widely employed, and tend to fill the unskilled, lower paid jobs in the industry. In contrast, white male employees are to be found in the occupations designated as requiring more skill. There is evidence that these occupations do require the acquisition of greater technical competence than the majority of unskilled jobs but, nevertheless, men's monopolization of them is also indicative of their ability to 'socially construct' their skills.

The findings show considerable variation in occupational structures between countries and, in particular, the proportions of the labour force in skilled occupations. The continuity of craft traditions and skills in the FRG is an important factor in explaining the high proportion of skilled workers here. Unfortunately, insufficient data is available to develop more fully the analysis of historical, cultural and institutional factors affecting the composition of the workforce. However, it can be asserted that the heterogeneity of the industry, combined with the segmentation of the labour force has been a factor affecting the lack of unity in the organization of labour, since the instance in which there is a larger core of skilled labour — in the FRG — is also the instance in which a centrally coordinated union represents the entire food processing industry.

Table 7.1 Employment in Food Processing Industry (000s)

	Total	Male	Female	Female employment as % of total
Austria (1983)	106.0	62.2	43.7	41.2
Canada (1979)	219.4	156.9	62.5	28.4
FRG (1982)	747.0	429.0	318.0	42.5
Netherlands (1982)	133.0	100.0	33.0	24.8
Sweden (1982)	78.7	48.2	30.5	38.7
Switzerland (1982)	56.9	36.2	20.7	36.3
UK (1982)	479.0	274.0	205.0	42.7

Sources: Statistisches Handbuch für die Republik Österreich, 1984, p. 139. Statistics Canada, Employment and Payrolls Section: Employment, Earnings and Hours, 1979. (Survey of firms with 20 employees or more). ILO Yearbook of Labour Statistics, 1984, pp. 395–410. Statistical Abstract of Sweden, 1985, p. 188. NB. The statistics relate to the food and drink industry except for Austria, FRG and Sweden, which include tobacco as well. The inclusion of the tobacco industry tends to slightly underestimate the percentage of female employment in the rest of the food processing industry.

Table 7.2 Employment in Food, Drink and Tobacco Industry 1975–1982

ISIC[1]	1975	1982	% change
31 Austria	109.6	106.7	− 2.6
311–312 Denmark	51.2	54.0	+ 5.5
313	11.9	10.7	− 9.5
31 FRG	702.0	747.0	+ 6.4
311–312 Italy	139.5	114.6 (1981)	− 17.9
313	21.7	—	
311–312 Netherlands	150.0	133.0	− 11.4
313	17.0	11.0	− 35.3
311–312 Switzerland	40.9	57.0	+ 39.1
313	8.0	8.7	
311–312 Sweden	48.9	47.1	+ 7.9
313	4.2	3.0	− 3.6
311–312 UK	555.0	479.0	− 29.3
313	130.0	113.0	− 15.7
311–312 Canada	167.7	175.1	− 13.1
313	30.1	31.1	+ 4.4
			+ 3.3

Note: [1] ISIC category 31 represents food, drink and tobacco, ISIC 311–312 food manufacturing and 313 drink.
Source: ILO, Yearbook of Labour Statistics, 1984, pp. 370–410.

Table 7.3 Trends in Women's Employment Since 1975

	Total	1975 Female employment	%	Total	Female employment	%	% change
Austria	106.614	43.491	40.8 (1983)	106.000	43.672	41.2	+ 0.4
Canada	195.500	50.048	25.6 (1979)	219.400	62.310	28.4	+ 24.0
FRG	702.000	267.000	38.0 (1982)	747.000	318.000	42.5	+ 19.0
Netherlands	167.000	33.000	20.3 (1982)	144.000	34.000	23.6	+ 3.0
Sweden	83.621	32.913	39.3 (1982)	78.700	30.457	38.7	− 6.7
UK	685.000	268.000	39.1 (1982)	592.000	233.000	39.3	− 13.1

Sources: Statistisches Handbuch für die Republik Österreich, 1976, p. 299 and 1984 p. 139. Statistics Canada. Employment, Earnings and Hours, Dec. 1975 and Nov. 1979. (Survey of firms with 20 employees or more). ILO Yearbook of Statistics, 1984, pp. 399–410. Statistical Abstract of Sweden, 1981, p. 63 and 1985 p. 188.
NB. The statistics relate to the food and drink industry except for Austria, FRG and Sweden, which refer to tobacco as well.

Table 7.4 Percentage of Women Employees in Food Processing Compared to Overall Participation in the Labour Force

	Women as % of employment in food manufacturing[2]	Women as % of manufacturing employment[2]	Women as % of labour force[2]
Austria	41.2 (1984)	27.1 (1983)	32.2 (1983)
Canada	28.4 (1979)	27.9 (1981)	40.6 (1981)
FRG	42.5 (1982)	30.3 (1983)	34.6 (1983)
Netherlands	24.8 (1982)	16.8 (1981)	34.0 (1983)
Sweden	38.7 (1982)	26.4 (1980)	43.0 (1980)
Switzerland	36.3 (1982)	27.5 (1980)	34.4 (1980)
UK	42.7 (1982)	24.1[3] (1981)	40.0[3] (1981)

Notes: [1] For sources see Table 1. [2] All figures in these columns apart from UK from ILO Yearbook of Labour Statistics, 1984, pp. 19–42 and 54–72. [3] Eurostat. Labour Force Sample Survey, 1981, 1983, p. 89.

Table 7.5 Composition of Manual Labour Force in Food Processing (Full-time Employment)

NACE			Skilled	Semi-skilled	Unskilled	N = 100
	FRG					
411–423	Manufacture,	Male	54.3	27.7	17.9	100
	confectionery of	Female	3.2	13.1	83.7	100
	food products	Total	35.8	22.5	41.7	100
424–428	Drink industry	Male	72.1	12.7	15.3	100
		Female	3.4	18.6	78.0	100
		Total	65.4	13.2	21.4	100
	Netherlands					
411–423	Manufacture,	Male	26.3	44.5	29.2	100
	confectionery of	Female	4.3	18.5	77.3	100
	food products	Total	23.4	41.1	35.5	100
424–428	Drink industry	Male	21.0	41.5	37.5	100
		Female	.	24.0	65.1	100
		Total	20.7	40.9	38.4	100

Note: . Data relating to an undersized sample (less than 10 items) or for which the standard estimate of the mean equals or exceeds 10 %.
Source: Eurostat. Structure of Earnings: Principal Results, Vol. 7 BR Deutschland 1978/1979, and Vol. 6 Nederland, 1978/1979, pp. 34–37.

Table 7.6 Composition of Full-time Manual Labour Force by Percentage of Women

NACE			Skilled	Semi-skilled	Unskilled	Total
	FRG					
411–423	Manufacture,	Male	96.8	76.7	27.4	63.8
	confectionery of	Female	3.2	23.3	72.6	36.2
	food products	N = 100	70,387	44,122	81,977	196,486
424–428	Drink industry	Male	99.4	86.2	64.3	90.2
		Female	0.6	13.8	35.7	9.8
		N = 100	42,488	8,599	13,917	65,004
	Netherlands					
411–423	Manufacture,	Male	97.5	94.1	71.4	86.8
	confectionery of	Female	2.5	5.9	28.6	13.2
	food products	N = 100	17,735	31,138	26,881	75,753
424–428	Drink industry	Male	98.3	98.1	94.5	96.8
		Female	1.7	1.9	5.5	3.2
		N = 100	1,445	2,854	2,675	6,974

Sources: Eurostat: Vol. 7 BR Deutschland, 1978/79, pp. 34–37.
Eurostat: Vol. 6 Nederland, 1978/79, pp. 34–37.

Table 7.7 Composition of Non-manual Labour Force in Food Processing

NACE		1	2	3	4	5	N = 100
	FRG						
411–423	Manufacture, confectionery of food products	4.0	14.6	44.3	28.2	8.6	84,566
424–428	Drink industry	4.1	14.1	54.3	20.1	7.3	32,045
	Netherlands						
411–423	Manufacture, confectionery of food products	4.0	14.6	14.2	52.0	14.3	38,188
424–428	Drink industry	2.0	16.4	19.4	42.1	19.8	5,156

1. Top Management Executives. 2. Other Senior Executives. 3. Assistants. 4. Clerical. 5. Supervisors.
Sources: Eurostat Vol. 7, BR Deutschland, pp. 312–315.
Eurostat Vol. 6, Nederland, pp. 312–315.

Table 7.8 Occupational Structure in the UK Food Processing Industry, 1981[a]

	Revised WOC	Food & Drink
1.	Managers and administrators	4
2.	Education professions	0[b]
3.	Health, welfare professions	0
4.	Other professions	3
5.	Literary, artistic, sports occupations	0
6.	Engineers, scientists etc.	2
7.	Technicians, draughtsmen	1
8.	Clerical occupations	8
9.	Secretarial occupations	2
10.	Sales representatives	3
11.	Other sales occupations	3
12.	Supervisors	1
13.	Foremen	5
14.	Eng. craft occupations (module)	4
15.	Eng. craft occupations (non-module)	1
16.	Construction craft occupations	1
17.	Other craft occupations	0
18.	Skilled operatives	6
19.	Other operatives	43
20.	Security occupations	1
21.	Skilled personal service occupations	2
22.	Other personal service occupations	4
23.	Other occupations	5
24.	Armed forces	0
25.	Inadequately described occupations	0
1.—25.	All occupations	100[c]
Notes: see p. 148		n = 61,598

Table 7.9 Composition of the Labour Force by Occupation and Gender in the UK Food Processing Industry, 1981[a]

	Revised WOC	Food & Drink		
		% males	% females	n = 100
1.	Managers and administrators	88	12	3,012
2.	Education professions	55	45	139
3.	Health, welfare professions	36	64	135
4.	Other professions	84	16	1,801
5.	Literary, artistic, sports occupations	11	89	300
6.	Engineers, scientists etc.	94	6	1,013
7.	Technicians, draughtsmen	78	22	569
8.	Clerical occupations	25	75	4,853
9.	Secretarial occupations	1	99	1,290
10.	Sales representatives	92	8	1,928
11.	Other sales occupations	52	48	2,025
12.	Supervisors	43	57	515
13.	Foremen	81	19	3,240
14.	Eng. craft occupations (module)	99	1	2,635
15.	Eng. craft occupations (non-module)	100	0	475
16.	Construction craft occupations	98	2	468
17.	Other craft occupations	96	4	117
18.	Skilled operatives	74	26	3,980
19.	Other operatives	56	44	25,892
20.	Security occupations	98	2	357
21.	Skilled personal service occupations	59	41	1,285
22.	Other personal service occupations	25	75	2,384
23.	Other occupations	78	22	2,900
24.	Armed forces	0[b]	0	0
25.	Inadequately described occupations	61	39	285
1.—25.	All occupations	37,767	23,831	61,598

Notes: [a] Figures of employees and self-employed are based on a 10 per cent sample of the 1981 Census of Population. [b] 0 = less than .5 per cent.

Notes to table 7.8: [a] Figures of employees and self-employed are based on a 10 per cent sample of the 1981 Census of Population. [b] 0 = less than .5 per cent. [c] Due to rounding, figures may not add up to 100.

Table 7.10 Canada. Average Wage Rates for Women and Men in Similarly Described Occupations in Food Processing, 1981

SIC classifications	Women	Men	Women's wage as % of male wage
Industry and Occupation			
Slaughtering & meat processing			
Boner, meat	9.22	10.15	90.8
Butcher	9.23	9.66	95.5
Packager, hand	9.28	9.32	99.6
Sausage tier	9.72	9.11	106.7
Dairy factories			
Dairy helper	305ʷ/h	358ʷ/h	85.2
Food tester	330ʷ/h	352ʷ/h	93.8
Packages, machine	9.03	7.95	113.6
Packer, liquid	345ʷ/h	359ʷ/h	96.1
Fish products			
Fish cleaner & cutter	9.27	7.96	116.5
Fish processing machine feeder	7.76	9.00	86.2
Freezer washer	6.07	9.65	62.9
Grader, fish	6.07	10.91	55.6
Packager, hand	7.72	10.01	77.1
Bakeries			
Baker, helper	7.76	9.30	83.4
Baker, sweet goods	6.36	8.45	75.3
Driver — salesperson	209ʷ/h	392ʷ/h	53.3
Oven person	6.61	9.09	72.7
Packager	7.41	8.87	83.5
Soft drinks			
Machine-tender crew	7.92	9.28	85.3
Packer, liquid	339ʷ/h	360ʷ/h	94.2

Note: ʷ/h = weekly wages. Otherwise hourly wages are reported.
Source: Labour Canada, Women's Bureau. Women in the Labour Force, Part 2.

Table 7.11 Trainees in Handwerk Trades in the Federal Republic of Germany: Food Industry

	Total	Male	Female	% Female
Baker, confectionery	28,479	26,584	1,895	6.6
Butcher	20,897	20,777	120	0.1
Cook	16,507	14,058	2,449	14.8
Small food traders and processors	31,414	222	31,192	99.3

Source: European Centre for the Development of Vocational Training (CEDEFOP) Training and Labour Market Policy Measures for the Vocational Promotion of Women in the Federal Republic of Germany, 1982.

Table 7.12: Hours of Work Per Week

	1981		1982		1983	
	Male	Female	Male	Female	Male	Female
FRG[1]	44.5	40.6	44.3	40.2	43.9	40.2
Netherlands	41.3*	40.1	41.1*	40.1	41.2*	40.1
UK	44.8	38.1	44.9	38.4	45.3	39.0
Austria[2]	n. a.	n. a.	n. a.	n. a.	37.8	34.9

Notes: [1] Figures refer to ISIC 31 (food, drink and tobacco). Where marked * they refer only to ISIC 311–312 (food and drink). [2] Figures based on quarterly 1 per cent census. Statistisches Handbuch für die Republik Österreich, 1984.
Source: ILO Yearbook of Statistics, Geneva, 1984, pp. 559–572.

Table 7.13 Part-time Employees in the UK Food Processung Industry: September 1981

Industry	Females				Males				Total
	F-T	%	P-T	%	F-T	%	P-T	%	N = 100
Food, drink and tobacco	175.0	26	99.2	15	385.7	58	9.2	1	669.3

Source: Department of Employment, Census of Employment Final Results for September 1981. Employment Gazette, December 1983, Volume 91, No. 12. Occasional Supplement No. 2.

Chapter 8

Agricultural Policy and the Associations of the Food Processing Industry

William D. Coleman

Agricultural policy is one of the most visible and controversial policy arenas in the body politic in most Western European countries and in North America. Discussion and debate over the Common Agricultural Policy (CAP) in the European Economic Community, over the role of marketing boards in Canada and the United States, and over what to do with agricultural surpluses described variously as 'butter mountains' and 'wine lakes' occur almost daily. The poignancy of the issues derives from the fact that the state has intervened directly and extensively into the agricultural economy spending huge sums of money. The three subsectors of the food processing industry that are central to the studies in this book — meat and meat products, dairy products, and processed fruits and vegetables — are all close to the farm gate. Most of their basic raw materials are purchased directly from agricultural producers. As a result, agricultural policies have affected their operation in fundamental ways. The subsectors have responded by seeking a greater say in the formulation of these policies and even a role in administering them. Such responses have been coordinated largely by the business interest associations representing the subsectors in the various countries. In the course of assuming these roles, the associations have themselves changed as organizations. Less traditional pressure groups, they have assumed governing capacities speaking to the new role of interest associations increasingly found in Western liberal democracies. The task of this chapter then is to outline the impact of agricultural policy on the organization and activities of business interest associations in the food processing industry.

More specifically, agricultural policy will be shown to have had contradictory effects on the 'organizational development' (Schmitter and Streeck, 1981) of food processing business associations. On the one hand, extensive regulation of the prices of agricultural products and in some countries of their supply has created opportunities for food processing associations to acquire status and to become extensively involved in both the making of policy and its implementation in the food processing industry. As private associations coming to perform some public functions, these associations have become more developed in the sense of increasing their autonomy from their members and becoming more of a neutral intermediary between the state and the sector.

On the other hand, agricultural policy in all of the countries in the study has often been organized differently depending on the commodity involved. This sub-division of policy by commodity has had the further effect of placing the subsectors of the food processing industry in different policy arenas. To the extent that this has occurred, food processing subsectors have become more closely tied with the corresponding group of farmers and less closely tied to one another. Depending on the degree of vertical and horizontal integration in the overall system of business interest associations, this partitioning of the industry will have a variable impact on organizational development. Associational systems that are well-integrated across major divisions of the economy will be able to minimize the damage to the organizational development to food processing associations. On the other hand, associational systems that are not well-integrated will leave the way open for serious problems in the way of coordination of action across subsectors in the food processing industry.

The contradictory forces on associations in the sector resulting from agricultural policy, some pushing toward development and some pushing against it, have both practical and theoretical implications. Practically speaking, the organization of business interest associations that is found places real constraints on the extent to which policies can be sector-wide in the food processing sector. In a theoretical vein, the opposing forces on the associations suggest a result that is different than from what might be expected according to some hypotheses about associational development. For example, Schmitter (1982, 1983) suggests a mode of interest intermediation is composed of two structures. A mode includes first of all, structures of representation, the patterns of organization in the associational system, which vary from 'pluralist' to 'corporatist'. Second, a mode is composed of structures of control; to wit, the relationships between associations and the state. These are seen by Schmitter to range from 'pressure' politics (associations are not involved formally in policy formulation and implementation) to 'concertation' (associations are so involved). The hypothesis is that associations drawn into concertation relations with the state will develop corporatist structures of representation and that those in pressure type relations will foster pluralist representation structures. Other combinations such as concertation and pluralist representation are felt to be less likely and inherently unstable. What is anomalous then about food processing associations, is that in several countries, this very combination of pluralist structures of representation coexisting with concertative relationships not only occurs with some regularity but also appears to be quite stable.

The argument in this chapter is presented in the following manner. First, the concept of organizational development is briefly discussed and then a general scheme for summarizing agricultural policy and the expected relationships between components of the schema and organizational development is presented. These concepts are then used for an analysis of agricultural policy and business interest associations in four states outside the European Economic Community — Austria, Canada, Sweden and Switzerland and for the EEC using examples drawn from the United Kingdom, West Germany and The Netherlands. The chapter concludes with a discussion of the theoretical implications of the contradictory effects of agricultural policy on the organizational development of business associations referred to above.

Organizational Development and Agricultural Policy

As it is presented in the introductory chapter of this book, the concept of the organizational development of associations refers to two aspects of associative action. First, it involves the capacity of associations and systems of associations to coordinate and organize a complex range of activity. Schmitter and Streeck (1981) argue that associations that have broad and inclusive domains in terms of product, territory and function and that possess structures through which associations and associational systems are integrated with one another, will be more capable of coordinating activity. Hence they are understood to be more developed. In such instances then, one expects to find peak associations integrating vertically the activities of first-order, direct membership associations in the sector and perhaps, well-institutionalized, regular horizontal ties among the associations. In Schmitter's terms (1982), associations and associational systems that are developed in this sense are said to have a 'corporatist' structure of representation.

Second, developed associations will have achieved a position of strategic interdependence between the state and their members, a certain measure of autonomy from both (Streeck and Schmitter, 1984). In order to gain such a status, associations need to have a certain symmetry in the sources of their resources: some being drawn from their members, some from the state and some from other environments such as trade unions or, in the instance of agricultural policy, farmers. In addition, the associations will have achieved an effective monopoly as intermediaries for a given sector or subsector. Critical in this process would appear to be the delegation of certain privileges from the state to the associations: guaranteed access to policy-making, the provision of institutionalized forums for the participation of associations in policy formulation and the assignment of certain aspects of policy for implementation by associations. Associations that are developed in this sense are said to be engaged in a 'concertative' relationship with the state (Schmitter, 1982).

How might the notion of organizational development be related to agricultural policy? Agricultural policy is a very broad concept and it is beyond our capacity to discuss the whole of what it entails in this chapter. Rather, we shall confine our discussion to those aspects of agricultural policy that take the form of economic regulation, that is the regulation of prices, rates of return, entry and output in an industry (Stanbury and Lermer, 1983). This subset of agricultural policy has been particularly critical to the organization of business interests in the food processing industry.

Agricultural policy in this more restricted sense can be disaggregated into several components each of which having an impact upon organizational development.

1. *Level of Government.* If the national government is primarily responsible for price and supply, national associations will be encouraged. If regional or local governments have this responsibility, regional or local associations will be strengthened. The presence of strong and autonomous regional associations will make the coordination of interests in the sector more difficult, and hence will hamper organizational development. If the responsibility lies with a supra-national government, coordination may be encouraged on the national plane in response to nationalist pressures.
2. *Mode of Price Determination.* If the price is fixed by government, organizational development will be encouraged through the formal involvement of associations in consultations on the appropriate level. If the price is fixed by farmers' organizations through a delegation of authority by the state, development will still be encouraged through the official recognition of food processors' associations as consultants. If the price is negotiated by interested parties (farmers, processors, consumers), organizational development may be promoted through official recognition of the parties to the process. Finally, if price is determined by market forces, no particular incentive to organizational development will occur.
3. *Type of Price Affected.* The price regulated may be that for the raw agricultural products, the wholesale price or the retail price of processed products. Greater associational coordination will be encouraged in the latter two cases because a larger range of interests will need to be involved.
4. *Determination of Supply.* If supply of raw agricultural products is determined by government agencies or farmers' organizations, food processing associations are likely to receive some formal status as consultants to the decision. Similarly, if supply is controlled through the regulation of imports, food processing associations are likely to be formally recognized participants in the decision. If supply is determined by market forces, further organizational development of food processing business associations will not be encouraged.

A. Dairy Products

The regulatory systems in place for both consumers' milk and manufactured dairy products are arguably the most developed and restricting in the whole food processing sector. Generally speaking, the price of milk paid to dairy farmers is fixed by the government or its delegate for the nation as a whole. Supplies of dairy products are tightly controlled using import controls, internal production quotas, and agreements which fix lines of supply between producers and processors. Accordingly, associations representing dairy processing firms have advanced furthest in acquiring governing capacities — the ability to control their members' behaviour through the assumption of state-certified responsibilities.

Although this is the general pattern found in our group of countries, several variations in the conduct of associative action may be identified. Furthermore, the use of private governments in the various states differs in some cases between the consumers' milk and the manufactured dairy products subsectors. We turn then first of all to consider the regulations and association responses in the area of consumers' milk. The seven countries in this chapter fall into four groups: Austria and Sweden, Switzerland and The Netherlands, Canada and The United Kingdom and West Germany.

Austria and Sweden are distinguished by the fact that associational involvement in agricultural policy is subsumed into the more general, society-wide corporatist policy networks found in those countries. Accordingly, the associations involved tend to be the national peak associations for business and labour and not sector-specific associations as will be the case in the other countries. In both countries, prices are set for the country as a whole. In Austria, the price paid to producers and the retail price are fixed (Traxler, 1983 a) while in Sweden, it is the wholesale price that is controlled (Pestoff, 1983). In both cases, the price is fixed by the government following consultation and negotiation with associations. In Austria, four groups are officially represented in this process (Traxler, 1983 a: 3–4): *Präsidentenkonferenz der Landwirtschaftskammern* (farmers), *Bundeswirtschaftskammer* (business), *Österreichischer Arbeiterkammertag* (workers).

The Swedish pattern for price setting varies a little from the Austrian case. Prices are set following formal, semi-annual price 'consultations'. These discussions are conducted between delegations of consumers and of farmers under the supervision of a state agency, the Agricultural Marketing Board. Unlike the Austrian case, the consumers delegation is not solely composed of trade unions but contains four members of parliament representing 'political' interests, representatives from wholesalers and food processors as well as four members from trade unions. The farmers delegation is really itself a combined delegation of farmers and processors because the producer cooperatives, whose association participates in these discussions, are the dominant force in the dairy processing industry (Pestoff, 1983: 11).

In both countries as well, separate quasi-public agencies have been created and delegated responsibility by the state for managing the supply of milk. In Austria, it is the *Milchwirtschaftsfonds* which is composed of the same four parties that were noted above as participating in the price negotiations (Traxler, 1983 a). In Sweden, a dairy price regulation association exists. As was the case in price negotiations, membership in the Swedish association is more varied than that found in Austria: its nine members include three nominated by the state, three from the producer cooperative movement including the branch associations responsible for dairy, one from the consumer cooperatives, and two from the private milk industry (Pestoff, 1983: 70). One of the government nominees is usually a representative from the trade unions. Business associations thus dominate the management of supply more in Sweden than in Austria where labour receives parity representation.

The extent of regulation of price and supply of consumers' milk is as extensive in Switzerland and the Netherlands as that found in Sweden and Austria. In both countries, the price paid to farmers for raw milk and the retail price are fixed. Competition is controlled by laying down which farmers sell to which processors and supply is managed through import controls. In both countries, the use of these policy instruments has led to the development of governing capacities by associations. The key difference is that these capacities have accrued to associations specific to the dairy sector rather than being absorbed by wider structures of interest intermediation.

In both Switzerland and Holland, the system of regulations is handled by state-recognized boards manned by private interest associations. In Switzerland the price of milk paid to farmers which determines all other prices is fixed by the *Bundesrat* following the advice of an expert commission. This expert commission includes association representatives of farmers, processors, wholesalers, retailers and consumers. The price regulations as well as measures controlling supply are administered by the Central Association of Swiss Milk Producers (ZVSM) which receives its authority from the state in Article 10 of the Milk Regulations attached to the federal law for promotion of agriculture and preservation of a *Bauernstand* (Farago et al.: 51).

In Holland, the farmers do not have as pre-eminent a position. The system there is managed by a special statutory trade association for the Dutch Dairy industry. This association is a vertical *Produktschap Zuivel* embracing the complete dairy sector from the dairy farmers to the retailers (van Waarden, 1983: 29). It devises rules for prices paid to farmers for milk and for retail prices.

The Canadian and British systems are similar to the previous two in that they involve associations specific to the sector and not more general peak associations. They differ as well in several respects. First, price negotiations are decentralized. In Britain, separate negotiations take place in England and Wales, in Scotland and in Northern Ireland. In Canada, consumers milk is understood to be a provincial responsibility. Second, in both countries, farmer-controlled marketing boards play a central role. For example, in England, the Minister of Agriculture sets the maximum retail price for consumers milk until the mid 1980s. With a few small exceptions, all farmers are required to sell their milk to the Milk Marketing Board. The Minister also sets the maximum wholesale price at which the board sells product to processors of consumers milk and to distributors. This leaves the MMB to make a decision about the prices to be paid to farmers for their milk, whilst, as we shall see below, the prices to be paid for individual uses of manufacturing milk are negotiated.

In Canada, prices for consumers milk are set by farmer-controlled marketing boards in each province. Like the British case, the major partners in the price-setting process are the farmers and processors. The explicit representation of consumer interests whether through trade unions, retailers or consumers groups that is found in the previous four countries does not occur.

In the Canadian case as well, there is additional cause for the organizational development of associations because of the use of policy instruments for controlling supply. In addition to the usual power of being able to tell farmers and processors who should buy from whom, the milk marketing boards have the power to tell farmers how much milk they can produce. The boards levy heavy fines when farmers exceed their quotas. In order to determine the total amount of milk that should be produced, the marketing boards are normally required by law to consult with the provincial processors' associations thereby affording these groups an additional public status (Coleman, 1984).

Finally, in the West German case, the prices for consumers milk are directly set by the market while being influenced by the intervention prices for butter and skim milk powder set by the European Economic Community. This topic brings us to the subject of manufacturing milk as a policy area.

The regulatory systems and therefore opportunities for growth of private interest governments vary somewhat for manufactured dairy products. In Sweden, the processes are identical to ones already described. In Austria, aside from the fact that prices are set by the four parties noted through their membership on the semi-autonomous Paritätische Kommission and not by the minister the system functions the same. The differences are more substantial in Switzerland. In effect, milk products there fall into three classes: butter, cheese, and other remaining products. In the latter, admittedly smallest, group, price and supply are largely determined by market forces although manufacturers all pay the same price to the farmers for their raw milk.

In contrast, butter and cheese are strictly controlled through the use of authorized private organizations. The Swiss Käse-union is the regulatory agency in the cheese industry. It is composed essentially of associations representing three groups: dairy farmers, cheese manufacturers, and cheese exporters (Farago et al.: 54). This organization sets the prices of the cheese, supervises its quality and actively promotes Swiss cheese on the internal and export markets. The companion organization for butter is BUTYRA, in law a cooperative. It administers a strong system of import controls which essentially close the Swiss market to outsiders. As one of several members of BUTYRA, processors' associations have a share in the public power delegated to it (Farago et al.: 56).

The Canadian case also differs for dairy products. The price of industrial milk is set by the provincial marketing boards based on intervention prices for butter and skim milk powder that the federal government through an agency called the Canadian Dairy Commission offers the processors for purchasing excess produce. Unlike consumers' milk then, the real power over industrial milk lies with the federal government. The supply of industrial milk is set by an organization called the Canadian Milk Supply Management Committee which is composed of representatives of the provinces and of the provincial marketing boards with the processors' associations given ex officio, nonvoting membership (Coleman, 1984). The involvement then of processors in industrial milk policy is somewhat less than in consumers' milk. Farmers organizations dominate more completely.

The most important difference in the area of manufacturing milk from consumers' milk for Britain, Germany and the Netherlands is that it is regulated by the European Economic Community. Generally speaking, in a commodity regime set up under the Common Agricultural Policy, three prices are used (Harris et al., 1983: Ch. 3):

1. *Target Price.* This price is the internal wholesale price, which, given normal marketing circumstances (which seldom occur in agriculture), would be obtainable.

2. *Threshold Price*. This is the minimum entry price set for imports so that target prices cannot be undercut by third country imports.
3. *Intervention Price*. This is the price that national intervention agencies are to pay for designated products. Because processors can always take advantage of this intervention price, it has an indirect effect upon the rest of the market for milk products.

The specific commodity regime for milk that has been in place since 1968 has two potentially contradictory objectives: ensuring a satisfactory income for milk producers and finding a balance between supply and demand for milk products. These objectives are pursued using the following instruments. A target price is fixed for milk of 3.7 % fat content delivered to the dairy. Intervention prices are then set for butter and skimmed milk powder at a level to ensure that the farmer receives close to the target price for milk. Finally, threshold prices are set for twelve different groups of milk products. These prices, in effect, determine the ceiling for EC internal market prices for these products. Imports coming in under the threshold price are taxed. In order to manage supply, particularly of butter and milk powder where intervention buying is open, export subsidies are paid, support is given for utilizing milk powder as animal feed, subsidies are paid on consumer butter sales and grants are given to processors for improving their storage capacity.

Room for maneuver at the national association level is somewhat constrained by these EC policies. Processors associations are afforded opportunities for acting as private governments primarily in the implementation of the policy. When it comes to policy formulation their primary activity is one of lobbying. The key operating agency for the CAP is the Commission of the European Communities. Under the Commission are a series of Management Committees for each commodity regime, ten specialist committees and finally Advisory Committees which parallel the management committees. The Management and specialist committees have as their members representatives from the Agricultural Departments of the member countries. The Advisory Committees are staffed by industry associations which must be organized at the European level. These are dominated by producers: 50 % of members are from the farmers and producers cooperatives associations, 25 % are representatives of consumers and trade unions, 25 % from wholesalers, retailers, consumers cooperatives and processors (Kirchner and Schwaiger, 1981: 51 ff). National processors associations are left with the task of lobbying their own Agriculture departments to develop positions in their favour and of providing input for their respective government representatives on the management committees.

In terms of acting as a private interest government, the most important venue for national processors' associations is the negotiation of manufacturing milk prices. The central issues in these negotiations are determining farmers' costs and the margin to be enjoyed by the processors. In the United Kingdom, these negotiations take place in England in a Committee composed of the Dairy Trades Federation (processors) and the Milk Marketing Board which purchases all the raw milk (with minor exceptions) from the farmers (Grant, 1983 b,

1983 c). In the Netherlands, the negotiations take place under the auspices of the statutory trade association of the dairy system.

The EC policy in addition creates problems for the integration of associative action in the food processing industry. As Harris et al. (1983: 247) note, divisions are created between first and second stage processors. First stage processors (such as dairy processors) who manufacture intervention products have a joint interest with farmers in seeking higher intervention prices. They have, after all, a guaranteed outlet and fixed margins. Second stage processors (such as dairy processors) find themselves caught between the high prices resulting from the CAP that protect farmers and first stage processors and the highly competitive retail market (see this chapter below). Furthermore, the complexity of the regulations discriminates against small firms (Harris et al., 1983: 249). Only the large firms can afford the resources to master the detail of EC policy. Smaller firms are forced to rely on associations or government departments which provide them with information that is less timely and specific than that gathered by large firms. This difference sets the stage for conflict between small and large firms in associations over the development of association personnel and resources.

B. Meat Products

As was the case in the milk sector, agricultural regulation in the meat processing industry differs depending on the type of meat involved. In this section of the chapter, three meat types will be considered: beef and veal, pigmeat and poultrymeat. The regulatory systems in place for these three products suggest that the seven countries in the study be divided into three groups:

1. Austria, Switzerland and Sweden — extensive regulation of beef and veal, and pigmeat and high associational development.
2. Canada — extensive regulation of poultrymeat and moderate associational development.
3. The EEC countries: Britain, Germany, the Netherlands — extensive regulation of beef and veal, moderate regulation of pigmeat, slight regulation of poultrymeat and little associational development.

In each of Austria, Sweden and Switzerland, the prices for beef and veal and pigmeat are essentially fixed. In Austria, the federal minister has relinquished his competence over meat pricing to the *Länder* authorities with the result that different price regimes are found in different regions. In some regions, the price paid to producers is the object of policy and in others both the producer price and the consumer price is regulated. Similar to milk, the wholesale price is fixed in Sweden. In Switzerland, it is the price paid to producers. In all three countries, supply is controlled through levies on imports and through intervention agents buying up and storing excess produce. In each case as well, the control over implementation of the policy has been delegated to para-state agencies run by interest associations with meat processors' associations included.

The system in Sweden is identical to that described for milk with associations being involved in semi-annual price negotiations and being members of price regulation associations (Pestoff, 1983). The Austrian system also parallels that found in milk. A special agency, the *Vieh- und Fleischkommission*, is responsible for administering the price systems, for approving imports and exports, for imposing import and export quotas and for concluding purchasing agreements with processing firms (Traxler, 1983 b: 39). This body has twelve members, 3 from the farmers chamber, 3 from the industry chamber and 6 from the two dominant trade unions — the same quadripartite structure found in the milk subsector.

In Switzerland, somewhat similar to the case of butter, a para-state cooperative, the *Genossenschaft für Schlachtvieh- und Fleischversorgung (GSF)*, is the key player in the system. A target or *Richtpreis* is set by the *Bundesrat* on the advice of the GSF, the Expert Committee on Meat and the Agricultural Advisory Commission. This price is set to ensure that farmers can meet their costs and receive a stable income. This target price serves as a guide to the GSF which sets an intervention price *(Übernahmepreis)* at which it will buy meat if no buyers are found. In fact only a minor portion of the meat goes through the GSF with most being sold directly by producers to meat packers and butchers (Senti, 1979). However, the intervention price of the GSF in effect sets the minimum price that farmers will obtain for their product. The GSF is composed of producers (9 votes), slaughterers (3), butchers and wholesale distributors (6) and consumers (2). In practice, the producers are counterbalanced by a coalition of the slaughterers, butchers and distributors thereby giving consumer organizations a crucial deciding role (Farago et al., 1984: 257 ff).

In Canada, the markets for beef and veal and for pigmeat are essentially open and unregulated (Coleman, 1984). The association that represents this subsector, the Canadian Meat Council, thus assumes no public functions in this policy area. However, the poultry industry which is more important in Canada than it is in most European countries (Harris et al., 1983: 84) is highly controlled. Prices paid to producers are fixed by provincial, farmer-controlled marketing boards in a system that parallels that described earlier for consumers' milk. The marketing boards also assign production quotas to individual farmers and purchasing quotas to processing firms. The overall supply is determined by two federal agencies, the Canadian Chicken Marketing Agency and the Canadian Turkey Marketing Agency which are in effect confederations of the provincial marketing boards. The same agencies also administer import quotas that are used to protect Canadian producers from American competition.

The adoption of this system of supply management has increased the public status of the processors' association, the Canadian Poultry and Egg Processors Council. Prior to the introduction of supply-management, this association was run by an employee of a large chicken processing firm out of his basement in his spare time. A decade later, the association employs five people, is an official adviser to the agencies controlling supply and is consulted regularly, albeit informally, on pricing.

In the CAP of the EEC, beef and veal production are almost as highly regulated as milk. A guide price is fixed each year for live animals and calves which is in turn supported by an intervention price. Although the system is quite complex, national intervention agencies are obliged to purchase specified categories of beef (Harris et al.: 110). In addition subsidies are available to processors for improving their own private storage facilities, import levies are used and export refunds are paid. In contrast, for pigmeat the instruments are more restricted and include the use of import levies, export refunds and aids to private storage schemes. In the poultry meat industry, only import levies are used. All of this policy is formulated and implemented at the European level by the Commission drawing upon its Management and Advisory committees. The evidence available (Grant, 1983 b; Hilbert, 1983) shows national meat processing associations in EEC countries assuming no public functions in the area of agricultural price regulation.

C. Fruit and Vegetables Processing

Generally speaking the agricultural regulation of fruits and vegetables is the least extensive of the three commodities being studied in this chapter. Among our seven countries, significant organizational development of processors' associations occurs in only three: Austria, Switzerland, and Canada. There is moderate regulation of prices and supply in these three countries as there is in the EC under the Common Agricultural Policy. However, as we have seen above, EC agricultural regulation creates opportunities for organizational development more for associations at the EC level than for national processors' associations. Finally, in Sweden, there is no agricultural regulation of fruits and vegetables.

Among the three more regulated countries, prices for raw fruits and vegetables are either fixed or negotiated in cartel-like fashion. In addition, three phase import regimes are used to control supply: in the first phase, imports are unrestricted (off season); in the second, imports are permitted only to cover requirements not satisfied by domestic sources; in the third, no imports are permitted because domestic needs are satisfied by internal production (peak of the harvest) (Rieder and Egger, 1983: 376).

The assumption of public functions by associations is most developed in Switzerland. Both the Swiss Fruit Association (SOV) and the Swiss Vegetable Union (SGU) have comprehensive vertical domains that include producers, processors and distributors (Farago et al.: 176). The associations are able then to coordinate price agreements between producers and processors (Rieder and Egger: 376). Unlike the milk and meat sectors, the Export Commission (*Fachausschuß*) which advises the Agriculture Ministry is also the body which regulates imports through the three phase system. Virtually all of its recommendations in this area are carried out by the state. This Expert Commission is effectively controlled by the SOV and SGU (Farago et al.: 264). Its chairman is always the adminstrative head of one of the two associations. Similar then to the milk and meat sectors, private interest associations essentially run agricultural regulation of fruit and vegetables in Switzerland.

Association involvement is more circumscribed in both Austria and Canada. In Austria, agreements on price are negotiated between individual firms and domestic producers. These agreements are normally preceded by negotiations of a target selling price between the relevant sections of the Agricultural and Industry Chambers. The target price is treated as a recommendation and is not always the same as the actual price paid (Traxler, 1983 b: 50). Decisions to liberalize or restrict imports are taken by the Agricultural and Forests Ministry after discussions with the Chamber organization.

The system differs somewhat in Canada. Similar to the other subsectors in Canada, the principal actors are farmer-controlled, provincial marketing boards. In 1980, there were 22 vegetable marketing boards and commissions (Prescott, 1980: 11). Where these three boards exist, farmers are required by law to sell all their produce to them. Some boards then are empowered to fix the price of the goods for selling to processors while others negotiate the prices with processors. Only in the latter case, do processors' associations become involved. They are recognized under the law as the 'official' representatives of the processing firms in the negotiations. Unlike the milk and poultry boards in Canada, the fruit and vegetable boards have no powers over supply. In those instances where the boards are not able to supply processors with raw products, processors import what they need and apply to have the duty remitted. These applications are prepared jointly by the national processors' and producers' associations and virtually always are approved by the government.

Under the CAP, separate arrangements exist for fresh and for processed fruits and vegetables. For fresh products, unlike beef and veal, and milk, virtually no intervention buying takes place. Instead a withdrawal price is set and producers are encouraged to withdraw products from the market when supplies are high. These products are purchased at the withdrawal price and then distributed free to charitable institutions, schools, prisons and hospitals (Harris et al.: 156). The market is also protected by border measures: *ad valorem* duties and minimum import prices.

Processed products are supported primarily by subsidy-type aids. Thus 'provided processors enter into contracts with producers to buy specified quantities at *minimum prices*, ... they can receive a processing aid designed to enable them to sell their production competitively with Third Country supplies on the EC domestic market.' (Harris et al.: 160.) Limited border protection is also available to the sector. The operation of these systems appears to open only limited consultation opportunities to processors' associations. Hilbert (1983: 170) reports that in West Germany the Federal Association of the Fruit and Vegetable Industry (BVOGI) participates in the Fruit and Vegetable Advisory Committee to the companion Management Committee of the Commission.

Conclusion

In the introduction to this chapter, following the work of Schmitter, two components of the study of associative action were distinguished, structures of representation and structures of control. An associational system or association is said to have 'developed' structures of representation if it can order and coordinate complex activities. Associational systems with this capacity are centralized, concentrated, non-competitive, vertically integrated and highly representative of their domains (Marin, 1983) and thus 'corporatist' in Schmitter's terms. Systems lacking these properties are termed pluralist. Similarly, developed structures of control occur when associations are capable of governing and directing their members and are integrated formally into the processes of policy formulation and implementation. In Schmitter's terms, 'concertation' between the state and associations is taking place. Where such integration does not occur, relations between groups and the state are said to take a 'pressure' form. In seeking to learn the conditions under which concertation is likely to occur, it has been hypothesized that a corporatist structure of representation is a necessary but insufficient condition. Furthermore, it is also hypothesized that systems where one of the components, representation or control, is undeveloped and the other is developed will be unstable and short-lived (Schmitter, 1982). The material presented in this chapter is useful for critically examining these hypotheses.

It is evident, first of all, that agricultural economic regulation has encouraged concertation between interest groups and the state. In each of the seven countries examined closely here, there were cases of interest associations participating regularly in the formulation of regulatory policy and in implementing the regulatory systems involved. At a minimum, associations representing farmers were involved, processors' associations were almost always involved, and consumers interests were occasionally involved. As expected, the involvement of trade unions or consumers' public interest groups appeared to be related to the type of price being controlled. Once wholesale or retail prices were being set, it was common for consumers interests to be represented. Within individual countries, it was clear that associations representing highly regulated subsectors achieved a greater public status than those in less regulated subsectors.

At the same time, in all of the countries except Austria and Sweden the supposedly unstable situation of a pluralist structure of representation and a concertation structure of control occurs. For example, in Switzerland, in all of our subsectors, private interest governments essentially devise and administer the regulatory system. However, these systems in each of the subsectors are run virtually independently of one another. The associational system in the food processing industry is highly fragmented and uncoordinated as was shown in Chapter 2. The same picture of a fragmented associational system is found in Canada with the added dimension of intense competition among associations in the system, an additional pluralist property. The instigator of this competition, the Grocery Products Manufacturers of Canada, not only competes for members with other associations in the subsectors but actively questions the *raison d'être* of the system of agricultural economic regulations in which they are involved.

Yet in both countries, there is no reason to assume that the coexistence of a pluralist system of representation and concertation is an uneasy state of affairs. Within each subsector, the associational systems are 'corporatist'. They are centralized, vertically integrated and there is no competition. They are highly representative of their membership. As a result across the several subsectors, relations between the state and industry are stable.

Only in Britain do we observe a move toward more corporatist structures of representation on a wider scale. The entry of the U. K. into the EC sparked the creation of the Food and Drink Industries Council, a peak association for dealing at the EC level on matters of policy. The FDIC has since entered into an office and director sharing arrangement with the Food Manufacturers Federation, a second industry peak association, being renamed the Food and Drink Federation[1]. None of the other EC countries, however, show increased integration in its associational system over the same time period. Perhaps Britain has needed a more concerted EC voice because of the particular problems of adapting its industry to the Community that come with being a late entry rather than a designer of the original policy.

The alert defender of the corporatism-concertation hypothesis will at this point pose the question: what about Austria and Sweden? In these countries, the expected correspondence between structures of representation and control is found. Corporatist associational systems coexist with concertation relations with the state. Yet there is nothing particularly distinctive about the food processing industries in these two countries that differentiates them from the other countries studied in this chapter. Undoubtedly the same processes that pull subsectors of the food processing industry apart in other countries are at work in Sweden and Austria. What is different is that the associational systems in these countries, which are corporatist on a society-wide scale, are able to contain and to override these disintegrative pressures.

The food processing industry is perhaps one where only the strong macro-social corporatist systems of an Austria or a Sweden are likely to maintain a degree of cooperation and coherence among its associations. Not only do policies on agricultural regulation differ by subsector in this industry, so do policies on quality control (Chapter 10). Spotty organization by labour robs the sector of another unifying force found in some other sectors (Chapter 6). The structure of the sector is one that encourages firms to expand vertically within a commodity group rather than horizontally across commodity groups. Only in systems like Austria and Sweden could such pressures be absorbed successfully from within.

In our view, then, the issue is not so much whether the corporatism-concertation hypothesis works but at what level the process operates. Concertation will only be stable as Schmitter and Marin suggest if the associational system involved is centralized, concentrated, non-competitive, vertically integrated and

---

[1] The two organizations merged in January 1986.

highly representative. However the associational system with those properties may obtain at the macro, the Meso or sectoral or even the subsectoral level in some instances. If the associational system is highly developed on the macro-social plane as is found in Austria and Sweden, the opportunities for concertation will be channelled upward to the national peak associations. In the absence of such macro-social development, the opportunities will be assumed at the first level (major sector — manufacturing, construction; sector — food processing, chemicals; subsector — meat products, agricultural chemicals) where a highly developed structure of representation is found. What is clear is that in the absence of independent factors promoting the development of associational systems at higher levels, the operative level in the food processing industry is the subsector.

Chapter 9

Retail Pressure and the Collective Reactions of the Food Processing Industry

Peter Farago

Several country teams participating in our project have found out during their research on business interest associations that retail pressure is one of the major problems that confronts the food processing industry. We therefore have decided to devote one chapter of our comparative reader to this topic.

Retail pressure has to do with the concentration process in food retail trading in many capitalist countries over the last 20 years. Today, retail chains can have such an importance on the market that they are able to get special conditions (discounts, additional payments etc.) from the industry. This possibility for the demand side to dictate its conditions successfully and irrespectively of the consequences for the supplier has been labelled 'retail pressure' *(Nachfragemacht)*.

Connected with retail pressure are several problems concerning the law on competition and competition policy starting with the exploitation of retailers' economic advantages up to the tolerance of cartels as an answer to the abuse of these advantages. In the context of our project, we are primarily interested in the industry's possibilities to react to the use of retail pressure by the demand side. In this article, I shall therefore not discuss in depth the debate on competition law and competition policies, but deal more extensively with the reactions of the food processing industry and its interest associations to pressure by the food retail trade. In a first, introductory section some selected indicators are presented on concentration processes in the food retail trade during the seventies; the discussion in this section is limited to the grocery trade (including multiples, co-operatives and independents) as the most important customer of the industry and neglects the specialists in the food retail trade (butchers, dairymen etc.), among other reasons because of lack of data. Furthermore, included in the comparative tables are mainly those western countries which are part of our project. The concrete use of retail pressure will be discussed in the following section. After the systematic evaluation of the industry's reactions to retail pressure in the third section, the final section of this paper contains some general considerations on the relations of processors and the retail trade in the food sector.

Structural changes in the Food Retail Trade and their Impact on Retail Pressure

The food retail trade as the food processing industry's most important marketing channel has in recent years undergone major structural changes. These changes manifest themselves in the rise of new forms of establishments, in the reduction of the number of outlets, in the growth of individual enterprises and the concentration of their market shares.

Traditionally and until the 1950s, food retail trading was dominated by a large number of small shops spread all over the country selling a more or less wide range of food. In addition to these small shops which procured their goods from the market or from wholesale organizations, there existed consumer co-operatives and a few multiples (firms which operate several outlets). This market structure underwent a profound change in the 1960s. The reasons for the changes are to be found — in addition to the rationalization efforts of the trade itself — in different, but partly complementary developments in the society (rise of agglomerations, changes in consumer habits as a consequence of motorization and employment of women etc.). Multiples could better meet the new needs emerging from such changes (continuous opening hours, comprehensive range of goods available in one shop, time-saving sales procedures, low prices) than traditional single shops. The latter tried to balance their competitive disadvantages by *different forms of integration:* retailers formed purchasing groups to rationalize the procurement and distribution of goods; or they engaged in voluntary chains founded by wholesalers for the same purposes. Thus, gradually a diversity of organizations emerged in the food retail trade:

> At one end of the spectrum are the very large buyers, namely, the largest multiple retailers, Co-operative societies and discount chains. At the other are the small unaffiliated independent retailers. In between these two extremes there is a range of department stores, variety stores, smaller multiples, mail order houses, independent retailers in voluntary groups and wholesalers of all kinds. (MMC 1981: 7)

However, the differences between these forms of organizations are, in practice, vanishing, and they are more and more resembling one another as the German Monopolies Commission states:

> Especially in retail trading the differences between the forms of organization and distribution have become more and more erased. This is particularly true for the different forms of voluntary chains whose structures have approached those of the multiples. (MK 1977: 17)

What counts for the food processing industry is the fact that growing market segments are supplied by centralized purchasing organizations — in whatever legal form — and that it, therefore, is confronted with a diminishing number of customers with a growing economic potential.

This structural change in food retailing basically takes place in all developed capitalist countries; however, its *shape* varies from one country to another. Unfortunately, the possibilities for international comparisons are somewhat limited because of the nationally divergent statistical bases. I therefore shall confine myself to a few important indicators. One such indicator is undoubtedly the development of the number of outlets shown in Table 9.1 for several European countries and Canada.

In almost all of these countries, the number of outlets has diminished remarkably; in the UK every second shop has disappeared during the period considered. Even in countries with a smaller absolute loss of outlets (like the Netherlands and Sweden), the density of outlets decreased (Table 9.2). Table 9.2 also shows that the density ratios in the different countries tend to equalize.

Special attention has been paid by the food processing industry to the fact that not all kinds of outlets have suffered equally from this decline. Outlets with small selling space have diminished, but those with a large one have expanded both in terms of selling space and of turnover (Table 9.3). This trend is expressed by a considerable increase in the average selling space per outlet (Table 9.4). The comparison of the average selling space and the turnover per square metre of the two largest Swiss retailers in Table 9.5 clearly shows that large outlets have better returns than small ones and thus benefit from important competitive advantages.

Corresponding to this trend favouring large outlets is the growth of concentration on the level of enterprises. The degree of this concentration is displayed in Table 9.6. In most of the countries mentioned, the five largest food retailing companies control from one third to two thirds of the market. The only exception is the Netherlands, where the market is dominated by a relatively large number of voluntary chains with minor market shares respectively.

Another important feature for the food processing industry is the fact that many large retailers are processing food in their own plants. We found such cases of *vertical integration* of some importance in Austria, Sweden and Switzerland. In all these countries, *consumer co-operatives* are not only the market leaders in retail trading, but they also are major food processors serving their shops partly or (like the Swiss MIGROS) mainly with their own products. Furthermore, in these countries there also are multiples which are, in one way or another, directly involved in processing (SPAR in Austria, ICA in Sweden, MERKUR in Switzerland). Thus, co-operatives and multiples are not only major customers to the food processing industry but also direct competitors.

With regard to the actual forms and effects of retail pressure the degree of concentration in the food retail trade is but a rough indicator. The direct relations between the industry and its largest customers are of greater importance in this context. Is there a one-sided dependence in the sense that processors rely on a few or even on only one retailer for their economic survival, and if so, to what degree, then, are they dependent? For it is only in such cases of one-sided dependence that processors can be put under pressure from retailers to the advantage of the latter. Quantitative data on such a concrete level are rare; I shall cite some of the most important ones that I have found.

Linda (1981) investigated the concentration on the demand side in several European countries taking large food processing companies as an example. Table 9.7 demonstrates that there are distinct variations from country to country. The share of products marketed through the ten most important customers is, on the average, the highest in Switzerland; only Belgium shows a comparable figure,

Germany and France are in the middle, and in Italy the concentration on the demand side is the lowest.

The figures given in Table 9.7 are averages. The extreme values reported in Linda's article are considerably higher. Based on the author's definition of dependence on retailers (processor sells more than 60 % to only 10 retailers, Linda 1981: 24), we can find processors which are 'not anymore independent units in the full sense of the word' (Linda 1981: 24) in each of the above mentioned countries except Italy. These companies are supposedly to a high degree exposed to the pressure of the retailers.

In Austria, which is not covered in Linda's research, the demand side concentration is well advanced, too. On average the two largest retailers hold a share of 23 % of the sales of branded goods as a whole; there are extreme cases with the processor selling up to 44 % of his production to only one retailer (Wüger 1983: 104).

The most pertinent data available on processor-retailer relations stem from an investigation carried out by Switzerland's largest retail company, MIGROS. The company's suppliers were asked for information about the importance MIGROS had for them as a customer.[1] One of the results of this study was that, on the average, 32 % of each supplier's turnover was marketed through MIGROS, the remaining 68 % being divided between 1475 other customers. If MIGROS cancelled its orders, the utilization of the supplier's capacity *(Auslastungsgrad)* would, on the average, fall from 89 % to 61 %. Furthermore, the MIGROS-suppliers sell about 1/5 of their articles (22 %) exclusively or to a large extent to MIGROS. Considering such figures it is not at all surprising that MIGROS itself concludes in this study that it has demand power. The company even admits that it knowingly uses its power vis-a-vis the suppliers and that misuse of this power may happen from time to time.

MIGROS is — as far as the existence and the use of demand power is concerned — nationally as well as internationally hardly a special case. This section showed that the concentration process in the food retail trade produced the necessary structural prerequisites for demand side power in several developed capitalist countries. The actual forms and contents of demand pressure will be discussed in the next section.

The Use of Retail Pressure

There is relatively little precise information on the way retail pressure is actually used. This has to do with the reluctance of firms affected to give details on this matter because they fear the retailers' counter-measures. However, the reports of the British Monopolies and Mergers Commission (MMC), the German Monopolies Commission (Monopolkommission, MK) and the Swiss Cartels Commission (Schweizerische Kartellkommission, SKK) include some evidence on the practice of retail pressure. The most complete, although not

[1] The study has been published in MIGROS-Sozialbilanz (1980), 16 ff.

systematic, inventory of such practices is to be found in the listing of 'facts leading to competition distortion', the so-called *'list of sins' (Sündenregister)* edited by the German Ministry of Economics (Bundeswirtschaftsministerium, 1975). Concerning the food sector, the list enumerates 20 relevant forms of retail pressure, the most commonly used being:

— special discounts for new orders	(Eintrittsgelder für Erstaufträge)
— promotion contributions	(Werbebeiträge)
— shelf-leasing	(Regalmiete)
— shifting of pricing	(Verlagerung der Preisauszeichnung)
— lengthening of the date of payment	(Verlängerung der Zahlungsfrist)
— claiming whole packages of special payments (particularly different discounts)	(Forderung ganzer Bündel von Sonderleistungen, insbesondere verschiedener Rabatte)

One case has been reported in which the retailer wanted the processor to give him investment loans on special terms *(Investitionsdarlehen zu nicht marktüblichen Konditionen)*. All these claims have been documented with specific examples. The above-mentioned British and Swiss reports prove that there are similar practices in these countries, too. Thus, the advantages the retailers seek to realize using their demand power mainly include discounts (including special payment conditions) and the transfer of costs to the disadvantage of the processor (promotion terms, shelf-leasing etc.). In certain instances, also a transfer of the entrepreneur's risk *(unternehmerisches Risiko)* is intended (e. g. compensation of turnover shortfalls — *Deckungsbeiträge bei Umsatzausfällen* — contracts of short duration, short-dated ordering). Another method which has been mentioned by the Swiss Cartels Commission is the threat of replacing branded goods by own label products (VKK 1983: 282); this threat presupposes the existence of considerable retailer-owned production capacities of the possibility of contracting with another processor.

Undoubtedly, the retailers are able to succeed in practice. They can do this mainly because of their position on the market. On the other side, they are also assisted by the competition between the processors; this competition often allows the retailers to have even far-reaching claims fulfilled by processors who want to utilize their capacities fully under any circumstances whatsoever. Several authors point to the fact that processors themselves have started to grant discounts and special conditions to retailers as a means of competition, but that they have been overridden by the raising of claims by the retailers. 'The industry held out its little finger to the purchasers, so they took the whole hand', as an official of the German sectoral trade-union put it.

What can happen if a processor refuses to agree with the claims of a retailer is exemplified in a report of the Swiss Cartels Commission:

When a processor refused to agree to the discounts a retailer claimed for a certain product, this retailer cancelled his orders for another product. Moreover, in defiance of the processor he sold the branded good in question below costs, financing the difference himself. As a reaction, another retailer boycotted the said article for some time; he assumed that the processor had granted special conditions to his competitor so that the latter could sell at exceptionally low prices. (VKK 1983: 287)

This example shows how easily certain measures taken by a retailer can affect actors initially not involved in a specific conflict.

All in all, the food processing industry is exposed to a considerable economic pressure from the retailers. The next section will deal with the forms and means the processors use to resist this pressure.

Collective Reactions of the Food Processing Industry to Retail Pressure

Although the structural changes in food retailing described in the first section of this article followed analogous trends in all countries included in our research project and although they resulted in high degrees of concentration (Table 9.6), not all of the food processing industry association officials interviewed by the different country teams were equally anxious about retail pressure. Especially in Canada and Sweden, the problem seems to be less urgent than in the other countries. This fact is due to a cumulation of different reasons. Firstly, the degree of integration of food processing and distribution is extraordinarily high in both countries; the market leaders in food processing and retailing belong in Canada as well as in Sweden to the same enterprises respectively. Secondly, in Canada the highly fragmented associational system of our sector impedes the articulation of problems affecting the entire food processing industry; and in Sweden the encompassing system of price regulations ensures, among other things, fixed retail prices, thus putting an end to the most important stimulus for the use of retail pressure, namely price competition[2]. In contrast to Canada and Sweden, association officials in Austria, Germany, the Netherlands, the UK and Switzerland complained a great deal about retail pressure. Therefore, this section deals only with the countries for which I have concrete information on the existence of the problem and on its articulation by the food processing industry.

With regard to collective reactions on retail pressure, I distinguish three possible fields of intervention:

— the market
— the public
— the state

Such interventions can be carried out by newly formed collective actors like cartels or similar organizations founded to tackle the specific problem or they can be carried out by organizations belonging to the associational system. In three of the countries studied there are, incorporated into the associational system, specialized sector-unspecific associations dealing mainly with problems in connection with retail pressure; these are the associations of the branded

---

[2] For more details on the situation in these countries, see Coleman (1984) and Pestoff (1983).

goods industry in Austria, Germany and Switzerland. An equivalent exists in the form of a foundation in the Netherlands.[3] In what follows, I shall deal with the above-mentioned fields of intervention one after the other, also discussing the role the different actors take.

1. The most important and most frequent collective *market* interventions are agreements on prices and conditions. There are different examples for such agreements in the countries studied. In Germany, based on the above-mentioned 'list of sins' the association of the branded goods industry *(Markenverband)* enacted voluntary 'rules of competition' which it had officially registered (MK 1977: 25 f.). These rules prohibited the association's members from meeting the retailers' claims for entry payments, investment contributions, special discounts and so on. In Germany, there also exists an agreement on conditions in the sweets industry *(Konditionenkartell der deutschen Süßwarenwirtschaft)* signed by 78 companies of the branch. This cartel is limited to conditions and does not cover prices. Agreements on prices and conditions also exist in Austria and Switzerland.

Most of these attempts to answer retail pressure by manufacturers' collective voluntary agreements failed or succeeded only partly (cf. for the example of Germany Hilbert 1983: 247). There are two reasons for this outcome: on the one hand, competition laws in most countries are very restrictive with respect to cartels and similar organizations or agreements. On the other hand, excess capacities on the side of the processors and the subsequent competition often prevent some firms from observing such agreements, this is true even in countries like Austria, where the laws are relatively favourable with respect to cartels (Traxler 1983 b: 52). Thus, manufacturers are tempted to ignore existing agreements for the sake of improving their market shares. Indeed, the failure of the German voluntary agreements was one of the reasons why British associations did not even try to set up such arrangements (Grant 1983 b: 104 f.).

One exception to the rule that agreements on prices and conditions in the food sector usually do not work has been observed in Switzerland. The example is instructive because it illustrates the specific conditions required for the successful formation of a cartel. First of all, it has to be remembered that the Swiss cartel law does not prohibit cartels or similar organizations unless they have been shown to misuse their market power. Consequently, there are many cartels in Switzerland. One of them is the cartel of the manufacturers of breakfast beverages[4]. This cartel has been explicitly legitimated as an answer to retail pressure. Its formation has been facilitated by the fact that there are only six important manufacturers of breakfast beverages in Switzerland, three of them being members of the cartel (VKK 1983: 263 ff.). Although the marked leader did not join the cartel because of the strength of its product (OVOMALTINE),

---

[3] For more details on these associations and the structure of national associational systems, see chapter 2 of this book.

[4] In Switzerland favourite breakfast foods are beverages based on dehydrated powder on a malt and chocolate base, commonly dissolved in cold or warm milk; the best known brand is OVOMALTINE.

it holds a favourable position with respect to the agreement, among other things because the latter uses its own conditions as a guideline (VKK 1983: 288 f.). The cartel entered the market in 1982 and was almost immediately successful. Special discounts to retailers have diminished remarkably and promotion contributions to the retailers have dropped partly by 200 % (VKK 1983: 284, 286). Nevertheless, there has been no evidence that consumer prices have gone up during the same period (VKK 1983: 279). The Swiss Cartels Commission has explicitly approved of the cartel of the breakfast beverages manufacturers as an appropriate reaction to the misuse of demand power by the retailers in this special market (VKK 1983: 318).

The example of the breakfast beverages cartel in Switzerland demonstrates that agreements on prices and conditions can be a useful answer to retail pressure. It also demonstrates, however, that special conditions are needed to make such a cartel successful: primarily, a legislation and jurisdiction which is favourable to or at least does not prohibit cartels; secondly, a high degree of concentration on the side of the industry facilitating the control of the cartel members by reducing their number.[5]

In addition to manufacturers' agreements on prices and conditions there are in several of the countries studied (Germany, the Netherlands, Switzerland) attempts to regulate the market by voluntary agreements between processors and retailers. However, up to now none of these attempts has been an outstanding success. This was not always the fault of the industry alone, as the example of the 'chart of fair competition' in Switzerland shows. The most important intention of this chart was a regulation of the frequent but controversial practice of selling goods below the cost price *(Verkauf unter Einstandspreis)*. The processors, represented by the association of branded goods manufacturers (PROMARCA), and several of the largest retailers already had signed the chart, but a few discounters holding considerable market shares refused. The other retailers, then, not willing to voluntarily concede their competitors advantages on the market, withdrew their consent. The chart had failed, in spite of the agreement of the processors (cf. more details in Farago 1984: 33 f.).

2. Processors' collective interventions in relation to the *public* have different forms and objectives. There is, for example, the possibility that several firms together publish concrete cases of retail pressure. However, it will normally be within the scope of the actions of interest associations to promote the manufacturing industry's position facing retail pressure in relation to the public. Frequently, such actions are designed to accompany association interventions at the state level, e. g. in the course of a new legislation; associations then will try to promote their point of view. Another purpose of public interventions is the general promotion of branded goods in competition with the own labels of the retailers. Interventions in the public sphere are common in all of those countries studied where retail pressure is a problem for the industry. They are, however, especially striking where they are managed by specialized organizations. The Swiss PROMARCA, for example, started a large (and expensive) promotion

---

[5] For more details on this cartel, see Farago (1984).

campaign stating that 'branded goods are the better choice'. The headline of this campaign ('What is a branded good?') hinted at one of the major problems of manufacturers in this field, namely the definition of the branded good vis-a-vis the own label products (which by the way often are produced by the same manufacturers) and the legitimation of the frequently considerable price differences between the two.

3. In the case of the *state* as a field of intervention, I distinguish two levels: legislation and implementation. With regard to *legislation* the collective action of processors is mainly concerned with problems of competition and cartel law. Such laws exist in all the countries studied; however, they differ remarkably in scope and restrictiveness. I have already mentioned the case of Switzerland as an example for a relatively loose cartel legislation. On the other hand, EEC regulations are relatively restrictive. Processors then are confronted with different legislative conditions and therefore are urged to react differently. Since in most countries cartels and other agreements on prices or conditions are generally regarded with scepticism, interventions by processors and their associations aim at extending the legal prescriptions to the retail trade rather than loosening them. In contrast, the Swiss PROMARCA's goal in the current revision of the cartel law is to prevent a partial or complete prohibition of cartels. So this association wants to keep the law as loose as possible whereas in other countries processors' associations try to tighten it.

But in these matters, too, the manufacturers not always succeed in speaking with one voice. In the UK, for example, attempts to intervene in the legislation have failed because of internal differences between 'those wanting legal regulation, those preferring voluntary agreements, and those wishing the current situation to continue without modification' (Grant 1983 b: 105). It is probably significant that successful interventions in the field of competition legislation are rather made by branded goods associations than by sector-specific ones.[6] This may have to do with the required specialized knowledge of this topic which the former have a better chance to acquire.

Interventions in the field of *implementation* are usually restricted to the activation of controlling bodies like the British Monopolies and Mergers Commission or the Swiss Cartels Commission. The reports of these bodies on retail pressure have often been initiated in response to the requests of manufacturers.[7] This does, however, not mean that these reports follow entirely the intentions of the manufacturers. The Swiss Cartels Commission, for example, has certainly — as mentioned above — approved of the cartel of the breakfast beverages manufacturers, but in the same report the Commision judged the effects of the cartel on competition as 'prevailingly negative', and it suggested the cancellation of several regulations on competition restrictions and specific types of discounts (VKK 1983: 319 f.; cf. also Farago 1984: 42 f.). The British report, too, was not cheered by the industry since it came to the conclusion 'that neither the reference practice, nor any particular form it may take, generally or invariably operates

---

[6] In the UK there is no equivalent to a *Markenverband*.
[7] The report of the German Monopolies Commission was initiated by the Government.

against the public interest' (Grant 1983 b: 103). And the German Monopolies Commission refuses to tolerate the legal restriction of discounts and other special conditions *(gesetzliche Einschränkung des Nebenleistungswettbewerbs)* proposed by the manufacturers in its report on the misuse of demand power (MK 1977: 13). The industry's influence on these bodies, then, is limited. This applies also to countries where — as in Germany and in Switzerland — there are specialized associations like the 'Markenverband'; these associations, too, are but one among many interest groups interviewed by the commissions.

Another possibility for interventions in the field of implementation is, in principle, bringing accusations of specific misuses of demand power. But even in countries where there is a legal base for such complaints, this happens only very rarely because processors fear retailers' reprisals (Hilbert 1983: 248). In Austria, it is possible for associations themselves to accuse those who engage in competition law violations which have a general importance. However, the problem of protecting the members against eventual countermeasures of the retailers persists.

All in all, the intervention possibilities for the food processing industry and its associations in the field of the state are quite restricted. The situation is somewhat different in those countries where interventions concerning the issue of competition law can be delegated to specialized sector-unspecific associations which have the possibility to accumulate a specific know-how. The question then arises under what circumstances such associations develop and why they exist in some countries and not in other ones. I cannot give an answer to this question since this would require more historical investigation than we have done in our project. I therefore have to leave it open for future research.

4. In spite of considerable personal and financial expenses in some countries the effects of collective interventions against retail pressure are surprisingly poor. Competition on the market and a lack of solidarity often prevent collective action even in cases where the legal regulations are somewhat looser than usual; the associations have hardly any influence on the reports of the official commissions; influence on legislation depends on several other factors in connection with the political system and is effective only in a middle- and long-term perspective; and the success of public relations campaigns is hard to measure anyhow. The only substantial result of processors' collective interventions in all these fields is the public discussion on retail pressure that they have stimulated and that they help to keep going on. The manufacturers thus join a growing critique vis-a-vis the large retail companies and their expansion. The problem of retail pressure and of its impact on the food processing industry, however, basically remains unchanged.

The lack of success of individual and collective reactions on retail pressure is a consequence of structural problems in the relation of the industry to the retail trade which cannot be solved by single measures. In the final section of this paper I shall try to outline these problems.

Conclusion: Structural Limits of Collective Reactions
to Retail Pressure

In the first section of this chapter, concentration in the food retail trade was designated as one of the main reasons for retail pressure, and its development was demonstrated. However, the high degree of concentration on the demand side is faced with a similarly high degree of concentration on the supply side. This has been pointed out not only by retail traders themselves (cf. e. g. Hunt 1983: 137) but also by independent experts like the British Monopolies and Mergers Commission (MMC 1981: 30 f.) and Burns (1983). This was also one of the results of our own project's investigation into the sectoral structure of the food processing industry (cf. chapter 4 of this book). In the food sector, we therefore find mainly 'large firms dealing with large firms' (Burns 1983: 372). Linda (1981: 27) refers to a *bilateral oligopoly*. The crucial issue here is that this general pattern is not in equilibrium. One of the two sides in this arrangement always was predominant, and this predominance has changed over the last 25 years (MMC 1981: 34 f.). Until the 1950s and the early 1960s, the already highly concentrated industry dominated the still traditionally small scale retail trade. The vivid memory of these golden times for processors shows up in a sentence of the Swiss PROMARCA's director who once remarked: 'The times of the proud branded goods manufacturer being able to dictate his conditions to the trade have gone.'

The relationship between processors and retailers began to change as soon as concentration grew on the retailers' side. From then on, new factors became important, in particular the retailers' higher flexibility in switching from one product to another. While the industry has to provide sometimes expensive infrastructures (research and development, product design, production and packing lines) specially designed for specific products which cannot always easily be used to produce other goods, the retailers' infrastructures (selling space, shelves etc.) are generally independent from specific products. The retailer, therefore, can relatively easily exclude a product from his range or replace it by another, similar one, if he does not want to accept the manufacturer's conditions.[8] This structural disequilibrium is aggravated in those cases — not rare, especially in the food sector — where a processor depends to a large extent on one single product which in turn is of no special importance to the retailer. The weakening of brand loyalties repeatedly referred to in the literature (e. g. MMC 1981: 32) is an additional factor facilitating the switch from one product to another for the retailer.

It is not the disequilibrium of industry and retail trade as such that is the new feature in the relations between the two but the shift of power from the industry to the retail trade. In this shift of power lies the explanation for the strength and the obstinacy with which the new situation is being publicly denounced by the

---

[8] Generally, and this applies in particular to the food sector, there are only a very few articles which are so strong on the market that a retailer could not renounce them without endangering his turnover.

losing side, namely the industry. However, the latter has contributed to the development with its generous policy of discounts, frequently at the expense of the small retailers. After all, trading relations with large customers have some rationalizing effects for the industry, too, in particular by the reduction of costs by the production of large quantities (MMC 1981: 33).

Since retail pressure mainly relies on the market structures and on a shift in the disequilibrium of the market powers, collective reactions on the market are of crucial importance for the food processing industry's defence against retail pressure. Reactions in the fields of the public and the state can only assist market reactions, but not replace them. Successes in these fields therefore produce but limited effects. In this paper it has been argued that processors can adopt two distinct strategies for market reactions: agreements on prices and conditions within the food processing industry or voluntary agreements between manufacturers and retailers. Both strategies have proved to be hardly successful. Agreements on prices and conditions are generally impeded by restrictive legal regulations and the economic situation of the sector (stagnating markets and excess capacities — *Überkapazitäten*); voluntary agreements between manufacturers and retailers can fail because of the divergent interests of the retailers as demonstrated by the example of the Swiss 'chart of fair competition'. These divergent interests stem from the rapid structural change of retail trading in the past years which has led to the rise of new forms of establishments, thus splitting the formerly more homogeneous retail sector. The heterogeneity of the retail sector makes its organization and the representation of its interests difficult. This may be one of the reasons why in several of the countries studied the associations of the retail trade have not succeeded in organizing and representing the entire domain in the same way as the associations of branded goods manufacturers. Significantly, the discounters which in the Swiss example refused to sign the 'chart of fair competition' did not belong to any of the associations of retail traders.

The food processing industry, therefore, is not only faced with the limits to collective reactions set by the market structure and the economic situation of the sector but also with the limits set by an *asymmetry in the organizational development of the industry and of retail trading* respectively which cannot be influenced by the industry and which seriously restricts or even prevents the solution of the problem of retail pressure by corporatist arrangements between manufacturers and retailers. There is some evidence, then, that retail pressure will remain an unsolved problem for the food processing industry in the near future.

Table 9.1 Development of the number of outlets

Country	Period	% Diff.	Source(s)
A	1973–1982	– 29 %	Selbstbedienung in Österreich 1982
CDN	1975–1981	– 22 %	Nielsen 1976, 1982
CH	1971–1980	– 29 %	VKK 1979, SWEDA 1980
D	1970–1980	– 37 %	LZ-Report 1980/81
GB	1971–1981	– 46 %	Burns 1983
NL	1975–1980	– 16 %	Centraal Registratiekantoor Detailhandel-Ambacht
S	1975–1981	– 17 %	Nielsen 1976, 1982

Table 9.2 Development of the density of outlets (Number of outlets per 1000 head of population)

Country	1970	1980	% Diff.
A	2.7	1.8	– 33 %
CDN	1.7	1.2	– 29 %
CH	2.4	1.5	– 38 %
D	2.8	1.5	– 46 %
GB	2.1	1.1	– 48 %
NL	1.3	0.9	– 31 %
S	1.6	1.1	– 31 %

Table 9.3 Development of the share of outlets and the share of turnover of shops with large selling areas, 1974–1980

Country	% of outlets	% of turnover
A	+ 24 %	+ 28 %
CDN	+ 32 %	+ 6 %
CH	+ 15 %	+ 19 %
D	+ 7 %	+ 12 %
NL	+ 13 %	+ 13 %
S	+ 6 %	– 5 %

Table 9.4 Development of the average selling space per outlet

Country	Period	% Diff.	Source
A	1973–1982	+ 102 %	Selbstbedienung in Österreich 1982
CH	1968–1977	+ 117 %	VKK 1979
D	1970–1979	+ 146 %	LZ-Report 1980/81

Table 9.5 Average selling areas and average turnover per square metre of the largest Swiss food retailing companies, 1981

Name	Average selling area per outlet, sq. m.	Average turnover per sq. m., SFr.
MIGROS	1258	13'400
COOP	394	11'700

Source: IHA 1982

Table 9.6 Degree of concentration in the food retail trade

Country	Year	Share of total food turnover of the largest food retailing company	of the 5 largest food retailing companies	Source
A	1980	17 %	61 %	Traxler 1983
CH	1982	24 %	54 %	UNILEVER/IHA
D	1982	8 %	29 %	G + L Top 200
GB	1982	14 %	49 %	AGB Share of trade report 1982
NL	1980	5 %	14 %	Het financieele Dagblad: Omzet-cijfers 1981
S	1978	29 %	67 %*	Pestoff 1983

* 4 largest companies

Table 9.7 Average share of 10 top buyers (in %) in the aggregate sales of the manufacturer/seller, 1978

B	59 %
CH	64 %
D	32 %
F	36 %
I	17 %

These figures are derived from a sample of big manufacturers/sellers in each country which answered the questionnaire from the European Association of Branded Goods Industries (AIM).
Source: Linda 1981

Table 9.2, Source: Nielsen, 1982. Table 9.3, Source: Nielsen 1976, 1982.

Chapter 10

The Food Industry and Quality Regulation*

BERT DE VROOM

In the last chapter it was noted that the food processing industry had had difficulty in coping with the economic pressures exerted by an increasingly concentrated retail sector. Another problem that the industry faces is increasing consumer concern about food quality, particularly in terms of the use of additives in food production. The long standing legislative frameworks set up in the first place in many countries in the nineteenth century address themselves to more traditional issues such as adulteration, contamination in the production and handling of food etc. They cannot, for example, readily cope with issues such as the presence in food of minute amounts of agrochemicals or antibiotics given to animals. New issues are therefore appearing on the quality control agenda, with the EEC and the US Food and Drug Administration playing an important role in highlighting problems and devising solutions.

Quality control is therefore an important and topical issue in its own right. However, apart from this substantive importance, it is also relevant to the main themes of this book. Quality control issues are ones that organizationally developed associations should be able to handle as intermediaries between their members and government. In a virtuous cycle of organizational development, one would expect to see associations acquiring new responsibilities in this area, and, hence, additional influence over their members' behaviour.

I. Quality Regulation: State Involvement

Quality and Competition

Competition between firms in the same sector may have different effects on product quality. Price competition may result in decreasing quality, when

* This study is an outcome of the research projects (a) 'Organization of Business Interests in The Netherlands', part of an international project (1980–1985) co-ordinated by P. C. Schmitter and W. Streeck, and supported by the Netherlands' Organization for Basic Scientific Research (ZWO); and (b) 'Business and Self Regulation', supported by the University of Leiden.

I thank in particular Wyn Grant for his quantity of quality information and his 'iron' patience.

producers for instance shift from using expensive raw materials to cheap ones, or skip quality control procedures at the factory level. Competition — in the sense of quality competition — on the other hand may also improve quality. According to Stigler (1975: 178) this mechanism is the typical historical sequence, because, as he argues, it is usual for profitable firms to compete by improving quality, reliability and safety. And indeed many firms (in particular large ones) have invested in quality control of products and manufacturing processes, in advertising quality(-image) of their products and in developing well-known brand names as a symbol and a guarantee of the 'high quality standards' of their products.

So, in the long run, quality improvement of a great number of products may occur. However, in the daily game of competition producers may be led by short term interests and short term profits and will possibly produce cheap, low quality or shoddy products instead of expensive high quality products. This may in particular be applied to mass products, and under conditions of declining income of the majority of (potential) consumers. In this game, swindling and adulteration are favourite 'strategies' used by 'unfair' competitors from ancient times until the twentieth century. In the end public scandals and public criticism may be the result and the quality image of the whole sector will be characterized by these scandalous incidents and shoddy goods. Giles (1976) for instance has pointed to lucrative adulteration activities in highly competitive areas in the eighteenth century, when pepper was adulterated with glove dust, or mustard, butter and coffee were mixed up with flour, grass, radish seeds or lard (p. 4). In the Dutch dairy industry adulteration became a serious problem by 1890: 'merchants and factories tried to enrich themselves by mixing cheaper margarine or water in the butter and selling it for prices of regular butter. In 1903 for example a much publicised lawsuit was held in England against a Gouda cheese with only 1.6 percent fat and 57 percent water' (Van Waarden, 1985: 206). Even today competition may lead to adulteration and swindling, as described for several cases below.

Quality Regulation and Collective Interest

A declining quality image of a sector may not only damage producers with high standards of reliability (when consumers change to other products) but also the sector as a whole (when, for instance, export markets are closed for products from certain countries). From this point of view one may assume there is a potential collective interest, at least among one group of 'fair' competitors, in regulating the behaviour of 'unfair' competitors, to exclude public scandals and to raise the quality image of the sector as a whole. This can be done either by organized business — existing or newly founded business interest associations — other private organizations, state agencies or a combination of these possibilities. Private regulation by business interest associations may be preferred by business, but will have to deal in this case with the classical dilemma, of, on the one side, manufacturers competing with each other on quality and price, and on the other side, a collective interest in raising the quality image and fighting unfair competition. It is an organizational problem how to combine competition and co-operation. This problem is even more serious since every firm can try to escape from a collective agreement on quality and make some short term profits (the well-known 'prisoners' dilemma), as can be illustrated with the following example.

Recently there has been an adulteration conflict between bacon manufacturers in the Netherlands. One manufacturer did produce and export bacon with much more water than was allowed by law and so he was able to make high profits. The other manufacturers protested against these adulteration practices with the result that a fine was imposed by a semi-state board of disciplinary law. The 'adulterator' has defended himself by claiming it was not bacon but only 'salted pork' and as such it did not fall under bacon quality regulation. Nevertheless these products were imported in other countries, labelled as bacon. It is a classical example of the 'free rider', using the quality image of a state licensed bacon hallmark to sell products that are not bacon in the eyes of the law. In this particular case the other competitors have waited eagerly for the definitive judgement: either the 'free rider' would be condemned or all bacon manufacturers would change to 'salted pork' (with a bad reputation for Dutch bacon in the long run).

Not only will the prisoners' dilemma of unfair competitors be a problem for private regulation by business interest associations, but also the definition of quality itself. In particular in heterogeneous sectors — heterogeneity with respect to size, technical equipment and the manufacturing technology of firms — one may assume different and conflicting views with respect to the specific tenor and purpose of quality regulation.

This was, for instance, the case in the Dutch meat processing sector. Since the second half of the 1970s this sector has to deal with overcapacity, decreasing sales and growing competition. Different tripartite committees (along the Dutch corporatist lines) have studied these sectoral problems[1]. One of the findings was the 'moderate quality image' of Dutch meat products (NEHEM, 1981: 31). In a joint study of the Ministries of Economic Affairs and Agriculture this aspect was underlined again: 'the quality level of certain meat products has decreased in recent years caused by a continuing keen price competition' (1981: 135). As a result a tripartite committee — composed of government, manufacturers and consumers — was called into existence to formulate quality norms for a state licensed quality hallmark for meat products[2]. Smoked sausage — a typical Dutch meat product — became the first product to be regulated. This initiative, however, caused a high conflict between different subgroups of sausage manufacturers: (1) those (mostly butchers) who produce sausages along traditional lines and based on artisanal techniques (real meat, natural guts, natural smoked,

---

[1] 'Commissie Onderzoek Vleessector' (Produktschap voor Vee en Vlees): Rapport, Augustus 1977. 'Struktuurcommissie Vleesindustrie' (NEHEM): Versterken Varkensvleesverwerkende Industrie, 1981.

[2] 'Werkgroep Kwaliteitsverbetering Vleeswaren' (Working Party Quality Improvement of Meatproducts).

no synthetic flavours, colours, perfumed essences, etc.); (2) bulk producers who use different basic materials (e. g. meat offal instead of real meat) and chemical additives (in general medium sized and large industrial manufacturers); and (3) Unilever which has the largest market share for smoked sausages (about 75 %) and which produces through the use of advanced technologies: continuous flow ('sausage without end'), artificial smoked (perfumed essences, etc.) and a synthetic gut.

Every subgroup wanted a quality definition in which only their products could fit, because every group thought their products were the best. The butchers were the first who decided to withdraw and to introduce their own 'Super quality' label. Between industrial manufacturers there was a more problematic situation. On the one side there was a group of manufacturers that wanted to exclude artificially smoked sausages and the use of artificial guts from the quality hallmark (in fact an attempt to keep the Unilever sausages outside the quality label). On the other side Unilever argued for just the opposite position. These different opinions caused an internal conflict in the business interest association of manufacturers of meat products (VNV)[3], which also represents the interests of both groups in statutory organizations charged with formulation and implementation of quality regulations. Unilever, however, has a strong position within the association and actually represents the VNV in the regulatory agency. Other member-firms of the VNV have accused their interest association of defending only the interests of large members (Unilever), since in the ultimate quality standard for smoked sausage 'artifically smoked sausages' and the use of 'artificial guts' were explicitly included, in other words 'Unox' sausages.

In reality, however, the quality standard looked more like a compromise of all interests. It was defined in such a way that it did not discriminate between different qualities. This is also reflected in the negative and oppositional response of industry. Unilever, for instance, ignores the ultimate state licensed hallmark of 'Quality Smoked Sausage', because it did not discriminate their own much promoted UNOX-label from other labels. If all sausages get the same quality label, as Unilever argues, negative effects in competition may be the result, since UNOX-sausages are more expensive than other labels. For this reason Unilever is still promoting its own factory label. Manufacturers of the second subgroup were dissatisfied because from their point of view a state licensed quality label for natural smoked sausages and manufactured with natural guts could possibly have given them a (small) benefit in their competition with Unilever. They feel that their interest association did not represent their interests and for this reason some (small) manufacturers have withdrawn. Within the association plans have been discussed to cope in future with this kind of conflict between large and small members. One idea was a change in organizational structure not based (explicitly) on size, since the potential conflict would then become manifest, but on regional sections in which smaller firms could have a better opportunity to discuss their problems and interests.

[3] VNV = Verening voor de Nederlandse Vleeswarenindustrie/Association for the Dutch Meat Processing Industry.

This case illustrates the conflicting elements in quality regulation and the problems in binding members with different interests to a voluntary quality regulation. Also Giles refers to a similar problem in the food processing industry in the UK. As early as the 1850s this industry, under pressure from public criticism on adulteration of food, undertook some voluntary reform, but 'it was not very successful due to the different conflicting views' (Giles, 1976: 5).

Only highly developed interest associations seem able to guarantee successful self-regulation under these circumstances, if the subject of self regulation is not closely linked to public interests and state intervention is marginal. I have described these conditions for private regulation of business interest associations in the field of quality for the pharmaceutical industry (De Vroom, 1985).

If quality regulation is needed, but interest organizations are not able to cope with this problem autonomously and consumers lose confidence in sectoral products, state intervention seems to be the only solution, as early state involvement in the Dutch dairy industry illustrates. About 1900 business interest associations started a voluntary system of quality control of butter, since adulteration of butter had become a serious problem and exports dropped dramatically. However, state intervention was needed for effective quality regulation. These voluntary associations were not able to control completely the behaviour of all firms in the sector. This is one reason why foreign purchasers did not have much confidence in this private quality control and why exports continued to diminish. In 1905 the state took over supervision of these private control institutions and quality hallmarks were guaranteed by the state. A couple of years later the same procedure was developed for other dairy products (Pluim Mentz and Verwayen, 1980: 5, 6).

Absence of Self Regulation

The problems of private quality regulation are probably one explanation for the absence of *pure* self regulation by business interest associations in the field of product quality. Pure self regulation can be understood as regulation of the

Table 10.1 Aspects of quality regulation

I.   Regulation of the *product*
     1. Formulation of a central framework (legislation) concerning quality in general;
     2. Formulation of standards concerning quality of specific products; and
     3. Operationalization of quality norms for specific products.
II. Regulation of *procedures*
     4. Implementation and administration of standards and norms;
     5. Control of the observation of the quality standards and norms;
     6. Supervision over implementation and control;
     7. Sanctioning of transgressors; and
     8. The handling of appeals.

Source: De Vroom, 1985: 131.

product (formulation of global framework of quality standards, specific quality standards and norms) and regulation of *procedures* to gain the intended outcome (implementation and administration of standards and norms; control of the observation of the quality standards and norms; supervision over implementation and control; and sanctioning of transgressors) by private organizations *without* state intervention (Table 10.1).

Pure self regulation in this sense we will find in hardly any economic area in society, except in some cases of, for instance, cartels. In most cases the state is involved to a certain extent, but the degree of state involvement may vary from one topic to another. With respect to food quality the data collected in the international research project on 'Business Interest Associations' shows that quality regulation of food is an important state activity and that private regulation hardly exists. Of different regulatory areas product quality and safety standards seem to be the most important objects of state intervention (Table 10.2). Among the interest organizations studied in the international research project on 'Business Interest Associations', there are only some minor examples in countries like the United Kingdom and Germany (Table 10.3).

Table 10.2 Objects of State Regulation in Different Countries[1] and Industrial Sectors[2]

Object of State Regulation	Score[3]	
	YES	NO
Product	36	20
Health and Safety	36	20
Prices	26	30
Competitive Practices	13	43
Environmental Effects	13	43
Profits	5	51
Investment	5	51

Source: International Research Project Business Interest Associations.
[1] The 9 countries of the Research Project.
[2] The 7 industrial sectors of the Research Project.
[3] Number of countries (maximum = 9) x number of sectors (maximum = 9). The food processing sectors are not included for Italy and Spain. Also machine tools is excluded for Spain. So the total maximum score is 56.

In Germany the *Bundesverband der Deutschen Fleischwarenindustrie* has some private regulations *(Verbandsrichtlinien)* for specific meat products *(Richtlinie für Fleischgerichte in Soßen, Richtlinie für Kohlroulade und Fleischspieße)* (Linke, 1980: 81). But these private regulations must be seen as a 'topping up' of a great number of state regulations in the sector.

In the United Kingdom there is the 'somewhat peculiarly British' (Dennis, 1980: 125) system of *Codes of Practice*. These Codes are methods of quasi-legislative control, more or less voluntarily applied. According to Dennis (1980) these codes for the food industry are drawn up as a result of agreement between manufacturers and enforcement authorities, or even unilaterally by industry if

Table 10.3 a Involvement of Business Interest Associations in Quality Regulation

Type of Regul. Involvement of BIA's Ctry/S	Self Regulation Pure Private Regulation	Consultation not-inst.	Consultation inst.	State Regulation Semi-State	'Delegation' Enforcement (Mon. Goods) in:
A M	—	—	X	X	—
D	—	—	X	X	—
CND M	—	X	—	—	—
D	—	X	—	—	—
D M	X	—	X	—	—
D	—	—	X	—	X
NL M	—	—	X	X	X
D	—	—	X	X	X
S M	—	—	X	—	X
D	—	—	X	—	X
CH M	—	—	X	—	X
D	—	—	X	—	X
UK M	X	—	X	—	—
D	—	—	X	X	—

Source: International Research Project on BIAs
M = Meat; D = Dairy

Table 10.3 b Number of Business Interest Associations involved in Consultation of Quality Regulation in the Dairy and Meat Processing Sectors in Six Countries (1980)

Country[1]	Formal Consultation in Legislation[2]							
	Dairy				Meat			
	0	1	2	3	0	1	2	3
Canada		1	2	1	2			2
Germany		4		2		1		1
Netherlands	9	3	2		5		1	2
Sweden				1	2			1
Switzerland				5				4
UK				2				1
Total	9	8	4	11	7	3	1	11

Source: International Research Project on Business Interest Associations.
[1] Only those countries are included that have sector specific business interest associations.
[2] 0 = never; 1 = rarely; 2 = occasionally; 3 = frequently.

'as is all too often the case enforcement authorities cannot agree amongst themselves on the constitution of the code' (Dennis: 125). The benefit for the industry is that codes can be 'simply written using understandable phraseology with an agreed meaning and are not therefore necessarily subject to the courts' interpretation of the word'. However, according to Coates (1984), there is no significant use of codes in food standards, unlike areas such as agricultural chemicals and farm animal welfare (Coates: 150). The relative absence of Codes of Practice — except in the cases of unfit meat and quality of bacon — in the food sector can be explained by the severe state regulation in this area.

Private regulation seems unnecessary, unless state regulation fails or is ineffective. This is, for instance, the case for 'unscrupulous trade in Unfit Meat' (terminology of the business interest association of British Bacon and Meat Manufacturers) (BMMA, 1982: 3). The BMMA has pressed the Minister for Agriculture, Fisheries and Food 'for rapid introduction of legislation to curb the unscrupulous trade', but in the absence of these new controls, the industry 'has continued in grave danger, and has frequently counselled extreme vigilance; once again, *we stress the need to observe the Code of Practice on Unfit Meat issued in 1981*' (BMMA, 1982: 3. Underlining BdV). In 1981 the manufacturers organized in the BMMA agreed on a 'Code of Recommended Practice for the Production of Bacon and Bacon Joints'. This code is the basis for the 'British Charter Quality Bacon', introduced in 1982: products meeting certain standards and produced in approved plants are to be allowed to carry the British Charter Quality Bacon symbol as an assurance to customers and encouraging more effective competition against imported products. It has, however, essentially a promotional character. Already in the 1970s the bacon manufacturers tried to introduce a regulation like this, but it failed because of problems with funding and with self-certification (information supplied by Meat and Livestock Commission).

Apart from these particular examples, regulation of quality has become in almost every industrialized country a state affair. Even historically private regulations have been incorporated in state regulations, such as for instance in Switzerland. Quality of milk in Switzerland is regulated by the *Milchlieferungsregulativ*. Historically this quality regulation was based on pure associational directions of two business interest associations in the dairy sector (ZVSM and *Schweiz. Milchkäuferverband*). Nowadays, however, these private regulations are incorporated in state regulation and so they have changed into compulsory regulation under state licence (Kaufman, 1971: 60). Also the examples of quality control of milk in Germany and the Netherlands are more or less incorporated in an overall state quality regulation system. For this reason these examples will be discussed in the paragraph, dealing with 'delegated' state regulation.

State involvement

State regulation of product quality is not new. In particular those products of direct importance for health and safety of (a part of) the population, such as food and drink have been dealt with by state intervention since early history. The original objects of regulation were adulteration and poisoning of food and drink. Already in ancient times, both Athens and Rome had laws to prevent the adulteration of wine. Also in the middle ages different local or central govern-

mental regulations were developed in several countries to prevent adulteration
and to control the quality of food:

> Municipal authorities in many places policed the fairs and marketplaces to protect
> purchasers of food. Inspection was practiced, and detailed regulations were enforced.
> For example, Augsburg in 1276 ordered meat that was not freshly slaughtered to be sold
> at a special stand, and the Florentines forbade the sale on Monday of meat that had been
> on sale the previous Saturday (Encyclopedia Britannica).

These early regulations were aimed at only a small number of specific
products which were highly valued and much in demand, like spices, coffee, tea
and bread, and which were for that reason a prime target for adulteration.

It was not until the nineteenth century that more comprehensive food
legislation and inspection procedures were introduced in western countries.
Next to improved technical conditions that made more elaborated quality
standards and better control procedures possible, it was essentially 'social'
conditions that were responsible for the rapid introduction of food legislation in
the last century. The Industrial Revolution had caused a tremendous increase in
urban population, faced with poverty and slum conditions. They did not have
the money to buy good food, nor the possibility to 'produce' their own food like
the agrarian population. Within these circumstances swindling and adulteration
by unscrupulous shopkeepers, entrepreneurs and manufacturers proved to be a
short term profitable business. Low paid urban people became dependent on
cheap, adulterated products. The establishment in the 19th century of consumer
co-operatives first in the UK (Rochdale) and later in other industrialized
countries, can be seen as a collective response of consumers to the practices of
swindlers and adulterators. The slum conditions of the urban population and the
bad quality of food caused at the same time public scandals and governments
were pressed by public opinion to intervene by legislation.

The present Food and Drugs Act in the United Kingdom has its roots in the
Adulteration of Food and Drinks Act of 1860. Modern food legislation in the
United States is based on acts prohibiting the adulteration of drugs (1848) and
food (1890). In most industrialized countries extensive food legislation was
introduced between 1870 and 1920, more or less depending on the level of
industrial development. In Italy the first food law, dealing primarily with public
health aspects, dates from 1888; in Belgium in 1890 an act on the adulteration of
foodstuffs was passed; in Germany in 1879 and in the Netherlands — with a
relatively late industrial take off — the food and drugs act (Warenwet) was
passed in 1919 together with the meat inspection act (Vleeskeuringswet) (Source:
Commission of the European Communities, 1980).

Benefits of State Involvement

From the point of view of (certain) food manufacturers and business interest
associations state involvement in quality regulation can have different benefits, as
discussed earlier. Firstly, since product quality is directly linked to competition,
quality regulation by business interest associations can result in serious internal

conflicts of interest and interest associations will be confronted with 'management of diversity problems'. Secondly, if business interest associations gain sufficient resources to act like 'private governments', they might lose their voluntary character and will probably become alienated from their members. In both cases state intervention can be helpful in defending the interests of 'respectable' producers against 'unfair' competitors, or defending the interests of 'established' firms against 'outsiders', and at the same time state regulation will relieve business interest associations of their 'management of diversity problems' *(Entlastung)*.

One example of defending interests of established firms against outsiders by means of state regulation is the *Canadian Dairy Products Act* of 1893. The ostensible purpose of this act was to prevent manufactures of imitation cheese and to control the labelling of cheese in favour of Canadian cheese makers:

> Preventing the manufacture of imitation cheese, of course, prevented such substitute products from reducing the demand for real cheese. The Act's labelling requirements made it necessary to mark any cheese made in Canada and destined for export as Canadian, and prohibited such labelling of any cheese not made in Canada. This effectively protected Canadian cheese-makers from United States cheese which at the time being was imported into Canada and then re-exported as a Canadian-made product, thereby benefiting from the superior international reputation of Canadian cheese (especially cheddar). (Anderson, 1981: 31.)

Another Canadian example of quality regulation as prevention of outsiders is the federal ban since 1923 on the sale of oleo margarine: 'probably the most salient example of regulation solicited by dairy processors and producers (represented by their Business Interest Association) for their own protection' (Anderson: 33). This ban remained in force until 1951, but thereafter 'processors succeeded in obtaining various provincial limits on the use of oleo margarine' (33).

Kolko (1967) has described how large meat processing firms in the United States have played an important role in the introduction of the Meat Inspection Act. On the one side their object was to prevent 'unfair competition' and 'unqualified' producers: they 'learned very early in the history of the industry that it was not to their profit to poison their customers, especially in a competitive market in which the consumer could go elsewhere' (Kolko: 99). But, on the other hand, the large meat processors wanted state regulation because they thought that regulation would 'primarily affect their innumerable small competitors' (Kolko: 107).

Not only in Canada and the United States but also in European countries quality regulation is used to exclude outsiders. For instance Germany uses the old Bavarian *Reinheitsgebot* (dating from the middle ages) to restrict the entry of foreign beers on to the national market. In France national quality standards for wine are used to close the market for wines from other countries. In the Netherlands meat processing firms are pressing national government to use national quality norms to prevent the import of Belgian meat products (NEHEM, 1981: 31). The use of national quality norms to prevent imports is, however, at variance with the principles of the European Community on free trade between member states (Rome Treaty). At the time of writing (1985) different cases are being discussed by the European Court.

Quality and Public Criticism

Business interests are not the only incentives for state involvement in product quality. Other important incentives are public criticism and the public interest with respect to product quality.

As a consequence of the importance of food for consumption and public health the food industry is very vulnerable to scandals and public criticism, caused either by unfair competitors or unqualified or irresponsible producers (and traders). Scandals can lead to drastic decline of consumption (even for high quality products). A well-known example from the pharmaceutical industry is the thalidomide scandal ('softenon') and public criticism of promotional activities of multinationals in third world countries. These scandals attracted much publicity and reduction of consumption. Another notorious scandal some years ago was the affair of Spanish olive oil, that caused the deaths of a great number of people. In 1984 in the Netherlands there was a scandal of food poisoning by shrimps: fourteen people died after having consumed shrimps. This calamity resulted in a temporary governmental prohibition on the sale of shrimps and a prohibition on home-scaling of shrimps. This affair was attended by much negative publicity with a serious collapse of consumption, not just of shrimps but also fish and mussels. The regular trade accused illegal traders of having caused this food poisoning affair, but at the same time they criticized the sudden and 'unfair' state involvement.

The threat of 'unfair' state intervention — e.g. very strict and inflexible rules, no influence by the industry — is the other side of the coin when the state gets involved and reacts to public scandals. This was also the pattern in the thalidomide-scandal: 'étatist' regulations and reduction of self regulation of the industry and institutionalized contacts with state agencies to a minimal level (De Vroom, 1985). In these cases state intervention goes beyond the initial objectives of the industry. A specific example of 'goal-displacement' — from the point of view of the industry — is the establishment by 1980 of a new state agency in the Netherlands: VKA (Food and Quality Affairs)[4]. At first industry was in favour of this new agency, because they thought it could promote a better quality image of food products and it could defend the interests of the industry against another state agency: the Ministry of Public Health and Environmental Control[5]. However, the agency did not develop in the way the industry had hoped for.

[4] VKA = Directie Voedings en kwaliteitsaangelegenheden van het Ministerie van Landbouw.
[5] The idea that the VKA would protect the interests of producers was based on the fact and experience that the Ministry of Agriculture always has defended their interests, especially the department VAAP (for production and marketing aspects of agricultural products). The director of the VKA characterized the VAAP as follows: 'if the industry is crying, the VAAP is crying with them; if the industry is laughing, the VAAP is laughing with them' (source: interview).

The VKA is moving in the direction of 'consumerism' and is acting now as an opponent of industry. The business interest association of meat manufacturers (VNV) is pressing the Minister of Agriculture to change the VKA. A spokesman of the VNV: 'the VKA is only listening to consumer organizations — those organizations do not represent consumer opinions but sell their opinions to consumers — and not to business interest associations, which do represent their members' interests'[6].

Interim Summary

Quality regulation of food products is predominantly a state affair in different countries. State involvement can, on the one side, be beneficial for certain groups of manufacturers to protect their interests against: *'swindlers'* selling products of very bad quality but suggesting that they are of the same quality as regular products (unfair competition), *'outsiders'* producing according to other quality norms than the established firms on a certain market (not necessarily low quality products) and *'unqualified or irresponsible producers'* producing without using essential quality norms. The first and last group can possibly cause scandals in the sector (e. g. food poisoning) and undermine the faith of consumers in products (also high quality products) of the whole sector. On the other hand state quality regulation can turn into 'étatism' and 'consumerism'. For that reason manufacturers will probably try to get involved in formulation and even enforcement of state regulation. But also the state may, for technical reasons and for problems of compliance, need the participation of business in regulation.

In the second part of this chapter I will discuss the way business interest associations in different countries and subsectors of the food processing industry are involved in quality regulation by the state.

II. Involvement of Business Interest Associations in State Regulation

In the foregoing paragraphs strong state involvement and the absence of pure private collective regulation is discussed. This does not mean that business interest associations are completely absent in the area of quality regulation. Business interest associations play an important role in this game. A distinction can be made between three types of involvement:

(1) business interest associations are involved in *consultation* procedures by the state (examples: Canada and United Kingdom);
(2) business interest associations are involved in *corporatist* or semi-state bodies (partly) responsible for formulation, enforcement and/or sanctioning of quality regulations (Austria, Netherlands, UK);
(3) business interest associations have got direct *delegated state power to enforce* state licensed quality regulations (Switzerland, Netherlands).

---

[6] Source: interview.

Involvement in Consultation

Involvement of business in consultation with respect to different legislative affairs is illustrated in Table 10.4. Out of 347 BIAs in 9 countries, 258 (74.3 %) BIAs are involved in consultation, of which 136 (39.2 %) frequently. 105 BIAs (30.3 %) even have a legal right to be consulted by the state, what may be seen as an indication of the importance of interest groups in legislative procedures. This seems in particular the case for Switzerland, Germany and the Netherlands, where by far the most BIAs have the legal right to be consulted by the state (see Table 10.5).

The involvement of BIAs in consultation is even stronger for the meat processing and dairy sector (Table 10.6). 45.5 % of all BIAs in the meat processing sector and 50 % of all BIAs in the dairy sector have a legal right to be consulted. Involvement in formal consultation in these sectors is somewhat below the average. This is probably due to the fact that in countries where BIAs can get a legal right to be consulted by the state other BIAs (without that right) probably are less involved in consultation procedures. If Tables 10.4 and 10.5 are compared, there seems some evidence for this hypothesis.

In the following paragraph the involvement of business interest associations in consultation will be discussed in more detail in relation to the examples of Canada and the United Kingdom, where consultation procedures are very important.

(a) Canada: The Intermediate Role of Business Interest Associations

Quality regulation of dairy and meat products is in Canada a governmental affair and is authorized by a network of federal, provincial and municipal legislation. This legislation includes statutes, 'regulations' (i. e. delegated legislation) and municipal bylaws. Formulation and implementation in the foodproces-

Table 10.4 Formal Consultation in Legislation of Business Interest Associations in Nine Different Countries

Country	Never	Rarely	Occasionally	Frequently
Austria	7	6	3	1
Canada	3	7	11	30
Germany	11	17	3	16
Italy	3	7	3	3
Netherlands	40	6	13	13
Spain	3	7	5	4
Sweden	12		6	15
Switzerland	5	9	2	39
United Kingdom	5	13	4	15
Total	89	72	50	136
	25.6 %	20.7 %	14.4 %	39.2 %

Source: International Research Project on BIAs.

Table 10.5 Legal Right of BIAs to be Consulted by the State in Nine Countries

Country	No	Yes
Austria	16	1
Canada	49	2
Germany	27	22
Italy	15	1
Netherlands	52	19
Spain	17	1
Sweden	33	
Switzerland		55
United Kingdom	33	4
Total	242	105
	69.7%	30.3%

Source: International Research Project on BIAs.

Table 10.6 Involvement of BIAs in Consultation in the Dairy and Meat Processing Sector in Six Countries[1]. (Number of involved BIAs in percentage of total number of associations in research project; 1980)

	Dairy Industry (N = 32)	Meat Processing (N = 22)	All Sectors (N = 347)
Involvement in Formal Consultation	71.9	68.1	74.3
Legal Right to be Consulted by the State	50.0	45.5	30.3

Source: International Research Project on BIAs.
[1] Only six countries, because these sectors have not been studied in Spain and Italy, and in Austria there are no sector-specific BIAs.

sing sector is as in most other countries to a great extent the responsibility of the Department of Agriculture and to a lesser extent the Department of Health and Welfare. However procedures exist in most instances for consulting industry via its business interest associations, especially regarding formulation of new regulations.

Unlike the UK-case Canadian consultation is less formalized and institutionalized. There are hardly any legal permanent bodies in which industry can be represented. None of the associations in the meat processing sector and only one in the dairy industry has the legal right to be consulted by the state. Consultation procedures are not predominantly informal but have an *ad hoc* character. They differ according to products, quality aspects, purpose of intended regulation, but also according to the state agency responsible for a certain quality regulation. Consultation in the dairy industry works more smoothly compared with the meat processing sector. Especially when quality regulation is aiming at 'fair competition', compared with 'consumer protection', consultation of the industry is more developed. Notwithstanding the not-formalized character, consultation is very important for regulation: 'No new policy or important change in the regulations would be adopted without extensive consultation with relevant policy sub-units.' (Coleman, 1984: 62.)

The important role of consultation for regulatory policy in Canada must primarily be explained by the relatively weak state. Particularly in the case of quality regulation the state needs product-specific information to formulate product standards, grading regulations, compositional norms, labelling and packaging regulations, etc. Information is not only necessary for technical reasons but also to ascertain the compliance capability of the industry (apart from compliance readiness: see Zald, 1978). The responsible state agencies in Canada do not have the necessary resources to collect all (technical) information needed, nor do they possess the capacity to guarantee compliance of the industry regarding intended regulations. To attain the intended outcome of regulation a classical exchange relation is developed between industry and the state: information and compliance readiness by industry in exchange for influence on regulation. Business interest associations have become the intermediaries co-ordinating this exchange. This function is also reflected in the intra-organizational structure of interest associations in the dairy and meat sector: member firms are organized in (relatively autonomous) sub-units and committees particularly dealing with regulations regarding 'fair competition' and 'consumer protection'. Coleman (1984: 56):

> (these sub-units and committees) are preferred means by the associations for dealing with the state on matters related to the policy of ensuring fair competition or protecting consumers. In a sense, they were called into being in order to develop and implement the regulations that are needed for accomplishment of these policy goals. They are the key units with which the state shares responsibility for the regulatory system with associations.

Leckie and Morris (1980) have given different examples of how industry is involved in the consultation process. One example is the 'hamburger-case'. With the growing consumption of hamburgers — commonly processed in plants — in the early 1970s an increasing public concern developed regarding the microbiological quality of ground meat, both in Canada and the United States. In the USA standards were set up at that time. In Canada after a couple of years the Health Protection Branch of the Department of Health and Welfare also proposed standards of ground meat, however — as Leckie and Morris emphasize — 'with no preliminary dialogue with the major interested parties' (p. 95), obviously something un-Canadian. The position of the industry was clear, it did not want strict mandatory bacteriological standards. The business interest association of the meat processing industry (Meat Packers Council) reacted along two different lines. Firstly the need for these standards was debated and secondly the possibility of compliance was questioned, implicitly indicating both compliance readiness and capability from the side of the industry: the question is 'whether consistent compliance would prove possible or practical and whether public health benefits would equal or exceed compliance costs' (Leckie and Morris, 1980: 95).

The general picture is that state agencies in Canada are dependent on the industry for information, laboratory facilities (e. g. Coleman: 'The Health Protection Branch simply does not have the resources to do the research required by itself' [p. 32]), and compliance. This can also be illustrated by the differences between the dairy and meat sector. State agencies are less dependent on the industry in the meat sector compared with the dairy sector, due to the different inspection systems. In the meat processing sector state-inspection is much more developed. Firstly there is a specific state agency — the Meat Hygiene Division of the Department of Agriculture — responsible for Meat Inspection Acts both on federal and provincial level. There are, secondly, specific regulations for inspection of meat and slaughterhouse on municipal level (Leckie and Morris, 1980: 148–78). In the Meat Inspection Act criteria for inspection — based on quality standards of meat — and for the method and frequency of inspection are formulated. Thirdly, one important feature of the inspection system is the daily inspection by governmental inspectors located in each meat processing plant.

There are no specific inspection regulations for the dairy industry, but inspection procedures are laid down in the Agricultural Products Standards Act (Anderson, 1981: 35). Inspection is not daily and in each plant, but occasionally and on a provincial level.

Coleman (1984) has pointed to the consequences of the different inspection systems for the relation between state and industry. The inspection system in the meat sector 'ensures that government secures itself much of the basic information it needs to run the system. It needs industry input only when new products or new processing procedures are being introduced' (p. 28). Location of inspectors in each plant also 'enhances compliance in that sub-sector and lowers the need for the state to involve associations in the implementation of the system' (p. 30). In contrast, in the dairy industry occasional inspections do not supply agencies with the necessary detailed information and so they 'are more dependent on the industries involved for information than in the case of meat' (p. 30). On the other hand 'compliance is more dependent on persuasion than coercion' (p. 30).

The relatively less dependent relation of the state regarding the meat sector is also reflected in less involvement in consultation, or at least in more criticism of consultation procedures and actual regulations. By way of contrast the dairy industry is more involved in and more satisfied with state regulation in the sector (Anderson, 1981: 73). The dairy industry is also legally represented by the Ontario Dairy Council in quasi state bodies such as the Milk Advisory Committee (part of the Milk Commission of Ontario). In this committee all policy questions affecting the milk industry from prices to quality standards for fluid milk are required by law to be vetted (Coleman, 1984: 63). Another example of stronger involvement of the dairy industry in quality control is the legally authorized possibility of factory owners and their representatives to enter upon the farm of any of their suppliers to test the quality of milk from any cow (Anderson, 1981: 32)[7].

---

[7] Laid down in the 'Ontario Milk, Cheese and Butter Act'.

The Canadian system — notwithstanding the relatively low organizational development of interest associations — has some important benefits for the industry. As a result of the 'weak state' (Coleman), state agencies are dependent on business interest associations to obtain information and compliance. The not-institutionalized consultation system seems also a 'guarantee' that not 'every interest group or individual' is automatically represented (a complaint of UK manufacturers with respect to their system), and that business interest associations in fact have a monopoly in consultation procedures. In different governmental studies the under-representation of consumers and other groups is also stressed (Anderson; Leckie and Morris).

(b) United Kingdom — Institutionalized Consultation

State regulation of food quality in the UK has two characteristics. On the one hand there is a separation between drafting and enforcement. National government is responsible for drafting (Ministry of Agriculture), whereas enforcement is completely delegated to local enforcement authorities, with some degree of autonomy from national government, and is largely concentrated on the point-of-sale (and not in the factory) and on individual products. On the other hand formulation and initiation of new regulations is based on consultation. Before making any regulation the Food and Drugs Act 1955 (consolidated in the 1984 Act) requires that the Minister first consults those who appear to have an interest in the subject. As a result different interest groups or representative organizations are routinely involved in the policy making process.

The UK consultation system differs in two respects from the Canadian case. *Firstly* it is not an informal, ad hoc procedure but is based on a comparatively high developed and institutionalized consultation system of legally authorized committees. The most important ones with respect to quality of food are the Food Standards Committee (FSC) and the Food Additives and Contaminants Committee (FACC)[8]. The FSC was established in 1947 and was a direct result of the Second World War. As Ward (1976) has described, during the Second World War a higher degree of control was required for foodstuffs generally, to cope with wartime conditions. Specific regulations and orders were made by the Minister of Food. Ward notes 'To advise on the provisions to be included in these orders, an Interdepartmental Committee was set up in 1942 'to advise the Ministry of Food, upon request, in regard to the standards that would be appropriate for foods for which the Ministry may decide to provide standards of quality' (Ward, 1976: 27). In establishing this committee the basis for the postwar regulation structure, based on consultation and formulation, was laid. Ward states:

> In 1947 it was decided to continue the existence of a consultative body to review the need for food regulations but to replace the Interdepartmental Committee by a 'Food Standards Committee' with measures of independence. The FSC was set up to 'advise

[8] Other committees are the Committee on Medical Aspects of Food Policy and the Committee on Medical Aspects of Chemicals in Food and the Environment and various sub-committees.

the Ministers of Food and Health and the Secretary of State for Scotland as to the provision to be made concerning the composition of foods (other than liquid milk) and the labelling and marking of any foods for which provision is made, by (a) Statutory Orders under the Defence (Sale of Food) Regulations; on (b) Regulations (other than Milk or Dairy Regulations) under the Food and Drugs Acts; for preventing danger to health, loss of nutritional value or otherwise protecting purchasers'. (Ward, 1976: 27).

Until 1959 the Committee was kept on a fairly tight rein by the Ministry, but in that year the FSC got a more independent status. Since 1959 the FSC has been made up of an independent Chairman and nine members, three from the food trade, three with appropriate scientific expertise and three members with special concern for consumer views. 'No members are appointed to act as, nor do they see themselves as, representatives of particular organizations, but they contribute as individuals, as appropriate in view of their personal appointment by Ministers' (Ward, 1976: 28, 29). In 1951 a sub-Committee was formed for food additives and contaminants, that since 1964 has operated independently under the name, Food Additives and Contaminants Committee.

Like the Statutory Trade Associations in the Netherlands and the *Milch-wirtschaftsfonds* in Austria (see below), the FSC and the FACC in the UK are based on the principle of 'consensus': 'The Committee is encouraged to attempt its sometimes complex tasks, involving apparently conflicting views, by one basic principle. This is that, in the long term, there can be no fundamental divergence of interest between the consumer and the industries which supply him with food' (Ward, 1976: 24). The committees invite manufacturers associations, local authority associations and consumer bodies to present their views on a proposed regulation. Thereafter advice is given to the Minister. Apart from this committee-channel, industry can also comment directly to the Minister. This institutionalized consultation system is very important for business interest associations and is also reflected in the internal structure (committees, etc.) and activities of these associations (Grant, 1983) (See also Table 10.3 b). *Secondly* the extensive consultation is not so much the consequence of a weak state, but is a typical British response to conflicting interests, as Ward (1976: 37) has argued: 'it is an expression of the British ability to create institutions to reconcile apparently opposed viewpoints and to provide pragmatic solutions which often prove practical and acceptable'. In other words consultation can be seen as a mechanism for the state to get consent and compliance for legislation in a debated area.

In the 19th century consultation was hardly developed. On the one hand interest associations of manufacturers or consumers did not (generally) exist, but there was a general feeling of consumers and reputable manufacturers that quality regulation was necessary and that this was the proper role of the state. On the other hand there was no real need for the legislator to consult other parties 'in an area which is coincident with theft and in which an intent which is criminally fraudulent is palpably evident' (Kinch, 1980: 118). In particular in the 20th century (after the second world war) when quality competition between manufacturers and consumer criticism was increasing, quality regulation became a debatable area in which different interest groups with opposed viewpoints

criticized quality and quality regulations. Against this background the introduction of consultation must be explained.

The British system also has some benefits for manufacturers and their
associations. *Firstly* business interest associations play an important role in
consultation procedures and have an institutionalized influence on legislation.
Like the Canadian case national government is also dependent on information
given by the industry. Unlike the Canadian situation there is an extensive
organization of local enforcement authorities (almost 500), which could give
information to the state. But as a result of the peculiar British *point-of-sale*
enforcement system, local authorities are not active on factory level: 'There is no
point in taking samples in a factory and he has no right to know what is put into
a product' (Painter, 1981: 36), so manufacturers keep a monopoly on product
information. Painter (a consultant in trading law to private food industry): 'they
[manufacturers] would be horrified if they thought that enforcement officers
were able to come into the factory to look into the mixing bowl ... they believe
that the enforcement officer would not understand their manufacturing problems and could use the information gained for purposes of prosecution' (p. 36).
However there is an increasing pressure from the European Community to
introduce in all member states procedures of representative sampling, which is
only possible at factory level. But the British consultation system is probably a
barrier to this EC-regulation. In a recent governmental review it is argued that
this is a 'complex matter', that only can be resolved along the lines of consultation: 'it is difficult to see how any such measure could be introduced except on a
very long time scale and with agreement by interested parties' (Review of Food
Legislation, p. 49). *Secondly* the extended system of local enforcement
authorities creates the possibility of 'joint-ventures' between manufacturers and
authorities. Both parties have a common interest in prevention of prosecutions
(Waters, 1980) and in precise and detailed rules. Because day-to-day enforcement is not in the hands of the rule-making authority, there is no threat of goal-
displacement as discussed before.

Corporatist Quality Regulation

Regulatory policies and structures in which private interest groups are made
legally co-responsible or sometimes even completely responsible for formulation
and implementation of state regulation can be — according to Schmitter (1982)
— labeled as 'corporatism'. In these cases involvement of business interest
groups goes beyond institutionalized consultation procedures, discussed before.
In, for instance, the described case of the Food Standards Committee in the UK,
the state has the ultimate responsibility for implementation and formulation and
the involved interest groups have essentially an advisory role. In 'corporatist'
arrangements business interest groups are more heavily involved in regulation.
Apart from involvement in regulation of the product, business interest associations also can become involved in regulation of procedures (see Table 10.1).

In this paragraph three examples of 'classical corporatism' are discussed in
relation to quality regulation. Classical corporatist arrangements have — in

general — a multi-partite character (on the one hand interest groups with different or opposite interests and on the other hand the state), and are based on the principle of co-operation and (long term) consensus between the involved parties. The three examples discussed here are quality regulation in the Dutch and Austrian food processing industry and quality regulation in the British milk sector. The examples of the Netherlands and Austria are not so surprising, since both countries are in political and sociological literature well-known prototypes of classical corporatism. Corporatist arrangements in the UK seem more astonishing. Grant (1985) has commented on this point that

> It should be remembered that corporatist arrangements (...) are the exception rather than the rule in Britain. There is a strong tradition of consultation with sectional interests, but it is unusual for the state to designate a particular organization as the representative of a particular category of interest and to delegate powers to develop and implement public policy to a private government (p. 186).

In the *Netherlands* the 1950 Act on Statutory Industrial Organizations has resulted in the voluntary establishment by industry (or government) of fourteen 'vertical' Commodity Boards *(Produktschappen)* and twenty-one 'horizontal' Industrial Boards *(Bedrijfsschappen)*. Up till now these commodity boards were only established in the food processing sector, whereas industrial boards were also set up in other sectors. The vertical structure of commodity boards (such as the Dairy Commodity Board or Commodity Board for Meat and Livestock) is based on participation of business and employees involved in production and manufacturing of a certain product from raw material (for instance milk, fresh meat or cattle) to end product (for instance cheese, butter or meat products). Industrial boards organize firms (employers) and employees producing or manufacturing the same kinds of products (mostly) using the same kinds of techniques (on factory or artisan basis), such as the Industrial Board for the Meat processing industry or the Industrial Board for Butchers.

Interest organizations of employees and of entrepreneurs/employers are equally entitled to appoint representatives to the executives of the boards, to a great number of task-specific committees, to control institutions of the boards, etc. In practice, however, most boards are predominantly run by sector-specific business interest associations, since the largest trade unions have withdrawn from these statutory organizations. This was a result of the 'revolutionary' sixties, when the 'conflict model' of society was considered by the majority of labour movement as more adequate then the 'harmony model' of corporatism. For most sector-specific business interest associations, however, commodity and industrial boards are important institutions for influencing national and supranational policies in favour of sectoral interests. In certain respects sector-specific business interest associations (can) use these boards as private governments with a state licence.

The importance of statutory organizations for business interest associations is also reflected in the internal structure and activities of the involved associations. In the meat processing sector nine business interest associations are involved in either the Commodity Board for Meat and Livestock or for Poultry or in the

Industrial Board for the Meat processing industry, or for Poultry and Eggs or for Butchers. These associations are the Dutch Meat Manufacturers' Association (VNV), Association of Dutch Meat Manufacturers' Association (VNV), Association of Dutch Baconmanufacturers (VNB), Central Association for Meat Wholesale (COV), Association of the Dutch Poultrymanufacturing Industry (NEPLUVI), Dutch Association for Trade and Manufacturing of Poultry (VHVP) and four different business interest associations of butchers (differentiated on religious criteria). In the dairy processing sector two business interest associations (industry) participate in the Commodity Board for Dairy Products, the Royal Dutch Dairy Union (FNZ) and Association of Dairy Industry and Milk Hygiene (VVZM).

Apart from representation in the executives of these boards, the relevant business interest associations are represented (either by staff or by members) in a great number of task-specific committees of these boards. For example, the Dutch Meat Manufacturers Association (VNV) represents their members in about 45 external committees, of which about half (21) are committees of the Commodity Board for Meat and Lifestock. A number of committees deal with particular aspects of quality regulation, such as the Committee for Improvement Meat Quality, 'Salmonella Committee', Foundation Dutch Meat Products Control, Committee for Meat Inspection, Advisory Committee for Meat Inspection Act, etc.

Apart from government regulation, the boards have autonomous powers to lay down binding rules (ordinances) relating to, for instance, the quality of raw materials and end products in the sector they are responsible for. Until 1980 there were about seventy quality ordinances set by these corporatist boards, covering products ranging from sauerkraut to Dutch gin. Since consumers are not represented in the executives of the boards, their interests seem to be of secondary importance in this kind of quality regulation. The relative unimportance of consumer interests and the importance of business interests is also expressed in promotional literature of these boards: 'the intention of these ordinances is to prevent distortion of competition, to improve sales possibilities and to offer the consumer good information and advice' (Agricultural Commodity Boards, 1979: 4). The accent on business oriented quality regulation by commodity boards is a consequence of historical and institutional characteristics. Quality regulation with respect to public health and consumer interests is predominantly the responsibility of the Ministry of Public Health, whereas the Ministry of Agriculture is responsible for commodity boards in the food processing sector. Historically quality regulation of the Ministry of Agriculture was primarily aimed at export (as discussed before) and was embedded in the Act on the Export of Agricultural Products *(Landbouwuitvoerwet)* of 1928. This orientation on export (business interests) is automatically incorporated in the commodity boards.

However, as a result of EC policy regarding quality regulation, both with respect to competition and consumer interests, since the early seventies it is no longer permitted to have different quality standards and regulations on national level for products destined for foreign and domestic markets. National governments were asked to adjust their national quality regulations to Community directives. In the Netherlands the Act on the Export of Agricultural Products was replaced in 1974 by the new Act on Quality of Agricultural Products *(Landbouwkwaliteitswet)*. At the same time a specific agency was established within the Ministry of Agriculture to deal explicitly with quality of food products (see notes 4 and 5). Another effect of EC-policy was the curtailing of the autonomous rule-making authority of commodity boards. Within the framework of national and supra national (EC) legislation and regulation, the corporatist boards still have some autonomous power to regulate specific issues, but above all they have become more heavily involved in operationalization and enforcement of EC regulations on sectoral level.

Notwithstanding the well-known corporatist character of *Austria*, quality regulation in the dairy and meat processing sector is to a large extent a state affair. This state regulation is based on three different acts: Food Act *(Lebensmittelgesetz)* (LMG), Act on Market Regulation *(Marktordnungsgesetz)* (MOG) and the Livestock Act *(Viehwirtschaftsgesetz)* (VWG). The LMG is the most important regulation system for food. Quality standards (both for dairy and meat products) are formulated on the basis of this act. Formulation and implementation of quality regulations is the responsibility of the Federal Ministry of Health and Environment Protection. Business interest associations are involved along corporatist lines in this state regulation via the 'Codexcommittee'. The Codexcommittee can advise the Ministry in matters of quality standards and is also involved in operationalization of standards into 'codex norms', which are laid down in the Austrian Codex Alimentaris *(Österreichisches Lebensmittelbuch)*, which is part of the LMG. Implementation, control, supervision and sanctioning of these codex norms is, however, a state affair and is done by the Federal Ministry of Public Health and Environmental Protection.

In the codexcommittee different interest organizations (of farmers, industry, consumers and trade unions), public research institutes and different state agencies, are represented. Industry is represented by the Association of Austrian Manufacturers *(Vereinigung Österreichischer Industrieller)* (VOI) and the Federal Chamber *(Bundeswirtschaftskammer)* (BWK), an industrial chamber functioning as a compulsory peak association of the whole economy. Since product-specific interests (for instance for meat or dairy products) are not organized in separate interest associations in Austria, the influence of these interests on specific quality regulation may be low. For instance the VOI organizes industrial firms of all sectors, but does not have product-specific (even no sector-specific) sub-units. The BWK on the other hand does have sector-specific sub-units. With respect to the dairy and meat-processing sector, the relevant subunit is *Fachverband der Nahrungs- und Genußmittelindustrie*, on federal level, and *Fachgruppe* on provincial level. Involvement in Codex-activities is a central task of the BWK and is considered as very important for regulation of competition (Traxler, 1983: 44).

Apart from the system of state quality regulation in Austria there are some other, additional quality standards for dairy and meat products. With respect to dairy products different types of market-regulations are laid down in the MOG, such as for protection of the domestic market, for supply and for quality: 'preparation of milk and milk products of faultless quality', by means of 'fixing of quality standards and the implementation of regular quality controls' (Traxler, 1985: 152). Implementation sanctioning of these regulations is delegated to the *Milchwirtschaftsfonds* (MWF), in which interest associations of farmers, business, and employees are represented. Business interests are represented by the already mentioned BWK. Like the Dutch corporatist statutory organizations the MWF is based on the principle of consensus: 'decisions must be reached either unanimously or by four-fifths majority' (Traxler, 1985: 153). So, quality standards are, like the other regulations, according to Traxler 'subject to political control of the interest associations involved' (153). The difference with the Dutch situation is however the absence of the large trade unions in the statutory organizations and the existence of relatively well organized business interest associations for product-specific interests.

The meat sector is much less regulated than the dairy sector (Traxler, 1983 b: 39). There are some market-regulations with respect to price, product and quality, based on the *Viehwirtschaftsgesetz* (VWG). Here again a tri-partite committee *(Vieh- und Fleischkommission)* has got some powers of implementation with respect to a number of regulations. This committee is installed by the Federal Ministry for Agriculture, and consists of interest groups of farmers, employees and business.

The last example of corporatist arrangement with respect to quality regulation is the dairy sector in the *United Kingdom*. The business interest association for the dairy sector — the Dairy Trade Federation (DTF) — is involved in quality regulation via a statutory organization: the 'Joint Committee'. In this Joint Committee the DTF negotiates with the Milk Marketing Board — a semi-state organization for farmers — on different aspects of milk. According to Grant (1985: 185) the composition and powers of the Joint Committee are laid down in a statutory instrument approved by Parliament and cover matters apart from prices for manufacturing milk such as allocation of supplies and quality control. Quality control — testing milk for butterfat and solids-not-fat — has been a private affair of the industry over many years. It was not until 1962 that the Joint Committee introduced a comprehensive scheme ('Milk Quality Payment Scheme') for regularly testing all supplies and paying the producer a price directly linked to the compositional quality, hygienic quality and for the presence of antibodies (MMB, 1981 a, 1981 b).

Enforcement of Quality Regulations by Business Interest Associations

Another variant of corporatist regulation — as defined before — is delegation of certain implementation tasks of the state to private organizations, or state licence for private organizations to fulfill regulatory tasks (that would otherwise have been done by the state). Since quality regulation is predominantly a state responsibility — as illustrated before — one may suppose that delegation to private organizations or state licence of private regulation is only possible under specific conditions. Apart from the presence of a collective interest in self regulation by business and absence of public ciritcism, the most important conditions seem to be: (a) capacity of private organizations to bind members to the regulatory policy of the organization; (b) resources to perform regulatory activities (know-how, professional staff, financial resources); and (c) relative autonomy from the state and the functional group (see also De Vroom, 1985: 130). Since these conditions have been discussed in other chapters of this book I will concentrate in this section on producing some results from the international research project.

Seventy business interest associations of 349 BIAs are involved in enforcement of quality in different industrial sectors and countries, as illustrated in Table 10.7. In Switzerland BIAs have a relatively high score with respect to involvement in enforcement of quality: 17 BIAs (32.1 %) of a total of 53 BIAs. Switzerland is followed by the Netherlands (26.4 %), Sweden (24.2 %), Germany (24.0 %) and Austria (22.2 %). In the other countries involvement of BIAs in enforcement is relatively low: UK (10.8 %), Canada (7.8 %), Italy (6.2 %) and Spain (5.3 %).

Out of 70 business interest associations involved in enforcement of quality, 17 associations (24.3 %) are active in this field in the dairy and meat sectors. These 17 associations we find in Germany (1), the Netherlands (9), Sweden (3) and Switzerland (4). For 12 associations enforcement of quality is only a minor activity, for the remaining 5 BIAs it is a major activity (see Tables 10.8, 10.9 and 10.10).

Table 10.7 Involvement of BIAs in Enforcement of Quality

Country	No Activity	Minor Activity	Major Activity	Involvement in % of Total Number BIAs
Austria	14	2	2	22.2
Canada	47	2	2	7.8
Germany	38	4	8	24.0
Italy	15	1		6.2
Netherlands	53	15	4	26.4
Spain	18	1		5.3
Sweden	25	5	3	24.2
Switzerland	36	11	6	32.1
United Kingdom	33	2	2	10.8
Total	279	43	27	20.0
	79.9 %	12.3 %	7.7 %	20.0

Source: International Research Project on BIAs.

Conclusion

Quality regulation (either state or private) is very important for business, especially to regulate competition. In this respect a distinction can be made between quality regulation to prevent 'swindlers', 'unqualified or irresponsible

Table 10.8 Business Interest Associations Involved in Enforcement of Quality Regulations in the Dairy Processing Industry

Country	Business Interest Associations	Minor Activity	Major Activity
Germany	Landesvereinigung der Milch-Wirtschaft in Nordrhein-Westfalen (LVNRW)	X	
Netherlands	Bond van Coöperatieve Zuivelfabrieken in Friesland (BvCZF)	X	
	Coöperatieve Zuid-Hollandse Organisatie van Zuivelverenigingen (CZOZ)	X	
	Zuid-Hollandse Zuivelbond (ZHZ)		X
	Gelders-Overijsselse Zuivelbond (GOZ)		X
	Vereniging van Zuivelindustrie en Melkhygiëne (VVZM)	X	
	Koninklijke Nederlandse Zuivel-Vereniging (FNZ)	X	
Sweden	Swedish Dairy Association (SMR)		X
Switzerland	Verband Schweiz. Schachtelkäsefabrikanten (SESK)		X
	Schweiz. Milchkäufer Verband (SMKV)	X	
	Schweiz. Genossenschaft der Weich- und Halbhartkäse Fabrikanten (SGWH)		X
Total	11	7	4

Source: International Research Project on BIAs.

Table 10.9 Business Interest Associations Involved in Enforcement of Quality Regulations in the Meat Processing Industry

Country	Business Interest Associations	Minor Activity	Major Activity
Netherlands	Netherland's Fats and Oilseeds-Trade Association (NOFOTA)		X
	Vereniging van Nederlandse Vleeswaren Fabrikanten (VNV)	X	
	Nederlandse Bond van Handelaren in en Bewerkeres van Slachtprodukten (NBHBS)	X	
Sweden	Federation of Swedish Food-Industries (SLIM)	X	
	Swedish Farmers' Meat Marketing Association (SCAN)	X	
Switzerland	Verband Schweiz. Fleischwaren-Fabrikanten (VSFF)	X	
Total	6	5	1

Source: Intern. Research Project on BIAs.

producers' (both representing 'unfair' competition) and 'outsiders' (foreign trade or producers from outside the domain of an organized collective interest).

Table 10.10 Number of Sector Specific Business Interest Associations[1] Involved in Enforcement of Quality in Dairy- and Meat Sector in Different Countries (1980)

Country	No	Activity Minor	Major	Total
Canada	8			8
Germany	7	1		8
Netherlands	13	6	3	22
Sweden	1	2	1	4
Switzerland	4	3	1	8
UK	3			3
Total	36	12	5	53
	67.9	22.6	9.4	100.0

Source: International Research Project on BIAs.
[1] In this table there are only those associations included which are selected for research with respect to the international research project on business interest associations. Countries without sector specific associations for Dairy or Meat (like Austria) are not included in this table.

Since quality regulation — from the point of view of business — is closely linked to competition, a collective interest in quality control may cause at the same time conflicting interests in the operationalization of a quality control scheme, as several examples have illustrated. Self regulation by business interest associations may, in other words, cause 'management of diversity problems' (case of 'smoked sausage'). Another problem of self regulation may be the lack of confidence of the public (of consumers) in self control of the industry. One way to overcome these conflicting problems is state regulation.

We have seen that, indeed, quality regulation in all the countries studied in the international research project is to a large extent a state affair. At the same time, however, the empirical data show a high degree of associational involvement in state quality regulation. There are two reasons for this involvement. Firstly interest associations can be necessary intermediaries between the industry and the state. On the one side only associations seem able to collect and mobilize technical know how (from their members), necessary to operationalize quality standards. On the other side state regulation can only be effective if there is a certain degree of compliance on the side of the industry, or as Zald (1978) has put it: 'the effectiveness of the application of sanctions and annunciation of norms depends on the compliance-readiness and compliance capability of target elements, the extent to which target element elites agree with norms and the costs of compliance' (p. 86). Business interest associations can play an important role in finding out the possibilities of compliance under their members. They can also be important in controlling the behaviour of members with respect to quality standards agreed on. Secondly business interest associations may be involved in state quality regulation to bring about regulations that are in favour of their members. As illustrated, this means in general legislation oriented to certain kinds of competition (unfair competitors and outsiders). Another objective of associational involvement may be the defence of (business oriented) quality regulation against 'consumerist' issues.

What, however, are the limits of associative action with respect to quality regulation? From the cases described in this chapter and from the data of the international research project, we can draw the conclusion that the shape of associational involvement in quality regulation does not reflect the characteristics of business interest associations, rather the characteristics of the state (or sector). For instance the important intermediary role of business interest associations in the Canadian food processing sector (relatively less developed associations compared with other countries) is primarily a result of the weak state. This is also expressed by the differences between the dairy and meat processing sector in Canada. In the meat processing sector the state is more involved (inspection) with the result of a less developed intermediary role for the business interest associations in this sector. We also found these sectoral differences in other countries studied.

The involvement of business interest associations in the UK food processing industry is a result of the well developed, institutionalized consultation procedures. In the Netherlands and Austria the existing corporatist structures enables associations to deal with quality regulation. Only in those cases where business interest associations have got a delegated power to enforce quality standards, are characteristics of the involved associations important for explanation.

Another and increasing limit on the involvement of business interest associations might be growing public concern, consumer pressure and consumer involvement in quality regulations. Recently, consumer interests have become more in the forefront of state regulation. Consumers have got institutionalized access to state agencies and national and supra-national (EC) regulations have more and more incorporated specific consumer interests with respect to quality in food.

What can we learn from quality control about organizational development? The chapter has shown that quality regulation is very much a state affair; even in Austria, with its neo-corporatist traits, quality regulation in the dairy and meat processing sectors is a matter for the state. In the Netherlands, the involvement of business interest associations in quality regulation is primarily the result of the existing corporatist structure in the food processing sector. Within this framework associations deal with different kinds of regulation. So far it's not quality as such but the semi-state structure that has had an important effect on associational development. More generally, associational involvement in quality control seems to be limited by two important factors — the implications of quality control for competition which creates conflicts of interest which associations find it difficult to manage; and public suspicion about self-regulation by interested parties. Where associational involvement is strong, as in Canada, this seems to be a reflection of the weak state, rather than a consequence of any strengths of the associations themselves.

In summary, the case of quality regulation provides some useful lessons about the limits of organizational development in food processing associations. A more general lesson to be drawn in relation to the debate about the emergence of a model of associative order is that there are some public policy issues which can be only partially dealt with through such a system of self regulation. There are times when state authority has to be exercised by the state itself in relation to private interests.

Chapter 11

Conclusions

WYN GRANT and WILLIAM COLEMAN

The International Institute of Management project on business interest associations was informed by the debate on neo-corporatism which engaged many social scientists from the mid-1970s onwards. In particular, the project was conceived in order to develop a systematic, comparative data base for the analysis of the willingness and ability of organized employers to contribute to corporatist bargains.

Before considering how the evidence presented on the food processing sector in this volume assists such an analysis, it is necessary to consider briefly what has happened to the broader debate on neo-corporatism. The debate has spawned an extensive literature and it is not proposed to summarize or review it here. The literature is often confused and contradictory, not least because there is no agreed definition of the phenomenon under discussion. However, it should be possible by the mid-eighties to stand back and ask what lessons can be learnt from a decade of academic endeavour.

One important gain is an improvement in our understanding of what might be called macro corporatism, that is, the negotiation of 'major socio-economic issues which affect the interests of classes as a whole.' (Cawson, 1986, p. 72). Having noted this improvement, one must not make ambitious claims for neo-corporatism. What is on offer is a middle range theory. As Cawson notes (1986, p. 32), corporatism is 'a partial theory of politics which cannot stand on its own as a theory of the state, still less one of society, as in writing about the corporate state, corporate society and so on.'

If, following Katzenstein (1985, p. 32) we view democratic corporatism at the macro level in terms of an ideology of social partnership shared by major producer groups in a society; a relatively centralized system of interest groups; and policy coordination through continuous bargaining, then these traits are found in a relatively small group of countries. All the countries possessing them (whether in terms of liberal or social corporatism, to use Katzenstein's terminology) are small ones: Austria, Belgium, Luxembourg, Norway, Sweden, Switzerland, and the Netherlands for the first couple of decades after the war. As Katzenstein shows in his work, there are good reasons why such countries should follow concertative strategies. Their survival in a highly competitive international market depends on their ability to fill specialized export niches, a strategy which depends on the maintenance of competitiveness through domestic cooperation, but also of social cohesion through the compensation of disadvantaged groups.

Some commentators might wish to add West Germany to the list; we would not. That is not to say that there are not corporatist traits present in the West German system. However, it is too easy to become fascinated by the relatively brief experience of 'concerted action' that occurred at the national level between 1967 and 1977. When one moves down to the sectoral level, one finds in the food processing industry, for example, an associative system of employers which does not lend itself to effective concertation (not even to mounting an effective defence against the unions without intervention from the peak association levels, as Hilbert and Voelzkow show in Chapter 6). The food processing industry is by no means exceptional in this respect. Streeck has shown (1983, p. 274) that organizations of employers in Germany are genuinely committed to a pluralist conception of representation and resent incorporation into the state.

Even in the smaller countries, there are signs of growing strain in corporatist arrangements. Wage solidarity has been difficult to maintain in Sweden, whilst the employers have regarded such ideas as wage-earner funds as changing the basis on which cooperation takes place. Austria has found it difficult to manage ecological protests within its corporatist system, demands that do not fit well within a framework of bargaining which is premised on the assumption that the maximization of production is a desirable and generally accepted goal. More generally, it has been argued that the smaller European democracies have postponed problems from the 1970s instead of tackling them, for example, labour hoarding by nationalized industries in Austria.

The defenders of neo-corporatist arrangements would, of course, maintain that the occurrence of particular strains within such structures should not be seen as an indication of their impending demise. Predicting the downfall of the Swedish system has, for example, some of the hallmarks of an academic 'end of the world' industry; when the predicted event fails to occur on schedule, it is merely postponed or explained away in terms of some psychologically satisfying but ultimately unconvincing rationalization.

Even so, neo-corporatist arrangements at the macro level do appear to be the property of small states in prosperous times. Whether they are prosperous because they are corporatist, or corporatist because they are prosperous, is a complex question. To date answers given suggest there is some kind of historical 'virtuous cycle' in which full employment, low inflation, social peace and corporatist bargaining feed off each other. However, such a cycle is capable of external interruption: supposing, for example (written in October 1986), a majority Peoples' Party (conservative) government was returned in Austria in November 1986. In the backwash of the resentment caused by the 1986 presidential election campaign, would everything go on as before?

Even if the corporatist arrangements in smaller states survive such external challenges, it does not mean that they offer a 'model' which can be transferred from one country to another. One thing that we do know from the accumulated research is that corporatist arrangements suddenly imposed from above are very unstable. They are more likely to succeed when they are built up from below as part of a long drawn out historical process. Moreover, they require special conditions for their successful survival which are found in a limited number of countries only.

Neo-corporatism as a macro phenomenon, then, appears to be a useful but limited form of explanation. It tells us something about how particular small countries, to date concentrated in Western Europe, govern themselves and, in particular, manage their economies. It is not an invention which has yet been exported to the less favourable climates of other small democracies such as New Zealand. The Swedes are, in any case, uncomfortable with the idea that they have corporatist arrangements, and the Austrians, although keen to circulate accounts of their paradigmatic case, do not claim that it is Austria's contribution to the enrichment of the art of government.

A second important outcome from the research carried out on neo-corporatism over the past decade is the growing recognition of the importance of corporatist arrangements at the meso or sectoral level. First signalled by Wassenberg (1982) and Cawson (1982), meso corporatism has attracted increasing attention from researchers. Several collections of studies have already appeared (Cawson, ed., 1985; Streeck and Schmitter, eds., 1985). Meso corporatist arrangements are found in virtually all western democracies, whether or not corporatism occurs at the macro level. To be sure, Traxler's chapter in this volume shows that macro corporatist arrangements, where they exist, will have a substantial impact on corporatist practices at the sectoral level. Where macro corporatism does not exist as in Canada or the United States, meso corporatist arrangements may tend to have a narrower scope and be weakened by the prevalent liberal values and ethos of competition among interest groups.

It is not enough, of course, to demonstrate that meso corporatist arrangements exist. One wants to know why they exist, how they operate, and who benefits and who loses from their existence. The studies of the food processing industry contained in this book allow us to examine such questions more closely.

Conditions Favouring Meso Corporatism

Generally speaking, the corporatist literature has identified three, sometimes interdependent, situations where meso corporatism becomes more likely:

1. Meso corporatism occurs as a defensive reaction by business to counter collective action by another producer group. The studies in this book have demonstrated that the critical other in such arrangements need not be labour. It may be farmers, or a professional group. Hence we may not be dealiing with tripartite concertative arrangements designed to secure the cooperation of labour, as is common with macro corporatism. There are often three partners, but in the food processing industry these are usually, the farmers, the processors, and the state (although other players may include the distributors, as in Switzerland, or the consumers, as in Sweden). Labour is, in many respects, a somewhat marginal player in the food processing industry. The industry is not

generally labour intensive, and there are many part-time and seasonal workers. (See the chapters by Hilbert and Voelzkow, and by Rainbird). This means that labour relations questions are not generally a high priority for employers.

2. Meso corporatism occurs in the context of positive adjustment or industrial policies for sectors threatened with decline or in the midst of an industrial crisis. In such instances, labour becomes the more likely partner, but examples of other groups such as farmers are available as well. (Atkinson and Coleman, 1985).

3. Meso corporatism represents in some instances an attempt by business to preempt state regulation in a particular sector through developing self-regulatory organizations that coopt or disarm particular opponents. One can see attempts of this kind in the food processing industry in relation to quality control issues (discussed by de Vroom in Chapter 10).

Processes of these kinds may be observed in any industry. A particular concern of this book was to see whether there was a 'spillover' effect from corporatist arrangements in agriculture into food processing with arrangements based in the agricultural sector also embracing food processors. As Cawson notes (1986, p. 113), 'almost everywhere agriculture has been the first industrial policy, seeking to rationalize production and stabilise cyclical fluctuations.' It is clear from the various chapters, especially that by Coleman, that there is a marked 'spillover' effect in dairy processing, a subsector particularly close to the farm gate. However, as indicated above, the relationship with agriculture may also lead to defensive meso corporatist arrangements by food processors seeking protection from the collective strength of farmers. Whatever the origins of a particular arrangement, it is clearly necessary to review the close relationship between agriculture and the food processing industry before proceeding any further.

Food Processing as a 'Shadow' Industry

Much of the food processing industry exists in the shadow of agriculture, an industry which has fewer employees and less output, but is much more effectively organized for political purposes. Small and Smith (1984) note that subsectors of the food processing industry such as dairying are more influenced by agricultural policy than industrial policy. They comment that (p. 185), 'the varying problems of the meat and dairy sector stem in large part from the EC *agricultural* policy.' Even so, the relationship between the two sectors is weaker than it once was. 'Food manufacturers are making much less extensive use of farm and food materials but correspondingly more intensive use of capital, packaging, and wholesaling and business services.' (Connor, Rogers, Marion and Mueller, 1985, p. 32). This particular observation arising from an American study has a more general applicability, indicating a growing division between primary food processing which uses agricultural products as its raw materials, and a secondary industry which receives many of its inputs from the primary sector. 'The primary processing sector is still closely linked to agriculture, whereas the secondary sector is becoming increasingly similar in structure to other branches of the manufacturing sector.' (OECD, 1983 a, p. 13).

What may be termed the political shadow status of the food processing industry manifests itself both in the organization of the state and the organization of the industry's associations. As Pestoff shows in Chapter 5, in all the countries studied, the food processing industry lies primarily under the jursidiction of the agricultural ministry. In only two cases does this ministry contain the word 'food' in its title. Such a finding points to the general tendency within such ministries to regard farmers as their principal client group and to consider the needs of the food processing industry with this orientation in mind. Food processing becomes isolated, then, from the mainstream of industrial policy making which is found elsewhere in government (e. g., in the Economics and Research and Technology ministries in West Germany), but is *also* a backwater when it comes to agricultural policy making. As a British food processing association official has complained, the policies of agriculture ministers 'have sometimes been of benefit to this or that part of the food industry but that has been almost entirely coincidental.' (Stocker, 1983, p. 251). Stocker argues that such state structural arrangements are important because they encourage giving priority to short-term farming policies over longer term strategic food policies. (Stocker, 1983, p. 253).

A similar bias in favour of agricultural as opposed to industrial interests arises in the realm of associative action. Agriculture, on the one hand, is well known for the effectiveness of its organizations and its ability to establish close links with politicians and civil servants and, on the other, for the willingness of farmers to resort to more unorthodox tactics such as blocking roads or violent demonstrations. It also cultivates close and politically helpful links with other industries, notably fertilizers, agrochemicals and the manufacturers of farm machinery. In comparison, food processing looks poorly organized. While it maintains links with the packaging and machinery industries, the ties are not nearly as strong as those the farming community has maintained and used with its suppliers.

More importantly, food processing is not generally well organized for representational purposes. There are exceptions, of course: the Austrian system is a model of cohesion, whilst the British system has moved incrementally towards a more effective set of arrangements. However, when compared to agriculture, the system of associations appears highly pluralist in character, reflecting the heterogeneity of the industry. There are large numbers of associations often serving very narrow interest categories. The domains of these associations often overlap, and there is sometimes direct competition for influence. Higher order associations are often poorly resourced, incomplete in their coverage, and with weak links to those associations they do organize.

As van Waarden notes in Chapter 4, such a chaotic system may well suit the larger transnationals in the industry, and can deal effectively with product specific, technical questions. However, its limitations are particularly apparent at the European Community level, where (as discussed in Pestoff's chapter) the industry's ability to express and follow through a collective position is seriously deficient when compared with agriculture or, even another manufacturing sector such as chemicals. The latter industry, also studied in the IIM project, has made a vigorous and effective response to the need for organization at the EEC level. In comparison, the food processing industry's level of organization would be viewed as more appropriate to a subsectoral organization in the chemical industry.

As van Waarden emphasizes, the most important characteristic of the food processing industry, and the most influential in explaining its pattern of associability, is its heterogeneity. Nevertheless, the industry *does* have interests as a whole, if only as a consequence of its political shadow status. However, because of the weakness of encompassing industry associations, the needs of the food processing industry end up being treated as an afterthought to those of agriculture. The 'industrial policy community' is not interested in the industry, and the priorities of the agricultural policy community lie elsewhere. For example, in 1984 when economies were sought in the CAP, the British Food and Drink Federation claims that 'DG VI [agriculture] swiftly moved in on the attack, in an attempt to claw back expenditures which were occurring outside the farm and commodity boundaries over which it presides.'

Why in the face of such common threats to the industry, has there not been mobilization to meet them? First, as van Waarden emphasizes, in many countries a substantial proportion of food processing is undertaken by farmers' cooperatives whose first loyalty is to their members. They are less likely to be interested in strengthening a distinctive food processing interest (although consumers' cooperatives are clearly in a different position). Second, as Coleman points out in his chapter on agricultural policy, in all the countries studied, agricultural policy was found often to be organized differently in the various subsectors. Hence, each subsector tends to develop bargaining links with the corresponding group of farmers, rather than with other food processors. Each subsectoral association, then, is likely to be preoccupied with the terms and conditions of its own particular deal, rather than with the broader picture.

While these arguments are clearly valid, there is one nagging question that remains. Farmers, too, are a very heterogeneous group, and yet this does not prevent them from organizing effectively. For example, they differ on the basis of whether they are arable or livestock farmers; on whether they are tenant farmers, individual owners, or agribusinesses; on whether or not they are members of a cooperative; on whether they are large scale or small scale farmers; on whether they have easy or difficult land; and on whether or not they sell directly to a food processor. Despite what would appear to be centrifugal interests, in most countries, they also recognize that they have a common interest as farmers. No doubt the existence of ministries of agriculture as focal points of identification is part of the story.

There is, however, a more general reason to take into consideration. No farmer is a significant enough producer to be able to exert direct influence on government; many food processing firms are. Hence, a firm like Unilever can contemplate conducting a large part of its relations with government on its own behalf through a specialized government relations division. Such an option is not open to farmers: to exert influence, they have to associate. Moreover, farmers exist in an industry in which prices and output are heavily influenced by state action. In contrast, although food processing does face substantial regulation in the area of quality control, most of the rules have been around a long time, and many of them fall into a 'category of pragmatic acquiescence.' (Connor, Rogers, Marion and Mueller, 1985, p. 418). Indeed, it is the disturbance of this stable environment by the increased interest of the EEC in quality related issues that has been one of the factors prompting some rationalization of food processing associations. Agriculture thus has very strong incentives to associate in terms of industry structure and government impact which are not present in the same way in food processing.

Does it matter that food processing has weaker associative arrangements than agriculture, other than for food processing manufacturers? It does in the sense that the food manufacturing industry faces, to an increasing extent, a number of problems which are of broader interest and importance. As Grosskopf comments (1983, p. 93):

> With the growing complexity of the food chain, and the development of increasingly significant horizontal linkages between its component parts and other sectors of the economy, the need for greater coherence in the formulation of policies for the food chain is increasing. Such coherence is necessary in order to ensure that individual measures are effective and is necessary if the relationship between the various agents in the food chain is to be regulated in a manner which is socially acceptable.

A particular problem area which confronts the industry is that of quality control, and in particular the growing public resistance to the use of additives in food products. This is a serious challenge to the industry because some food products could not be made without additives (e. g., margarine would consist of separate layers without emulsifiers); others would have a shorter shelf life and hence become more expensive and less attractive to consumers; whilst yet others would be unattractive purchases without added colours. Against this, some manufacturers are now following a marketing strategy of emphasizing the additive free character of their products.

As de Vroom shows in his chapter, regulation of quality has generally become a state matter, although seventy business associations in the industry are involved in the enforcement of quality standards. The determining factor is not the characteristics of the association, but rather state weakness, or its weakness in relation to a particular sector. Hence, the weaknesses of the associational system could be said to have contributed to a missed opportunity for organizational development in relation to quality control. Moreover, although associations may be able to influence the formulation and implementation of regulations on traditional adulteration and contamination issues, they may be less able to cope with the newer wave of criticisms of food additives.

Meso Corporatism: Who Benefits?

Business firms enter into meso corporatist arrangements in the food processing industry, then, largely in order to defend themselves against effective and strong farmers' organizations and their supportive agricultural departments. Among the most effective of these arrangements are those found in the dairy industry, a subsector in which sectoral conditions seem to 'wash out' national divergences in approaches to industrial policy. As Cawson notes (1986, p. 110), 'Meso corporatism seems to be almost everywhere characteristic of [the dairy industry], and in particular milk production and marketing.' As Manchester explains (1983, p. 8), 'Instability is inherent in fluid milk markets. Institutions must be created to deal with it.' Milk is a highly perishable commodity, which may experience fluctuations in supply which are not related to variations in demand. Governments throughout the world have recognized the need for orderly marketing structures. However, because there are a number of interests involved (farmers, processors, government, final consumers), whatever framework is created must involve a bargaining process in which the negotiators are able to secure the compliance of those they represent (whether or not with the assistance of state backed sanctions). In short, conditions are propitious for meso corporatism.

As is apparent from the material presented in this book, many of these arrangements are highly intricate pieces of political design, representing carefully constructed balancing arrangements between potentially opposed interests which have evolved over half a century or more. However, one must not allow a fascination with process to obscure questions about outcome. One may observe a tendency in such arrangements for, once again, the interests of food processing to be overshadowed by those of farming. Preventing economic, political and social turbulence in the farming community is often placed before having an efficient and successful dairy processing industry.

In order to ask who benefits, it is necessary to first ask how they benefit. In other words, what are the criteria for assessing corporatist arrangements? In practice, an emphasis is often placed on security and stability. For example, security of supply for manufacturers, security of income for farmers, plus a stable decision making environment which can handle potential conflicts of interest. The broader objective is the preservation of social peace by, for example, ensuring that family farmers do not go out of production; that rural creameries stay open; and that the consumer can be sure that his or her favourite milk product will be available on the supermarket counter (or, in Britain, on the doorstep). Such a stable and secure environment for the industry can be justified on a number of grounds. For example, it permits the heavy investment required in specialized transport fleets, and encourages continuing investment in dairy herds and in processing plants. It also allows the routinization of safety procedures, and industry involvement in the maintenance and development of quality standards.

Such arrangements do generally seem to have been successful in stabilizing and improving farm incomes; what is less predictable is the effect they have had on profits in the dairy processing industry. In Canada, Jacek (1986) shows that dairy processors capture very favourable profits compared to other sectors. In Britain, returns in the industry are below those in manufacturing as a whole. Part of the problem is that of disentangling the effect of the meso corporatist arrangements themselves, and of other relevant factors such as the degree of protection against foreign competition. The relationship between meso corporatist arrangements and company profitability is, Jacek's pioneering article aside, a neglected area which would repay further attention by researchers.

For most dairy enterprises, lower returns than the manufacturing average are probably an acceptable state of affairs. They know what conditions are like in the industry, and some of them are farmer cooperatives in any case. Single product firms have a stake in the long run viability of the sector; they are likely to be willing to trade short run profits for long run viability. Conglomerates, however, have different interests. Rather than being tied to the long-run interests of the sector as a whole, and pursuing appropriate strategies through associative action, they are likely to switch investment to more profitable areas (see Cawson, 1986, p. 111).

In practice, however, they may use the options of both exit and voice (or, more precisely, exit with voice). Relatively few dairy firms are conglomerates, but in the British case, one firm (Express Dairies) was acquired by a conglomerate (Grand Metropolitan). Grand Metropolitan became worried about the fact that it made less profits on its dairying activities than, say, on its gaming casinos or its private health clinics. The corporation placed the blame in its 1984 annual report on the 'the panoply of controls and constraints on commercial freedom in the UK stemming from our own Government's control of the liquid milk margin coupled with the monopoly powers and commercial activities of the Milk Marketing Board.'

Grand Metropolitan found two solutions to this problem. It sold a large part of its dairy business to a specialist food processing company. And, in conjunction with other dairy companies through the Dairy Trade Federation, it pressed for an inquiry into the impact of the Milk Marketing Board's own dairy products business on the independent companies. The subsequent government commissioned inquiry, the Touche Ross report, found that the MMB's dairy products division was not operating like a normal commercial enterprise. Its main purpose appeared to be to secure an outlet for the milk produced by farmers.

This particular case, from a liberally inclined country with a neo-liberal government, is cited because it raises wider issues. First, it shows that meso corporatist arrangements in dairying are open to criticism from businesses which are not part of the prevalent sectoral consensus. Second, it at least raises the possibility that the corporatist arrangements in dairying are part of a long shadow cast from the farming sector, a shadow which stunts the growth of dairy processing, whilst allowing farmers to benefit from a secure outlet for their produce.

In short, as Burns comments (1983 b, p. 61), 'the political power of the farming community leads to market power via government action.' Various support schemes have the effect of passing 'the excess capacity of the agricultural sector on to first stage processors.' (1983 b, p. 69). The task of ensuring that this capacity is taken up by processors leads to a variety of arrangements which, whatever their merits, represent a substantial departure from the traditional model of the autonomous capitalist utilizing different factors of production to make a competitive product which maximises his or her profits. For example, in the British and Austrian systems, there is an annual allocation of 'relevant farms' to each milk buyer who is obliged to accept all production from these farms.

As Schmitter and Streeck anticipated (1981, p. 236), the dairy example illustrates how business interest associations have been able 'to acquire the capacity to procure the compliance of their members with negotiated aggreements on matters which would otherwise be entirely under their discretion as private owners.' Capitalists behave in a way which is considerably at variance with the supposed logic of free market capitalism. What one sees in such subsectors as dairying is a classically corporatist approach in the sense that 'organization is both constrained by and shapes the nature of the interests concerned.' (Cawson, 1986, p. 11). Moreover, for all the emphasis in the preceding discussion on the overshadowing of food processing by farming, there may be elements of a non-zero-sum game in the sense that both farmers and processors (and, less likely, consumers) may be better off than they would be under a completely free market. To return to our initial question, the entry into meso corporatist arrangements by business firms often represents a defensive reaction in the face of the superior organizational capacity of farmers and a state bureaucracy sympathetic to them.

The Analysis and the Schmitter-Streeck Model

It was intended that this book should say something that was of interest to academics and practitioners interested in the food processing industry. However, its main purpose was to provide a sectoral test of some of the main issues and ideas set out by Schmitter and Streeck in their research design (1981). Such is the richness and complexity of this document that it was necessary to highlight certain themes from it in this book, as discussed in the introduction.

The first general point to emerge is that some of the language of analysis developed by Schmitter and Streeck needs to be refined. This is particularly apparent in relation to the concepts of 'logic of membership' and 'logic of influence'. As van Waarden makes clear in his chapter, what were initially seen as competing imperatives influencing associative action have a symbiotic relationship with one another. When these two sets of variables are operationalized, it is difficult to separate them. Moreover, it is clear that the logic of membership is strongly influenced by the logic of influence. The institutional characteristics of the interested category (logic of membership) may be significantly shaped by the actions of public interlocutors (logic of influence). For example, product markets are influenced by government's role as a customer, by product regulations etc. etc. In many sectors, then, product markets do not exist independently of government; they are shaped by government, although clearly the extent of government influence will vary from one subsector to another.

The symbiosis between the two logics helps explain a second finding that imposes a qualification on the initial hypothesis. On the one hand, as is apparent from the chapters by Traxler, van Waarden and Pestoff, the ability of the food processing industry to organize as a whole to handle complexity through its associations is relatively poor. And yet, as Jacek shows in his chapter, the other aspect of organizational development, relative autonomy, is present in a number of individual associations. Private interest governance does not have a clear relationship with the structure of sector wide associational systems, and occurs even in fragmented, competitive and flat horizontal systems. This contrast leads Jacek to pose an interesting speculative theoretical question: can associational systems remain heterogeneous and yet perform important public policy duties?

This theme is echoed in Coleman's chapter where he draws attention to the widespread occurrence of the supposedly unstable situation of a pluralist structure of representation and a concertation structure of control. Farago (Farago et al., 1986) discusses the same phenomenon at length in his review of associative action in Switzerland. In systems where there is macro corporatism (e. g., Austria and Sweden), concertation will be channelled up to the national level, i. e., the country approach will prevail over sectoral imperatives. In other cases, the sectoral, or, more often, subsectoral needs for concertation, appear to overcome national inhibiting factors. In the majority of the countries, then, sector (or subsector) influence wash out country approaches. These findings have important implications for the emerging debate about the relative importance of sectoral imperatives and national patterns (dominant ideologies, institutional capabilities etc.) in industrial policy (see, for example, Deubner 1984; Grant, Paterson and Whitston, forthcoming) and tentatively reinforce the case for the relevance of a sectoral or subsectoral approach.

In summary, upon reflection, the original question has not been correctly posed. If one is to test the hypothesis that associational system structures are more or less conducive to the assumption of public policy functions by associations, in sectors as diverse as food processing, one has to examine associational systems in subsectors as well as business associational systems as a whole. Indeed, such an emphasis has been present throughout this book.

In those systems where encompassing and integrated associational systems are lacking, the focus must be on the associations *in the sector or subsector* rather than on the associational system at large. If there are to be private interest governments within a sector/subsector, the sectoral/subsectoral association will need to have a familiar list of properties. It must organize the whole sector or subsector and speak for virtually all of the enterprises in it. It will suffer no competitors and be sufficiently differentiated to give voice to the range of interests within its domain. At the same time, it will possess the organizational means, whether through its committess or its board of directors, to integrate and find a consensus among these various interests. The association will possess a professional, technically expert staff that will generate its own informational base and become a reliable source of advice for the state. Forgoing most of the bluster and hyperbole of the lobby group, it will be prepared to act as a partner with the state in policy making. All of the evidence presented in this book suggests that in the countries with a more pluralistic system of interest groups, differences of these kinds still occur between associations that have become participants in the policy process as opposed to those that remain pressure groups on the outside.

Subject to these qualifications, the original organizational development hypothesis offered by Schmitter and Streeck (1981, p. 124) retains its credibility in the light of the research reported in this book. It will be recalled that associations are more likely candidates for neo-corporatist arrangements (we would add at the macro *or* meso level) the more:
— *encompassing* they are in scope and purpose
— *specialized* and *coordinated* they are internally
— *balanced* and hence *secure* is their supply of resources
— *autonomous* they are in their actions and their capacity to look to the longer term even in the face of pressing short term problems.

A key component of any neo-corporatist arrangement must be the formal organizational properties of the interest associations involved. The particular formal ways business interests are mediated by associational structures has a profound impact on the likelihood of neo-corporatist arrangements and, perhaps more importantly, on their success.

The companion assumption presented by Schmitter and Streeck (1981, p. 124) states that greater organizational development of associations indicates that associative action is more important to business than other means for defining and expressing its interests. The studies contained in this volume are less convincing in this regard. If we distinguish for the moment between associative action, on the one hand, and the maintenance of informal, collusive relationships with senior officials and politicians on the other, it is not self-evident that business persons would prefer the former over the latter, or that the former would obtain for them greater political power than the latter. What we can say is that working through associations and associational systems that are more organizationally developed offers business more opportunities to share in political power than when these are less developed such as occurs under pluralist conditions. Whether it provides greater access to political power than the opportunity to take part in the occasional private dinner with a head of government is less clear.

From the point of view of a conventional study of political influence, associative action is a complementary alternative to the use of government relations divisions or social networks linking politicians and business persons. (See Grant, 1984b; Useem, 1984). What this study has shown is that, in response to the extension of state responsibilities, and the considerable influence of organized farmers on policy making, food processing firms become drawn into meso corporatist arrangements. Under these conditions, it is unlikely that business can handle its relations with the state through more informal network based relationships. The incidence of meso corporatist arrangements varies nationally, by subsector, and by issue area. Even so, they are sufficiently frequent in occurrence, wide ranging in scope, and significant in terms of the issues with which they deal, to merit systematic attention. Although not incompatible with pluralist approaches, such a blurring of the public and the private, and the emergence of new forms of negotiation and partnership both between primary producers and processors and between industry and the state, can more usefully be explored within the frameworks of analysis deployed in this volume.

References

Almond, G. (1983) 'Corporatism, Pluralism and Professional Memory', *World Politics*, 35: 245–60.

Anderson, R. D. (1981) 'Government Regulation of the Canadian Dairy Processing, Distributing and Retailing Sector', Economic Council of Canada, Working Paper No. 25.

Ashby, A. W. (1983) 'The Economic Environment of the Food Industry', pp. 51–65 in J. Burns, J. McInerney, A. Swinbank (eds.), *The Food Industry: Economics and Policies*. London: Heinemann.

Atkinson, M. M. and W. D. Coleman, 'Corporatism and Industrial Policy', pp. 22–44, in A. Cawson (ed.) *Organized Interests and the State: Studies in Meso-Corporatism*. London: Sage.

Beechey, V. (1982) 'The Sexual Division of Labour and the Labour Process: a Critical Assessment of Braverman', pp. 54–73 in S. Wood (ed.), *The Degradation of Work? Skill, Deskilling and the Labour Process*. London: Hutchinson.

Bengtsson, L., A. C. Eriksson, P. Sederblad (1984) 'The Swedish Employers' Confederation and Centralized Collective Bargaining in 1980, 1981 and 1983'. University of Stockholm, Research Project 'The Associative Action of Swedish Business Interests', Research Report No. 10.

BMMA (1982) British Bacon and Meat Manufacturers' Association, *Annual Report, 1982*.

Brown, W. (ed.) (1981) *The Changing Contours of Industrial Relations*. Oxford: Basil Blackwell.

Bundeswirtschaftsministerium (1975) 'Wettbewerbsverzerrungen — Beispielkatalog des Bundeswirtschaftsministeriums'. Sonderdruck aus *Wettbewerb in Recht und Praxis*, January 1975, 24–32.

Buksti, J. (1983) 'Bread and Butter Agreement and High Political Disagreement', *Scandinavian Political Studies*, 6(n. s.)(3): 261–80.

Bunyan, J. (1678) *The Pilgrim's Progress*. London: Nath. Ponder.

Burns, J. A. (1983 a) 'The UK Food Chain with Particular Reference to the Inter-Relations Between Manufacturers and Distributors', *Journal of Agricultural Economics*, 34(3): 361–78.

Burns, J. A. (1983 b) 'Changes in the Relations Between Food Processing and Agricultural Production, Food Distribution and Consumption', pp. 52–72, in *OECD Food Industries in the 1980s* (Paris: Organization for Economic Cooperation and Development).

Cawson, A. (1982) *Corporatism and Welfare*. London: Heinemann.

Cawson, A. (1985) 'Introduction', pp. 1–21 in A. Cawson (ed.) *Organized Interests and the State: Studies in Meso-Corporatism*. London: Sage.

Cawson, A. (1986) *Corporatism and Political Theory*. Oxford: Basil Blackwell.

Cawson, A. (ed.) (1985) *Organized Interests and the State: Studies in Meso-Corporatism*. London: Sage.

Coates, D. (1984) 'Food Law. Brussels, Whitehall and Town Hall', pp. 144–60 in D. Lewis and H. Wallace (eds.) *Policies into Practice*. London: Heinemann.

Cockburn, C. (1983) *Brothers. Male Dominance and Technological Change*. London: Pluto Press.

Coleman, W. D. (1984) 'The Political Organization of Business Interests in the Canadian Food Processing Industry'. Berlin: International Institute of Management Discussion Paper IIM/LP 84–6.

Coleman, W. D. and W. Grant (1984) 'Business Associations and Public Policy: a Comparison of Organizational Development in Britain and Canada', *Journal of Public Policy*, 4(3): 209–35.

Coleman, W. D. and H. J. Jacek (1982) 'The Role of Business Interest Associations in the Canadian Food Processing Industry', paper presented to the Conference on the Food Processing Sector, Wroxton, England.

Coleman, W. D. and H. J. Jacek (1983 a) 'Business Interest Associations in Canada: A Preliminary Overview', paper presented to a Workshop of the Organization of Business Interests Project, Firenze.

Coleman, W. D. and H. J. Jacek (1983 b) 'The Role and Activities of Business Interest Associations in Canada', *Canadian Journal of Political Science*, 16(2): 257–80.

Commission of the European Communities (1980) *Symposium on Enforcement of Food Law* (Rome, 12–15 September 1978). Brussels: Commission of the European Communities.

Connor, J. M., R. T. Rogers, B. W. Marion and W. F. Mueller (1985) *The Food Manufacturing Industries*. Lexington: D. C. Heath.

Cox, G., P. Lowe and M. Winter (1985) 'Changing Directions in Agricultural Policy: Corporatist Arrangements in Production and Conservation Policies', *Sociologia Ruralis*, 25(2): 130–54.

Dennis, P. O. (1980) 'Constraints of Legislation', in P. O. Dennis, J. R. Blanchfield and A. G. Ward *Food Control in Action*. London: Applied Science Publishers.

Deubner, C. (1984) 'Change and internationalization in industry: towards a sectoral interpretation of West German politics', *International Organization*, 38(3): 501–35.

DiMaggio, P. J. and W. W. Powell (1983) 'The Iron Cage Revisited; Institutional Isomorphism and Collective Rationality in Organizational Fields', *American Sociological Review*, 48(2): 147–60.

Doran, A. (1984) *Craft Enterprises in Britain and Germany*. London: Anglo-German Foundation.

Easton, D. (1965) *A Systems Analysis of Political Life*. New York: Wiley.

Elias, P. (1985). 'Changes in Occupational Structure, 1971–81.' Paper presented to Edinburgh Survey Methodology Group seminar on the Uses of Surveys and Censuses for Monitoring Industrial and Occupational Change.

Elias, P. and B. Main (1982) Women's Working Lives: Evidence from the National Training Survey.' Institute for Employment Research research report, University of Warwick.

Farago, P. (1982) 'The Organization of Business Interests In The Swiss Food Processing Industry: a First Approach', paper presented to the Conference on the Food Processing Industry, Wroxton, England.

Farago, P. (1984) 'Nachfragemacht und die kollektiven Reaktionen der Nahrungsmittelindustrie. Eine Fallstudie über Möglichkeiten und Grenzen der Organisation von Wirtschaftsinteressen am Beispiel des Verhältnisses von Industrie und Handel in der schweizerischen Lebensmittelbranche.' European University Institute Working Paper No. 110/84, Firenze.

Farago, P. (1985) 'Regulating Milk Markets', pp. 168–81 in P. Schmitter and W. Streeck (eds.) *Private Interest Governments* (London: Sage).

Farago, P., H. Ruf and F. Wieder (1984) 'Wirtschaftsverbände in der Schweizer Nahrungsmittelindustrie.' Forschungsprojekt: Die Organisation von Wirtschaftsinteressen in der Schweiz. Bericht No. 1, Soziologisches Institut der Universität Zürich.

Farago, P., H. Kriesi, M. Buser, H. Ruf and P. Rustenholz (1986) *Wirtschaftsverbände in der Schweiz*. Zürich: Verlag Rüegger.

FDIC (1982) 'FDIC Statistical Digest', *FDIC Bulletin*, No. 22 (November): 38–42.

Gardner, C. (1986) 'Out of the Frying Pan', *New Society*, 75(1203): 95–96.

Gilb, C. F. (1981) 'Public or Private Governments?', pp. 464—91 in P. C. Nystrom and W. H. Starbuck (eds.), *Handbook of Organizational Design: Volume 2 — Remodelling Organizations and their Environments*. Oxford: Oxford University Press.

Giles, R. R. (1976) 'The Development of Food Legislation in the United Kingdom', pp. 4–13 in Ministry of Agriculture, Fisheries and Food, *Food Quality and Safety: a Century of Progress*. London: H.M.S.O.

G+L Top 200 (1981) *Die Umsatzkonzentration im Lebensmittelhandel 1981*. Frankfurt: Glendinning and Lehning GmbH.

Grant, W. (1983 a) 'Representing Capital: the Role of the CBI', pp. 69–84 in R. King (ed.) *Capital and Politics*. London: Routledge.

Grant, W. (1983 b) 'The Organization of Business Interests in the UK Food Processing Industry'. Berlin: International Institute of Management Discussion Paper IIM/LMP 83–11.

Grant, W. (1983 c) 'Gotta Lotta Bottle: Corporatism, the Public and the Private and the Milk Marketing System in Britain', paper presented to the European Consortium for Political Research Joint Sessions, Freiburg.

Grant, W. (1983 d) 'Private Organizations as Agents of Public Policy', paper presented to the Sixth Colloquium of the European Group for Organizational Studies, Firenze.

Grant, W. (1984 a) 'Is Corporatism Necessarily Interventionist? A Discussion of the Thatcher Government in Britain', paper presented to the conference on 'The *Ständestaat* in Historical and International Perspective', Ludwig Boltzmann Institut für Historische Sozialwissenschaft, Salzburg.

Grant, W. (1984 b) 'Large Firms and Public Policy in Britain', *Journal of Public Policy*, 4: 1—17.

Grant, W. (1985) 'Private organizations as agents of public policy: the case of milk marketing in Britain', pp. 182–96 in W. Streeck and P. C. Schmitter (eds.) *Private Interest Government: Beyond Market and State*. London: Sage.

Grant, W. (ed.) (1985) *The Political Economy of Corporatism*. London: Macmillan.

Grant, W., W. Paterson and C. Whitston (forthcoming) *International Industry, National Governments and the EEC*. Oxford: Oxford University Press.

Grant, W. and W. Streeck (1985) 'Large Firms and the Representation of Business Interests in the UK and West German Construction Industry', pp. 145–73 in A. Cawson (ed.) *Organized Interests and the State: Studies in Meso-Corporatism*. London: Sage.

Grosskopf, W. (1983) 'Structural Adjustments in the Food Industries of the Federal Republic of Germany', pp. 108–11, in *OECD Food Industries in the 1980s*. Paris: Organization for Economic Cooperation and Development.

Hammarström, O. and B. Viklund (1980) 'The Role of Government in Regulating Work Life'. Arbbetslivscentrum, Stockholm (typescript).

Harris, S. (1984) 'The CAP and its Impact on the EEC's Food Industries', pp. 1–22 in A. Swinbank and J. Burns (eds.) *The EEC and the Food Industries*. Reading: Department of Agricultural Economics and Management, University of Reading.

Harris, S., A. Swinbank and G. Wilkinson (1983) *The Food and Farm Policies of the European Community*. New York: Wiley.

Hartmann, G., I. Nicholas, A. Sorge and M. Warner (1983) 'Computerised Machine-Tools, Manpower Consequences and Skill Utilisation', *British Journal of Industrial Relations*, 21(2): 221–31.

Hilbert, J. (1982) 'Business Interest Associations in the West German Food Processing Industry', paper presented to the Conference on the Food Processing Sector, Wroxton, England.

Hilbert, J. (1983) 'Verbände im produzierenden Ernährungsgewerbe der Bundesrepublik Deutschland — Eine Studie zu Strukturen, Problemen und Wirkungen der "Organisation von Wirtschaftsinteressen"'. Typescript, University of Bielefeld.

Hunt, I.J. (1983) 'Developments in Food Distribution', pp. 127–42 in J. Burns, J. McInerney, A. Swinbank (eds.), *The Food Industry: Economics and Policies*. London: Heinemann.

IHA (1982) 'Kennziffern des schweizerischen Lebensmittel-Detailhandels 1982'. IHA Institut für Marktanalysen.

Jacek, H.J. (1983 a) 'The Organization and Activities of Business Interest Associations in North America: a Comparative Study of their Relations with the State and Organized Labour'. Paper prepared for the annual meeting of the American Political Science Association, Chicago, Ill.

Jacek, H.J. (1983 b) 'The Functions of Food Processing Associations as Agents of Public Policy', paper presented to the Sixth Colloquium of the European Group of Organizational Studies, Firenze.

Jacek, H.J. (1986) 'Pluralist and Corporatist Intermediation, Activities of Business Interest Associations, and Corporate Profits: Some Evidence from Canada', *Comparative Politics*, 17: 419–37.

Jackson, R.J. and M. P. C. M. van Schendelen (1985) 'Politics and Business: Partners and Antagonists? A Comparative Approach', paper presented to the European Consortium for Political Research, Barcelona Joint Session of Workshops.

Katzenstein, P.J. (1985) *Small States in World Markets*. Ithaca: Cornell University Press.

Kaufman, H. (1971) 'Die öffentlich-rechtlichen Aufgaben der ZVSM', dissertation, University of Freiburg.

Kinch, A. (1980) 'Preliminary Summing Up: Similarities and Differences between National Enforcement Systems' in Commission of the European Communities, *Symposium on Enforcement of Food Law*. Brussels: Commission of the European Communities.

Kirchner, E. and K. Schwaiger (1981) *The Role of Interest Groups in the European Community*. Aldershot: Gower.

Kolko, G. (1967) *The Triumph of Conservatism*. Chicago: Quadrangle Books.

Korpi, W. (1981) 'Sweden: Conflict, Power and Politics in Industrial Relations' in P. B. Doeringer et al. (eds.) *Industrial Relations in International Perspective: Essays on Research and Policy*. London: Macmillan.

Korpi, W. (1983) 'Political Democracy as Threat to Capitalism — a Comparison between Pluralism, Neo-Corporatism and a Power Resource Perspective' in J. Matthes (ed.) *Krise der Arbeitsgesellschaft?* Verhandlungen des 21. Deutschen Soziologentages in Bamberg 1982.

Laski, H. (1931) *Introduction to Politics*. London: Unwin Books.

Lecher, W. (1981) *Gewerkschaften in Europa in der Krise*. Köln: Bund Verlag.

Leckie, K. and J. Morris (1980) 'Study on Government Regulation in the Red Meat Industry', Working Paper No. 8, Economic Council of Canada.

Linda, R. (1981) 'Concentration and Competition in Food and Drink Manufacturing and Distribution', pp. 1–37 in H. W. de Jong (ed.) *The Structure of European Industry*. Brussels: Martinus Nijhoff.

Linke, H. (1980) 'Rechtsvorschriften', pp. 41–88 in *Fleischwarenhandbuch 1*. Hamburg: B. Behr's Verlag.

LZ-Report (1980/81) 'Lebensmittel-Zeitung: Markt- und Strukturzahlen der Nahrungs- und Genußmittelbranche.' Report 1980/81.

Manchester, A. C. (1983) *The Public Role in the Dairy Economy: Why and How Governments Intervene in the Milk Business.* Westview Press.

Marin, B. (1983) 'Organizing Interests by Interest Organizations: Associational Prerequisites of Cooperation in Austria', *International Political Science Review*, 4(2): 197–216.

Maunder, P. (1980) 'Food manufacturing', pp. 80–105 in P. S. Johnson (ed.), *The Structure of British Industry.* St. Albans: Granada.

MIGROS-Sozialbilanz (1980) 'Eine Darstellung der gesellschaftsbezogenen Ziele und Tätigkeiten der MIGROS-Gemeinschaft.' Zürich: MIGROS-Genossenschafts-Bund.

Ministeries van Landbouw en Visserij en van Ekonomische Zaken (1981) *Voedings en Genotmiddelenindustries (Bedrijfstakverkenning 1980).* Den Haag: Staatsuitgeverij.

MK (1977) *Monopolkommission, 1977: Mißbräuche der Nachfragemacht und Möglichkeiten zu ihrer Kontrolle im Rahmen des Gesetzes gegen Wettbewerbsbeschränkungen.* Sondergutachten der Monopolkommission, Band 7. Baden-Baden: Nomos.

MMB (1981 a) *The Quality of our Milk,* Information Service Leaflet No. 5. Thames Ditton: Milk Marketing Board.

MMB (1981 b) *Testing Milk for Quality,* Information Service Leaflet No. 24. Thames Ditton: Milk Marketing Board.

MMC (1981) *Monopolies and Mergers Commission: Discounts to Retailers.* London: H.M.S.O.

NEHEM (Nederlandse Herstructureingsmaatschappij) (1981) *Versteken Varkensvleesverwerkende Industrie.* 's-Hertogenbosch.

Nielsen (1976) 'The Grocery Marketing Scene: a Nielsen World-wide Review'. No. 2, 1976.

Nielsen (1982) 'The Grocery Marketing Scene: a Nielsen World-wide Review of Significant Industry Trends'. No. 6, 1982.

Nilsson, C. (1982) 'Working Hours Policy and the Institutional Framework for this in Sweden'. Report for the project, Arbeitszeitpolitik, University of Bielefeld (typescript).

OECD (1983 a) *OECD Food Industries in the 1980s.* Paris: Organization for Economic Cooperation and Development.

OECD (1983 b) *Positive Adjustment Policies in the Dairy Sector.* Paris: Organization for Economic Cooperation and Development.

Offe, C. (1981) 'The Attribution of Public Status to Interest Groups: Observations on the West German Case', pp. 123–58 in S. Berger (ed.) *Organizing Interests in Western Europe.* Cambridge: Cambridge University Press.

Offe, C. (1985) *Disorganized Capitalism: Contemporary Transformations of Work and Politics.* Cambridge: Polity Press.

Offe, C. and Wiesenthal, H. (1980) 'Two Logics of Collective Action: Theoretical Notes on Social Class and Organizational Form', *Political Power and Social Theory*, 1: 67–115.

Olson, M., Jnr. (1968) *The Logic of Collective Action: Public Goods and the Theory of Groups.* New York: Shocken.

Organization for Economic Cooperation and Development (1984), *Main Economic Indicators* as printed in Agriculture Canada, *Food Market Commentary*, 6(1): 51–53.

Painter, A. A. (1981) 'Enforcement: a Re-think?', *FDIC Bulletin*, No. 18 (July): 32–40.

Pestoff, V. (1981) 'Dilemmas Facing Producer Cooperatives in Sweden', AASBI Stockholm, Research Report No. 7.

Pestoff, V. (1983) 'The Associative Action of Swedish Business Interests: The Organization of Business Interests in the Swedish Food Processing Industry', Research Report No. 8, Department of Political Science, University of Stockholm.

Phillips, A. and B. Taylor (1980) 'Sex and Skill: Notes Towards a Feminist Economics', *Feminist Review*, No. 6: 79–88.

Picchio del Mercato, A. (1981), 'Social Reproduction and the Basic Structure of the Labour Market', pp. 193–209 in F. Wilkinson (ed.) *The Dynamics of Labour Market Segmentation*. London: Academic Press.

Pluim Mentz, J. P. and B. Verwayen (1980) *Landbouwkwaliteitswet*. Edite Schuurman and Jordens. Zwolle: Tjeenk Willink.

Prescott, D. M. (1980) *The Role of Marketing Boards in the Processed Tomato and Asparagus Industries*. Regulation Reference. Ottawa: Economic Council of Canada.

Rainbird, H. and Grant, W. (1984) 'Non-Statutory Training Organizations and Training Policy in the Food and Drink Industry', Institute for Employment Research, University of Warwick.

Rieder, P. and U. Egger (1983) *Agrarmärkte*. Zürich: Verlag der Fachvereine.

Roberts, B. C., R. Loveridge, J. Gennard, J. V. Eason (1972) *Reluctant Militants: a Study of Industrial Technicians*. London: Heinemann.

Rokkan, S. and Urwin, D. (1983) *Economy, Territory, Identity: Politics of West European Peripheries*. London: Sage.

Ryan, P. (1981) 'Segmentation, Duality and the Internal Labour Market' in F. Wilkinson (ed.) *The Dynamics of Labour Market Segmentation*. London: Academic Press.

Sanderson, M. E. and Winkler, J. T. (undated) 'Provender and Prophylaxis: The Emergence of Nutrition as a Political Issue', typescript, Cranfield Institute of Technology.

Schmitter, P. C. (1982) 'Reflections on Where the Theory of Neo-Corporatism Has Gone and Where the Praxis of Neo-Corporatism May Be Going', pp. 259–79 in G. Lehmbruch and P. C. Schmitter (eds.) *Patterns of Corporatist Policy-Making*. Beverly Hills: Sage.

Schmitter, P. C. (1983) 'Neo-Corporatism', 'Consensus', 'Governability' and 'Democracy' in the Management of Crisis in Contemporary Advanced Industrial/Capitalist Societies.' Paper presented to the OECD Expert Group on 'Collective Bargaining and Economic Policies: Dialogue and Consensus', Paris.

Schmitter, P. C., W. Streeck, and A. Martinelli (1980) 'The Organization of Business Interests in Advanced Industrial Societies — a Project Proposal', Berlin: International Institute of Management.

Schmitter, P. C. and Streeck, W. (1981) 'The Organization of Business Interests. A Research Design to Study the Associative Action of Business in the Advanced Industrial Societies of Western Europe.' Berlin: International Institute of Management Discussion Paper IIM/LMP 81–13.

Selbstbedienung in Österreich (1982). 'Selbstbedienung in Österreich. Entwicklung 1967–1982. Der österreichische Lebensmittel-Einzelhandel mit Selbstbedienung, 15. Bericht.' Wien: Österreichisches Institut für Verpackungswesen an der Wirtschaftsuniversität Wien, Arbeitskreis 'Selbstbedienung'.

Senti, R. (1979) *Organisation des schweizerischen Schlachtvieh- und Fleischmarktes*. Diessenhofen: Röegger.

Small, D. B. and L. D. Smith (1984), 'The Food, Drink and Tobacco Sectors', pp. 174–212, in N. Hood and S. Young (eds.) *Industry, Policy and the Scottish Economy*. Edinburgh: Edinburgh University Press.

Staber, U. and H. Aldrich (1983) 'Trade Association Stability and Public Policy', pp. 163–78 in R. H. Hall and R. E. Quinn (eds.), *Organizational Theory and Public Policy*. London: Sage.

Stanbury, W. T. and G. Lermer (1983) 'Regulation and the Redistribution of Wealth', *Canadian Public Administration*, 26(3): 378–401.

Stigler, G. J. (1975) 'Can Regulatory Agencies Protect the Consumer?' in G. Stigler, *The Citizen and the State: Essays on Regulation.* Chicago: University of Chicago Press.

Stocker, T. R. (1983) 'Pressures on Policy Formation', pp. 240–56 in J. Burns, J. McInerney and A. Swinbank (eds.) *The Food Industry: Economics and Policies.* London: Heinemann.

Stocker, T. R. (1985) 'Nutrition — the Food Industry's Role', *FDF Bulletin,* 1: 8–16.

Stoffaës, C. (1985) 'Explaining French Strategy in Electronics', pp. 187–94 in S. Zukin (ed.), *Industrial Policy: Business and Politics in the United States and France.* New York: Praeger.

Streeck, W. (1983) 'Between Pluralism and Corporatism: German Business Associations and the State', *Journal of Public Policy,* 3(3): 265–84.

Streeck, W. and P. C. Schmitter (1984) 'Community, Market, State and Associations? The Prospective Contribution of Interest Governance to Social Order'. European University Institute, Working Paper No. 94. Firenze.

Streeck, W. and P. C. Schmitter (eds.) (1985) *Private Interest Government: Beyond Market and State.* London: Sage.

SWEDA (1980). *Der schweizerische Lebensmittelhandel. Stand Januar 1980.* Zürich: Litton Business Systems, Dep. Sweda International.

Swinbank, A. and J. A. Burns (1984) 'The EEC and the Food and Drink Industries: a Summary of Themes', pp. 155–69 in A. Swinbank and J. A. Burns (eds.) *The EEC and the Food Industries.* Reading: University of Reading Department of Agricultural Economics and Management.

Traxler, F. (1982) 'Evolution gewerkschaftlicher Interessenvertretung, Entwicklungslogik und Organisationsdynamik gewerkschaftlichen Handelns am Beispiel Österreich.' Wien/Frankfurt.

Traxler, F. (1983 a) 'Prerequisites, Problem-Solving Capacity and Restrictions of Self-Regulation: A Case Study of Social Autonomy in the Austrian Milk Economy', paper presented to the Sixth Colloquium of the European Group for Organizational Studies, Firenze.

Traxler, F. (1983 b) 'Branchenprobleme, Unternehmeninteressen und ihre Organisation in der Nahrungs- und Genußmittelzeugung', Institut für Konfliktforschung, Wien (typescript).

Traxler, F. (1984) 'Bedingungen und Folgen kollektiven Unternehmerhandelns. Eine Analyse des Zusammenschlusses von Unternehmern in Interessenverbänden'. Wien, typescript.

Traxler, F. and Moser, U. (1984) 'Industrial Policy and Interest Associations: a Comparision of the Role of Organized Labour and Organized Capital in Austria's System of Corporatist Modernization'. Paper prepared for the EGOS conference on 'Trade Unions in Europe: the Organizational Perspective', Amersfoot.

Traxler, F. (1985) 'Prerequisites, Problem-Solving Capacity and Limits of Neo-Corporatist Regulation: a Case Study of Private Interest Governance and Economic Performance in Austria', pp. 150—167 in W. Streeck and P. C. Schmitter (eds.), *Private Interest Government.* London: Sage.

UNILEVER/IHA (1982) ,Der schweizerische Lebensmittel-Detailhandel 1982, inkl. Food-Umsatz Fachhandel.'

Useem, M. (1984) *The Inner Circle.* New York: Oxford University Press.

Visser, J. (1984) 'Dimensions of Union Growth in Postwar Western Europe', European University Institute Working Paper No. 89, Firenze.

VKK (1976) 'Die Nachfragemacht und deren Mißbrauch', pp. 57–93 in *Veröffentlichungen der schweizerischen Kartellkommission 1976.* Zürich: Orell Füssli.

VKK (1979) 'Die Konzentration im Lebensmitteldetailhandel', pp. 273–389 in *Veröffentlichungen der schweizerischen Kartellkommission 1979*. Zürich: Orell Füssli.

VKK (1983) 'Die Wettbewerbsverhältnisse auf dem Markt für Frühstücksgetränke', pp. 261–320 in *Veröffentlichungen der schweizerischen Kartellkommission 1983*. Zürich: Orell Füssli.

De Vroom, B. (1982) 'Quality Policy in the Dutch Meat Processing Industry: Problems of Associative Action', paper presented to the Conference on the Food Processing Sector, Wroxton, England.

De Vroom, B. (1985 a) 'The Rise of a New 'State' and the Development of Interest Associations: The Case of Business Interest Associations on EC-level', typescript, University of Leiden.

De Vroom, B. (1985 b), 'Quality Regulation in the Dutch Pharmaceutical Industry. Conditions for Private Regulation by Business Interest Associations', pp. 128–49 in W. Streeck and P. C. Schmitter (eds.) *Private Interest Government: Beyond Market and State*. London: Sage.

Van Waarden, F. (1982) 'Statutory Organization of the Agricultural Industry in the Netherlands', typescript, University of Leiden.

Van Waarden, F. (1984) 'Bureaucracy Around the State: Varieties of Collective Self Regulation in the Dutch Dairy Industry', European University Institute Working Paper No. 108, Firenze.

Van Waarden, F. (1985) 'Varieties of Collective Self-Regulation of Business: the Example of the Dutch Dairy Industry', pp. 197–220 in W. Streeck and P. C. Schmitter (eds.) *Private Interest Government: Beyond Market and State*. London: Sage.

Ward, A. G. (1976) 'Advising on Food Standards in the United Kingdom', pp. 22–41 in Ministry of Agriculture, Fisheries and Food, *Food Quality and Safety: a Century of Progress*. London: H.M.S.O.

Wassenberg, A. F. P. (1982) 'Neo-Corporatism and the Quest for Control: the Cuckoo Game', pp. 83–108, in G. Lehmbruch and P. C. Schmitter (eds.) *Patterns of Corporatist Policy-Making*. London: Sage.

Waters, A. M. (1980) 'Food Law Enforcement System in the UK' in Commission of the European Communities, *Symposium on Enforcement of Food Law*. Brussels: Commission of the European Communities.

Weber, H. (1983) 'Die Organisation von Wirtschaftsinteressen in Maschinenbau', Universität Bielefeld, Fakultät für Soziologie, typescript.

Wheelcock, V. and Fallows, S. (1985) 'Implications of the COMA Report on Diet and Cardiovascular Disease for British Agriculture', Food Policy Research, University of Bradford.

Wüger, M. (1983) 'Handel und Industrie — Eine Analyse ihrer wirtschaftlichen Beziehungen', *Österreichisches Institut für Wirtschaftsforschung, Monatsberichte*, 2/1983: 98–106.

Young, B., L. N. Lindberg and R. Hollingsworth (1985) 'The Governance of the American Dairy Industry: From Regional Dominance to Regional Cleavage', paper presented at the conference on The Regional Organization of Business Interests and Public Policy, McMaster University, Hamilton, Ontario, May 1985.

Young, S. (1984) *An Annotated Bibliography on Relations Between Government and Industry in Britain, 1960–82, Volumes 1 and 2*. London: Economic and Social Research Council.

Zald, M. N. (1978) 'On the Social Control of Industries', *Social Forces*, 57(1): 79–102.

Zysman, J. (1983) *Governments, Markets and Growth*. Oxford: Martin Robertson.

Index